Introduction to the Literary Art of the Gospel of John

Introduction to the Literary Art of the Gospel of John

A Biblical Approach

Paul Jaesuk Jo

WIPF & STOCK · Eugene, Oregon

INTRODUCTION TO THE LITERARY ART OF THE GOSPEL OF JOHN
A Biblical Approach

Copyright © 2022 Paul Jaesuk Jo. All rights reserved. Except for brief quotations in critical publications or reviews, no part of this book may be reproduced in any manner without prior written permission from the publisher. Write: Permissions, Wipf and Stock Publishers, 199 W. 8th Ave., Suite 3, Eugene, OR 97401.

Wipf & Stock
An Imprint of Wipf and Stock Publishers
199 W. 8th Ave., Suite 3
Eugene, OR 97401

www.wipfandstock.com

PAPERBACK ISBN: 978-1-6667-3555-0
HARDCOVER ISBN: 978-1-6667-9274-4
EBOOK ISBN: 978-1-6667-9275-1

05/23/22

Unless otherwise indicated, Scripture quotations are taken from the (NASB®) *New American Standard Bible*®, Copyright © 1960, 1971, 1977, 1995 by The Lockman Foundation. Used by permission. All rights reserved. www.lockman.org.

To my dear wife, Jiyoun,
who sacrifices so much in every way to see
Christ glorified in our home and
who loves the Lord with a faithful heart.
To my precious daughter, Kelly,
who is the joy, treasure, and greatest gift in our lives.

Contents

Abbreviations | ix
Introduction | 1

1 Contextualizing the Literary Art of the Gospel of John | 12
    Critical Theories according to Meyer H.
        Abram's Four Categories | 12
    Modern Literary Theories | 23
    Summary | 43

2 Old Testament Poetics as the Literary Background of John | 44
    Apostle John as the Author of the Gospel | 45
    Jewishness of the Gospel of John | 52
    Selected Testimonies on the Excellence of
        the Old Testament Poetics | 60
    Summary | 69

3 The Gospel of John in Light of the Poetics
   of Old Testament Poetry | 71
    Parallelism | 72
    Repetition and Variation | 78
    Terseness | 85
    Double Meaning | 90
    Imagery | 95
    Summary | 101

4   The Gospel of John in Light of the Poetics
    of Old Testament Narrative | 102
        Point of View | 103
        Character and Characterization | 110
        Plot | 118
        Gaps and Ambiguities | 127
        Narrative Time | 132
        Summary | 140

5   The Gospel of John in Light of the Poetics
    of Old Testament Prophets | 141
        The Word of the LORD | 145
        Prophetic Self-consciousness | 151
        Prophetic Persuasion | 158
        Prophetic Mode of Speaking | 163
        Summary | 167

Bibliography | 169
Subject Index | 195
Scripture Index | 205

Abbreviations

AB	Anchor Yale Bible Commentary
ABR	*Australian Biblical Review*
ABRL	The Anchor Bible Reference Library
ACCS	Ancient Christian Commentary on Scripture
ACW	Ancient Christian Writers
ANTC	Abingdon New Testament Commentaries
AThR	*Anglican Theological Review*
AUS	American University Studies
BASP	*Bulletin of the American Society of Papyrologists*
BDAG	Danker, Frederick W., Walter Bauer, William F. Arndt, and F. Wilbur Gingrich. *Greek-English Lexicon of the New Testament and Other Early Christian Literature.* 3rd ed. Chicago: University of Chicago Press, 2000 (Danker-Bauer-Arndt-Gingrich)
BDB	Brown, Francis, S. R. Driver, and Charles A. Briggs. *Enhanced Brown-Driver-Briggs Hebrew and English Lexicon*
BECNT	Baker Exegetical Commentary on the New Testament
BETL	Bibliotheca Ephemeridum Theologicarum Lovaniensium

BibInt	*Biblical Interpretation*
BibInt	Biblical Interpretation Series
BJS	Brown Judaic Studies
BLS	Bible and Literature Series
BNTC	Black's New Testament Commentary
BOSHNP	Berit Olaam Studies in Hebrew Narrative & Poetry
BRev	*Bible Review*
BSac	*Bibliotheca Sacra*
CBC	Cambridge Bible Commentary
CBQ	*Catholic Biblical Quarterly*
CCGNT	Classic Commentaries on the Greek New Testament
CGTSC	Cambridge Greek Testament for Schools and Colleges
ConBNT	Coniectanea Biblica New Testament Series
CTR	*Criswell Theological Review*
DBIm	*Dictionary of Biblical Imagery.* Edited by Leland Ryken, James C. Wilhoit, and Tremper Longman III. Downers Grove: InterVarsity, 1998
DOTWPW	*Dictionary of the Old Testament: Wisdom, Poetry & Writings.* Edited by Tremper Longman III and Peter Enns. Downers Grove, IL: InterVarsity, 2008
DRev	*Downside Review*
EAJT	*East Asia Journal of Theology*
EncJud	*Encyclopedia Judaica.* Edited by Fred Skolnik and Michael Berenbaum. 2nd ed. 22 vols. Detroit: Macmillan Reference USA, 2007
ETL	*Ephemerides Theologicae Lovanienses*
EvQ	*Evangelical Quarterly*
ExpTim	*Expository Times*
FOTL	Forms of the Old Testament Literature

HALOT	*The Hebrew and Aramaic Lexicon of the Old Testament.* Ludwig Koehler, Walter Baumgartner, and Johann J. Staggmm. Translated and edited under the supervision of Mervyn E.J. Richardson. 5 vols. Leiden: Brill, 1994–2000
Herm	Hermeneia—A Critical and Historical Commentary on the Bible
HSM	Harvard Semitic Monographs
HUCA	*Hebrew Union College Annual*
ICC	International Critical Commentary
IDB	*The Interpreter's Dictionary of the Bible.* Edited by George A. Buttrick. 4 vols. Nashville: Abingdon, 1962
IDS	*In die Skriflig*
Int	*Interpretation*
HBT	*Horizons in Biblical Theology*
JAAR	*Journal of the American Academy of Religion*
JBL	*Journal of Biblical Literature*
JETS	*Journal of the Evangelical Theological Society*
JNSL	*Journal of Northwest Semitic Languages*
JPOS	*Journal of the Palestine Oriental Society*
JSNT	*Journal for the Study of the New Testament*
JSNTSup	Journal for the Study of the New Testament Supplement Series
JSOT	*Journal for the Study of the Old Testament*
JSOTSup	Journal for the Study of the Old Testament Supplement Series
JSPSup	Journal for the Study of the Pseudepigrapha Supplement Series
JSS	*Journal of Semitic Studies*
JTSA	*Journal of Theology for Southern Africa*
JQR	*Jewish Quarterly Review*
LCL	Loeb Classical Library
LEC	Library of Early Christianity
LNTS	Library of New Testament Studies

L&N		Louw, Johannes P., and Eugene A. Nida, eds. *Greek-English Lexicon of the New Testament Based on Semantic Domains*. 2nd ed. New York: United Bible Society, 1989
NAC		New American Commentary
NCB		New Century Bible
Neot		*Neotestamentica*
NIB		*The New Interpreter's Bible*. Edited by Leander E. Keck. 12 vols. Nashville: Abingdon, 1994–2004
NIDB		*The New Interpreter's Dictionary of the Bible*. Edited by Katharine Doob Sakenfeld. 5 vols. Nashville: Abingdon, 2006–2009
NICNT		New International Commentary on the New Testament
NICOT		New International Commentary on the Old Testament
NIDNTT		*The New International Dictionary of New Testament Theology*. Edited by Colin Brown. 3 vols. Grand Rapids: Zondervan, 1975–1978
NIDOTTE		*New International Dictionary of Old Testament Theology & Exegesis*. Edited by Willem A. VanGemeren. 5 vols. Grand Rapids: Zondervan, 1997
NovTSup		Supplements to Novum Testamentum
NPEPP		*The New Princeton Encyclopedia of Poetry and Poetics*. Edited by Alex Preminger and T. V. F. Brogan. Princeton: Princeton University Press, 1993
NPNF1		*Nicene and Post-Nicene Fathers*, Series 1
NPNF2		*Nicene and Post-Nicene Fathers*, Series 2
NovT		*Novum Testamentum*
NovTSup		Novum Testamentum Supplement
NTC		New Testament Commentary
NTS		*New Testament Studies*
OTM		Oxford Theological Monographs
PAS		*Proceedings of the Aristotelian Society*
PNTC		The Pillar New Testament Commentary

PRSt	*Perspectives in Religious Studies*
RNBC	Readings: A New Biblical Commentary
SBG	Studies in Biblical Greek
SBLDS	Society of Biblical Literature Dissertation Series
SBLSymS	Society of Biblical Literature Symposium Series
SJ	Studies in Judaism
SJT	*Scottish Journal of Theology*
SNTSMS	Society for New Testament Studies Monograph Series
SNTSU	*Studien zum Neuen Testament und seiner Umwelt*
SP	Sacra Pagina
ST	*Studia Theologica*
SVTQ	*St. Vladimir's Theological Quarterly*
SwJT	*Southwestern Journal of Theology*
TDOT	*Theological Dictionary of the Old Testament*. Edited by G. Johannes Botterweck and Helmer Ringgren. Translated by John T. Willis et al. 16 vols. Grand Rapids: Eerdmans, 1974–2018
THL	The Humanists' Library
TJ	*Trinity Journal*
TLOT	*Theological Lexicon of the Old Testament*. Edited by Ernst Jenni, with assistance from Claus Westermann. Translated by Mark E. Biddle. 3 vols. Peabody, MA: Hendrickson, 1997
TynBul	*Tyndale Bulletin*
VT	*Vetus Testamentum*
VTSup	Vetus Testamentum Supplement
WBC	Word Biblical Commentary
WUNT	Wissenschaftliche Untersuchungen zum Neuen Testament
ZAW	*Zeitschrift für die alttestamentliche Wissenschaft*
ZNW	*Zeitschrift für die neutestamentliche wissenschaft und die Kunde der älteren Kirche*

Introduction

A FREQUENT DESCRIPTION OF John is that it is a pool in which a child can play and an elephant can swim.¹ It is a testimony to the Gospel's ability to convey truth in both simplicity and profundity and its effectiveness to render significance both to simple readings and deep theological inquiries. Its unfathomable reservoir has challenged scholars throughout the ages, yet it is simple enough to touch a child's heart.

Commentators in the history of the church have variously recognized the lofty nature of the Gospel of John. Augustine depicted it as the eagle from the imagery of four beasts in Revelation 4:7 and said that John "soars like an eagle above the clouds of human infirmity, and gazes upon the light of the unchangeable truth with those keenest and steadiest eyes of the heart."² Clement of Alexandria pointed to the depth of John's message in his designation of the Gospel as the "spiritual Gospel."³ In his homilies on the Gospel of John, John Chrysostom spoke on the voice of John as

> what is wonderful, this sound, great as it is, is neither a harsh nor an unpleasant one, but sweeter and more delightful than all harmony of music, and with more skill to soothe; and besides all this, most holy, and most awful, and full of mysteries so great, and bringing with it goods so great, that if men were exactly and with ready mind to receive and keep them, they could no

1. Morris, *Gospel according to John*, 3.
2. Augustine, *Cons.* 1.6.9.
3. Eusebius, *Hist. eccl.* 6.14.7.

longer be mere men nor remain upon the earth, but would take their stand above all the things of this life, and having adapted themselves to the condition of angels, would dwell on earth just as if it were heaven.[4]

For Chrysostom, the language of John was not confusing but "sweeter and more delightful than all harmony of music." On the same note, Martin Luther expressed his favor of this Gospel when he said that the Gospel is "unique in loveliness, and of a truth the principal gospel, far, far superior to the other three."[5]

The Gospel of John, however, unravels many complex features to its students as they look deeper. In *The Fourth Gospel,* Edwyn Hoskyns stated that the Fourth Gospel is "strange, restless, and unfamiliar,"[6] and C. K. Barrett said it is "simple in outline," but "complicated in detail."[7] It has been the task of interpreters throughout history to wrestle with these peculiar features of the Gospel in order to make sense of them.

As the higher critical methodologies began to dominate biblical scholarship since the Enlightenment, the focus of inquiries therefore shifted from the text itself to the history of the text. This dramatic change in biblical scholarship altered the attitude toward the Gospel and cast a negative light upon the beauty and the literary magnificence of John. Some have doubted the ability of the apostle to write a logical literary work, saying that he was a careless, old-aged, muddle-headed, confused, and even an insane writer.[8] Others posed serious doubts about the integrity of the book, with strong convictions in the hypotheses of disarrangements, sources, and multiple editors.[9] As the concern for the history of the text almost completely occupied Johannine scholarship in the modern period, the traditional view on the authorship of the Gospel found no acceptance among scholarly circles and investigation into John's literary fineness has become an irrelevant issue.

---

4. John Chrysostom, *Hom. Jo.* 1.1.

5. Dillenberger, *Martin Luther,* 19. For various attestations of the Gospel of John throughout history, see Kealy, *John's Gospel.*

6. Hoskyns, *Fourth Gospel,* 20.

7. Barrett, *Gospel according to St. John,* 11.

8. For these views, see Schmiedel, *Johannine Writings,* 203; Renan, *Life of Jesus,* 55; Schneider, *Die Aechtheit des Johanneischen Evangeliums,* 3; J. Wellhausen, *Das Evangelium Johannis,* 5.

9. For the history of development of these theories, see Teeple, *Literary Origin of the Gospel of John.*

The literary nature of the Scripture, however, came to take the center stage in scholarly discussions once again since the mid-twentieth century, and the Gospel of John began to be treated as a literary whole. Numerous studies explored this new direction,[10] but R. Alan Culpepper's publication of *Anatomy of the Fourth Gospel: A Study in Literary Design* (1983) became the watershed moment in Johannine study. His seminal work made the case to see the Gospel in essential unity and to approach the text as a "mirror" to reflect the real world of the reader instead of a "window" to see the historical situations behind the text.[11] With this understanding of the text, compositional history became irrelevant and complex features of the text came to have meanings. He stated, "According to this model, dissection and stratification have no place in the study of the Gospel and may distort and confuse one's view of the text. Every element of the gospel contributes to the production of its meaning, and the experience of reading the text is more important than understanding the process of its composition."[12] This emphasis on the wholeness of the Gospel and the primacy of the interaction between the reader and the text was certainly a welcome one for Johannine studies.

However, Culpepper's approach to the Fourth Gospel as a "mirror" with the application of narrative criticism used for fictions raised questions about the historicity of the story of the Gospel. Culpepper himself was aware of the dilemma of accepting the truth claim of the Gospel and the issue of fictiveness his method raises. In his conclusion, conjecturing too great of difference between the world of the Scripture and ours, he said the only way of reconciling the difference was to ask the question whether "'his story' can be true if it is not 'history.'"[13]

The truth claim of the Scripture is substantially at odds with the fictiveness of the novel, and the dilemma created by this difference perhaps should be admitted as irreconcilable and interpreting the former with the methodology of the latter as problematic. Thomas D. Lea recognized the issue when he said that "readers need an assurance that the events narrated in the fourth gospel actually occurred in order to derive spiritual benefits from them. That type of assurance will not be developed in

---

10. Cf. Stibbe, *John as Storyteller*, 9.
11. Culpepper, *Anatomy of the Fourth Gospel*, 3–5.
12. Culpepper, *Anatomy of the Fourth Gospel*, 5.
13. Culpepper, *Anatomy of the Fourth Gospel*, 235–36.

the approach Culpepper has taken."[14] Robert Scholes, James Phelan, and Robert L. Kellogg voiced their concern when they commented, "In the middle of the twentieth century, our view of narrative literature is almost hopelessly novel-centered."[15]

In addition to this novel-centered approximation, other literary critical theories invited new readings on the Gospel—such as rhetorical criticism, structuralist criticism, reader-response criticism, and deconstructionist criticism. While these reading strategies advanced Johannine studies considerably, serious confusions on the nature of biblical literature have ensued. As the proponents of these literary methodologies gradually detached the author from the text, the locus of meaning dissipated from the author, and Scripture's authoritative voice was called into question. The effect of these multiple readings of the text (un)intentionally converged with the postmodern understanding of Scripture. The meaning resided in the pluralistic readings of the text and to ask for authorial intent was to commit an "intentional fallacy."[16] Meyer H. Abrams very well demonstrated this attitude: "Whether the author has expressly stated what his intention was in writing a poem, or whether it is merely inferred from what we know about his life and opinions, his intention is irrelevant to the literary critic, because meaning and value reside within the text of the finished, free-standing, and public work of literature itself."[17] At the turn of the twentieth century, Robert Kysar raised a concern for this hermeneutical trend: "Still, there will be no such thing as a single authoritative interpretation of John—no such thing as a true reading of the text. Instead, the church will be forced to recognize the validity of a wide variety of interpretations, and truth found in a range of readings arising from a multicultural body of readers."[18]

In this light, Culpepper's own acknowledgement is particularly important for the purpose of the present study. Although he made use of the literary conventions of the modern day novel, he remarked that "it would be preferable if we could utilize literary categories which are peculiarly suitable for the study of the gospels rather than those which have been developed from the study of other literary genres, but perhaps

---

14. Lea, "Reliability of History in John's Gospel," 396.
15. Scholes et al., *Nature of Narrative*, 8.
16. Wimsatt and Beardsley, "Intentional Fallacy," 31–55.
17. Abrams, *Glossary of Literary Terms*, 83.
18. Kysar, "Coming Hermeneutical Earthquake," 188.

some progress toward that ability can be made by a study such as the present one."[19] What is at stake in Johannine study is to hear John in light of "literary categories which are peculiarly suitable" for him.

The apostle John stands in the long tradition of the Old Testament writers who as spokespersons for God delivered the divine messages in order to convict, condemn, persuade, and comfort the people of God. His writing style did not arise out of vacuum, nor was its immediate Greco-Roman literary world solely responsible for its intrinsic beauty and power. In his literary study of the Gospel of John, Mark W. G. Stibbe recognized the importance of applying literary conventions true to the Gospel and said that the narrative is "composed according to Hebrew and Graeco-Roman storytelling conventions."[20] While the influence of Greco-Roman conventions on John cannot be denied, and their concepts are undoubtedly useful to New Testament interpretation, it is questionable whether the Greeks captured all the fine nuances of literary and rhetorical traditions represented in the Old Testament. When examined, John's style discloses a closer affinity to his Hebraic root.

In recent years, the Gospel's Jewish character has gained scholarly consensus. Especially with the discovery of the Dead Sea Scrolls, its Jewishness is now at the center stage of discussion. Craig S. Keener stated, "The strongest argument for John's Jewishness is the fact that he deals with very Jewish issues in his work, some of which ... would make no sense outside a Jewish context."[21] He continued, "Though John's audience, like most Greek-speaking Jews, shared many aspects of the larger Mediterranean culture, the Fourth Gospel drives home apologetic points of special interest for a specifically Jewish audience. These points are clearest in the narrative structure of the main body of the Gospel."[22] Rudolf Schnackenburg discerned the Semitic nature of the Gospel:

> The technique of the discourses uses a number of effects which have already been noted in the epistles: antithesis, verbal links through key-words, concatenation of ideas by means of recourse to earlier ones, *inclusio* whereby the thought is brought back to

---

19. Culpepper, *Anatomy*, 9.

20. Stibbe, *John as Storyteller*, 67. Stibbe's study, however, focused on the Hellenistic literary conventions.

21. Keener, *Gospel of John*, 1:173.

22. Keener, *Gospel of John*, 1:174.

its starting-point, parallelism and variation—on the whole, the instruments of Semitic rather than Greek rhetoric.[23]

Thomas L. Brodie noted the important point that John's Gospel rests on the vast literary tradition of the Old Testament,[24] and Michael Fishbane said that the Hebrew Bible is "the repository of a vast store of hermeneutical techniques" and that these "have yet to be thoroughly investigated and systematized."[25] It is, therefore, fitting to search for the context of the literary design of John within the vast hermeneutical techniques of (and certainly the *art* of presenting truth in) the Old Testament.

Many studies in the relationship of the Fourth Gospel with the Old Testament focused their attention on explaining the *contents* of the Gospel in light of the Old Testament,[26] but the investigation into the *form* of the Gospel in light of Old Testament poetics (especially in their entirety in scope) is still lacking. If one is to understand the literary techniques of John—not just in part but in useful thoroughness and, hopefully, in completeness—and to have a *native* light shining upon its distinctive features, then all the aspects of Old Testament poetics must be identified and applied. Such endeavor will render invaluable insights into the true nature of the Fourth Gospel.

Meir Sternberg emphasized the importance of studying the form and said that the "question of the narrative as a functional structure" is a fundamental question and that "our primary business as readers is to make purposive sense of it, so as to explain the *what*'s and the *how*'s in terms of the *why*'s of communication."[27] Gail O'Day echoed this view when he said "any study of Johannine revelation that ignores the form, style, and mode of Johannine revelatory language will always miss the mark."[28] Without the proper understanding of the form of the Gospel, the fine turns of the narrative will always be susceptible to misunderstanding or remain unnoticed at best.

At the 2001 Annual Meeting of the Society of Biblical Literature, Harold W. Attridge in his presidential address introduced the idea of

---

23. Schnackenburg, *Gospel according to St. John*, 1:116.
24. Brodie, *Quest for the Origin*, 39.
25. Fishbane, *Biblical Interpretation in Ancient Israel*, 14.
26. For example, see the discussions in Porter, *Hearing the Old Testament*, and McKnight and Osborne, *Face of New Testament Studies*.
27. Sternberg, *Poetics of Biblical Narrative*, 1.
28. O'Day, *Revelation in the Fourth Gospel*, 47.

"genre bending" and published it in the following year in his article "Genre Bending in the Fourth Gospel."[29] There have been many proposals as for the genre of John's Gospel,[30] but Attridge observed that its form is fluid and thus suggested that it is a "kaleidoscopic Gospel."[31] On the nature of the Gospel, he asked this penetrating question: "Why does the Fourth Gospel exhibit so much interest in playing with generic conventions, extending them, undercutting them, twisting traditional elements into new and curious shapes, making literary forms do things that did not come naturally to them?"[32] It is an intriguing question, and he opined that the answer lies "in the intense reflection in the text on the process of transformation inaugurated by the Word's taking on flesh."[33] When considered, this remark certainly agrees with the contemplative style of John. His observation concerning the convergence of multiple genres in the Fourth Gospel is particularly important for the present study. He said:

> Despite some organizational similarities and a uniform linguistic tone, Johannine discourses are generically quite diverse, with parallels to a wide range of literary patterns and generic forms. The Gospel seems to delight in that diversity, in what Hebrews might call the 'multiple and manifold' ways that words work in order to express the significance of the Word. To use the categories of some of our colleagues who work with social-science models, the Word is honored by the manifold variety of the words used to express it, words that charm, words that challenge, words that evoke, and words that provoke.[34]

John's words are expressed in "multiple and manifold" ways characteristic in Hebrew thoughts and so they necessarily cross many generic

---

29. Attridge, "Genre Bending in the Fourth Gospel," 3–21.

30. The Johannine Gospel has been proposed as a bios (Aune, *New Testament in Its Literary Environment*; Burridge, *What Are the Gospels?*; Talbert, *What Is a Gospel?*; Votaw, *Gospels and Contemporary Biographies*), as a drama (Brant, *Dialogue and Drama*; Parsenios, *Departure and Consolation*; and Parsenios, *Rhetoric and Drama*), as a historiographical writing (Bauckham, "Historiographical Chracteristics," 17–36; Bauckham, *Testimony of the Beloved Disciple*), and as a novel (Brant, "Divine Birth and Apparent Parents," 199–211; Wills, *Quest of the Historical Gospel*). These references are indebted to Larsen, "Introduction," 13.

31. Attridge, "Genre Bending in the Fourth Gospel," 18.

32. Attridge, "Genre Bending in the Fourth Gospel," 20.

33. Attridge, "Genre Bending in the Fourth Gospel," 20.

34. Attridge, "Genre Bending in the Fourth Gospel," 10–11.

boundaries. The following comment is also significant for understanding John's style. He said:

> In the imagination of the fourth evangelist, genres are bent because words themselves are bent. The evangelist's strategy was not unprecedented in antiquity. Fiddling with generic convention is the stuff of which literature great and small was made . . . The fourth evangelist has something of the literary artist and the popular philosopher in him, but the motivation for his genre bending is his own. His appropriation of a variety of words, of formal types of discourse, is not so much, as this essay originally suggested, a way of using a variety of forms to convey a message. Rather, the use of most of these forms suggests that none of them is adequate to speak of the Word incarnate. John's genre bending is an effort to force its audience away from words to an encounter with the Word himself.[35]

Genre is a rhetorical convention, but John does not confine his style to just one form because the subject matter for him is too great to be grappled with. Perhaps, he found none of them adequate, so he freely mingled many rhetorical conventions that were available to him in his persuasion strategy. The Gospel of John is therefore "genre bending" and defies category. But at the same time, John's Gospel is best understood within its own social, cultural, and literary milieu, because, according to C. John Collins, genre is a communicative and social act.[36] As such, various Old Testament literary poetics belonging to its narrative, poetry, and prophecy sections (categories into which all of Old Testament writings fall into) reveal together John's style most fittingly.

The term *poetics*, in this study, refers to the compositional artistry of a literary work. As Adele Berlin explained, poetics concerns "the building blocks of literature and the rules by which they are assembled."[37] In speaking of Old Testament poetics, this study aims at discovering how certain forms of the Old Testament texts work to produce meanings. Poetics of the Old Testament has been a subject of much investigation itself

---

35. Attridge, "Genre Bending in the Fourth Gospel," 21.

36. Recognizing that there is so much confusion about what genre is, C. John Collins, following Carolyn Miller, defined genre as "a social and communicative act, with its associated linguistic, rhetorical, and literary conventions and expectations." Collins, *Reading Genesis Well*, 48.

37. Berlin, *Poetics and Interpretation of Biblical Narrative*, 15. Structuralists, however, use the term in a more technical sense. For an example, see Funk, *Poetics of Biblical Narrative*, 5.

in recent decades through studies in classical rhetorical conventions and modern literary theories.

The best way to understand Old Testament poetics, however, is to pay close attention to the text itself. Several Old Testament scholars during last several decades have published important studies in understanding how biblical narrative and poetry work. Some of the notable ones are: Robert Alter's *The Art of Biblical Narrative* (1981; revised and updated edition in 2011) and *The Art of Biblical Poetry* (1985; revised and updated edition in 2011); Shimon Bar-Efrat's *Narrative Art in the Bible* (1989); Adele Berlin's *Poetics and Interpretation of Biblical Narrative* (1983); J. P. Fokkelman's *Reading Biblical Narrative* (1999) and *Reading Biblical Poetry* (2001); James L. Kugel's *The Idea of Biblical Poetry* (1981); and Meir Sternberg's *The Poetics of Biblical Narrative* (1987). Gleanings from these studies are invaluable in identifying the poetics of the Old Testament and using them to consider John's narrative art.

This study seeks to recognize the Old Testament poetics of (and the compositional artistry in) narrative, poetry, and prophecy. Poetry is usually terser and more elevated than prose,[38] and the prophets convey direct divine messages through unique speech forms. Although these are distinctive Old Testament forms, one should note that they often exist embedded within each other. Old Testament writers frequently mixed poetry and prose (narrative) styles, and prophetic writings make use of both poetry and narrative to deliver God's message.[39] For this reason, when this study considers all these forms collectively to examine John's style, it will illumine his literary style far better than any singular consideration.

Five chapters constitute the major part of this book. The first chapter provides the context for studying the literary art of the Gospel of John. The first part of this chapter discusses Meyer H. Abrams's four categories of critical theory and it shows their relations to the discussion of John's literary art. The following section traces the rise and development of major literary theories (rhetorical criticism, narrative criticism, structuralist criticism, reader-response criticism, and deconstructionist criticism) particularly in their applications to the

---

38. Kugel, *Idea of Biblical Poetry*, 69.

39. The distinction between poetry and prose, especially in the Prophets, is often problematic. For example, see Holladay, "Prototypes and Copies," 351–67. Narrative and poetry are difficult to separate in the Old Testament. For example, there are narrative poetry in passages such as Judges 5 and Psalm 105. Berlin, *Poetics and Interpretation*, 13.

Johannine study. While there are additional ways of reading the Gospel, they are not included in this chapter because they are more ideological than methodological in consideration.[40]

Chapter two establishes reasonable grounds for using Old Testament poetics in the study of the literary art of the Gospel of John. From the discussions of the first chapter, this chapter takes the position that the Scripture is a communication between the author and the audience and that it is through the medium of the text (whether heard or read) and it concerns God and his message. This chapter shows that the traditional apostolic authorship is defendable, both internally and externally, and such view of the authorship provides the ground for understanding the Gospel's Jewish poetics. This chapter then highlights the Jewishness of the Fourth Gospel in terms of its Semitisms, centrality of Hebrew Scripture, Jewish hermeneutics, and contents. Lastly, the discussion turns to the selected testimonies on the excellence of the Old Testament poetics throughout history.

Chapters three, four, and five constitute the main discussion of the Old Testament poetics and their application in the Gospel of John. Each of these chapters centers on one of the major forms of the Old Testament writings and they follow a similar format.

Chapter three focuses upon the poetics of Old Testament poetry. This chapter examines the major facets of Old Testament poetry (parallelism, repetition and variation, terseness, double meaning, and imagery) and shows how they are evident in the Fourth Gospel.

Chapter four looks into the poetics of Old Testament narratives. Statements about the narrative character of the Old Testament provide here a general context for the discussion of this chapter. The main section observes the Old Testament narrative poetics (point of view, character and characterization, plot, gaps and ambiguities, and narrative time) to show how John follows in the footsteps of the biblical narrators in telling his story. Additionally, insights from discourse analysis are supplemented here because (1) linguistic elements are crucial in shaping the narrative and (2) such techniques are similarly present in the Old Testament through the Hebrew language.

Chapter five deals with the poetics of prophetic writings of the Old Testament. With a general introduction for the writing prophets of the Old Testament, this chapter expounds the major areas of prophetic

---

40. Cf. Carter, "Ideological Readings of the Fourth Gospel," 203–19.

poetics. Since they were spokespersons for God, commissioned to the people to convict and persuade them, this chapter recognizes that rhetoric is an important element in the discussion of the prophetic discourses. This chapter examines several important elements in prophetic writings (word of the LORD, prophetic self-consciousness, prophetic persuasion, and prophetic mode of speaking) and shows how they are the defining characteristics of John's narrative voice.

1

Contextualizing the Literary Art of the Gospel of John

A STUDY OF THE literary art of the Fourth Gospel requires a proper context. *New Oxford American Dictionary* defines context as "the circumstances that form the setting for an event, statement, or idea, and in terms of which it can be fully understood and assessed."[1] In order that the nature of this study "be fully understood and assessed," one needs to relate it properly to pertinent areas that form its setting. A study in the literary art is best understood in relation to, and in comparison and contrast with, its proper contextual setting.

Critical Theories according to Meyer H. Abram's Four Categories

Meyer H. Abrams (1912–2015) is an American literary critic known for his study of the Romantic period in English literature and also as the general editor of *The Norton Anthology of English Literature* from 1962 to 2000. In his *The Mirror and the Lamp: Romantic Theory and the Critical Tradition* (1953), Abrams recognized that there are four elements in any work of art—artist, work, universe, and audience[2]—and classified

---

1. *New Oxford American Dictionary*, s.v. "Context."

2. Roman Jakobson also presented these four elements in his linguistic communication model. Jakobson, "Closing Statement," 350–77.

literary theories into four categories of mimetic, pragmatic, expressive, and objective theories. Literature always exists somewhere among these four coordinates, and, as Abrams noted, "any reasonably adequate theory takes some account of all four elements."[3] But the case is that, as it will be demonstrated below, many theories have the tendency to be given over to one theory at the expense of neglecting the others.

Mimetic Theory

According to Abrams, mimetic approach evaluates literature on how well it imitates the external world, or on how the two categories of imitation and external world are related to each other.[4] Plato (ca. 427–ca. 347 BC), often considered as the founder of western philosophy, engaged himself with matters of literary criticism and paid attention to this concept of imitation in literature. Since then, mimetic theory came to dominate literary criticism in the western world until the eighteenth century.[5]

Plato believed that poetry did not belong to art. By art he meant any skillful action or creation, such as what fishers, sculptors, or doctors do. Since poetry was a product of inspiration or "divine possession," he believed that it did not belong to the category of art. On the lips of Socrates in *Ion*, Plato said, "as the Corybantian revelers when they dance are not in their right mind, so the lyric poets are not in their right mind when they are composing their beautiful strains: but falling under the power of music and metre they are inspired and possessed."[6] Plato believed that poetry was an *imitation* of arts. He illustrated this idea from the example of a carpenter. A carpenter makes a bed or a table from the idea he has, and the artist who paints it is only copying the creation of the carpenter.[7] In like manner, he believed that poetry was twice removed from reality, and thus its importance is only secondary. Plato saw that the reality (idea) and the appearance of reality are different and believed that the poets are only imitators of the latter. It is noteworthy that Plato had the highest regard for truth. He did not place much value on Homer or Hesiod because of their fictiveness. If anything is to be beneficial in educating young men,

3. Abrams, *Mirror and the Lamp*, 6.
4. Abrams, *Mirror and the Lamp*, 8.
5. Adams and Searle, *Critical Theory Since Plato*, 8.
6. Plato, "Ion," 1:289.
7. Plato, "Republic," 1:852–55.

he believed that it had to be grounded in truth. Concerning Homer and Hesiod, he said that they have a "fault which is most serious . . . the fault of telling a lie, and, what is more, a bad lie."[8]

Aristotle (384–22 BC), on the other hand, did not see reality as external from material things and held that poets imitate reality itself in their literary creation. In *Poetics*, which is his extensive and probably most influential treatment of poetry, he treated poetry as an art, as he discussed the constituents of plot, characters, diction, thought, spectacle, and melody. He said that poetry imitates the actions of men and originates from the human nature that desires to imitate. He said: "The instinct of imitation is implanted in man from childhood, one difference between him and other animals being that he is the most imitative of living creatures, and through imitation learns his earliest lesson; and no less universal is the pleasure felt in things imitated."[9] For this reason, Aristotle attributed imitation as the essential characteristic of a poet,[10] and held a positive view on the function of poetry. In his view, poetry is beneficial because it describes what could happen, while history concerns itself with what already happened in the past. In other words, as the latter concerns singular incidents in history (singular in nature); the former, deals with what is philosophic and universal in nature because it describes what is possible.[11] According to Aristotle, what is important, therefore, is not just the exactness of the copy of the reality, but the production itself which serves to educate and benefits the readers.

Another important person in the discussion of mimetic theory is Erich Auerbach. In his book *Mimesis*, he traced the representation of reality in western literatures from the fourth century BC to the twenty-first century AD. Auerbach made keen observations on how literatures represented reality, and he is credited as bringing the literariness of Scripture to the forefront of biblical studies.[12] Among his discussions, the following

---

8. Plato, "Republic," 1:641. For a fuller discussion of Plato's mimetic theory, see: Melberg, "Plato's 'Mimesis,'" 10–50.

9. Aristotle, *Poet.*, 1448b. This observation of human desire for imitation paved the way for modern (theological) approach to mimetic theory, especially of French René Girard (1923–2015). Girard applied the literary concept of mimesis to anthropological understanding of human desire and violence. Kaplan, *René Girard*. For a bibliography of Girard's books and articles, see: Swartley, *Violence Renounced*, 321–22.

10. Aristotle, *Poet.*, 1448b.

11. Aristotle, *Poet.*, 1451.

12. Alter and Kermode, *Literary Guide to the Bible*, 4.

observations about the reality of Scripture provide important insights for the study of its literary art.

First, he made an important distinction between the fictive "make-believe" world of literature and scriptural reality. Pointing out that the Scripture was not created for "realism" but was "oriented toward truth," he said that without believing it, "it is impossible to put the narrative of it to the use for which it was written."[13] Auerbach articulated correctly the difference between fiction and Scripture. Clarence Walhout observed this point and said that the "authorial stance" makes all the difference in the distinction of fiction and history, because "the historian claims—asserts—that the projected world (the story) of the text . . . actually occurred."[14]

The second characteristic of scriptural mimesis, according to Auerbach, is its figurative interpretation of history. Observing this unique feature of Scripture, he said that "an occurrence on earth signifies not only itself but at the same time another, which it predicts or confirms, without prejudice to the power of its concrete reality here and now."[15] Scripture narrates countless stories through the span of millennia, but these stories are all connected to each other, with their significance for their own contexts. The divine sovereignty of God makes this kind of representation of reality possible, and this aspect of scriptural reality is what makes Scripture powerful and most effective for all generations. Some foreshadow and others fulfill while being true to the "concrete reality here and now."[16]

The third characteristic of the scriptural representation of reality is that it is "fraught with background." Auerbach said that Scripture has

> the externalization of only so much of the phenomena as is necessary for the purpose of the narrative, all else left in obscurity; the decisive points of the narrative alone are emphasized, what lies between is nonexistent . . . the whole, permeated with the most unrelieved suspense and directed toward a single goal (and to that extent far more of a unity), remains mysterious and "fraught with background."[17]

---

13. Auerbach, *Mimesis*, 11.
14. Thiselton and Walhout, *Responsibility of Hermeneutics*, 69.
15. Auerbach, *Mimesis*, 490.
16. Auerbach, *Mimesis*, 490.
17. Auerbach, *Mimesis*, 9.

On the contrary, Auerbach noted that Homer's style was an externalized and uniformly illuminated style. The unique power of scriptural representation of reality comes from this character of being "fraught with background." The writers of Scripture never convey reality through a uniform externalization, but embraces the "nonexisten[ces]" for a single purpose. Such gaps in Scripture are, therefore, normal and expected.

Pragmatic Theory

While mimetic theory emphasizes the relationship of the text to the reality, pragmatic theory focuses on the readers' association with the text. Abrams named this aspect "pragmatic," because this approach "looks at the work of art chiefly as a means to an end," and considers the author "from the point of view of the powers and training he must have in order to achieve this end."[18] Although mimetic theory of literature held dominance in literary criticism from Plato to the eighteenth century, the pragmatic view of the text was never absent. The idea that poetry must delightfully and effectively instruct the hearers was always present.

Plato's rejection of false stories was based on his recognition that the poetry must have positive effects upon the hearers.[19] Aristotle recognized that acts of imitation are pleasant, even when the objects of imitation are not pleasant. He held this view because "it is not the object itself which here gives delight" but it is the audience who "draws inferences" and learns from them.[20] Horace (65–68 BC) said that "It is not enough that poems be showy and beautiful; they should also be affecting and interesting, and should carry away the mind of the auditor wherever they wish."[21] A writer known as "Longinus" also stated that sublime poetry "transports" the audience.[22] These classical writers placed importance on the *function* of poetry to affect and instruct the readers. The craft of the poetry had to fulfill this purpose.

In *An Apology for Poetry*, Sir Philip Sidney (1554–1586) held this affective (pragmatic) purpose of poetry and said that the final goal of poetry is to "lead and draw us to as high a perfection as our degenerate

---

18. Abrams, *Mirror and the Lamp*, 15.
19. Plato, "Republic," 641–43.
20. Aristotle, *Rhet.*, 1371b.
21. Horace, *Art of Poetry*, 18.
22. Longinus, "On the Sublime," 125.

souls, made worse by their clay-lodgings, can be capable of."[23] The poet accomplishes this goal by *delighting* the mind because without it, he reasoned, men "would fly as from an stranger."[24] James Beattie (1735–1803) recognized that pleasing is an end of poetry, but the purpose is to instruct, because pleasing without instruction is, he reasoned, most dangerous and poisonous because of its "alluring qualities."[25] Richard Hurd (1720–1808), however, made a decisive break in the theory of literature as he held a hedonistic view that instruction is a means for pleasure and that poetry is "the art of treating any subject in such a way as is found most delightful to us."[26]

The emphasis on the art's aesthetic effect upon the observers reached its height in the eighteenth century with Immanuel Kant's *Critique of Judgment*. Although others have already noted the concept of aesthetics before,[27] the idea reached its full maturity in Kant's *Critique*. Kant believed that there are three elements that give satisfaction: "pleasure," "beautiful," and "good." He believed that pleasure and good are attached to purposes, but said that beautiful is completely free. Art may be beautiful with no other ends attached to it. Recognizing something as beautiful, he said, "I am concerned, not with that in which I depend on the existence of the object, but with that which I make out of this representation in myself."[28] With this concept, the reader's role in the evaluation of literature becomes most important. His theory of beauty as autonomous and as the end in itself without any external attachment paved the way for the objectivist's view of literature. What is beautiful is a "disinterested satisfaction,"[29] and it is not subjected to any other objective end.

Walter Pater (1839–1994) carried this concept of beautiful to the extreme. In the Preface to *Studies in the History of the Renaissance*, he expressed his radical view:

> What effect does it really produce on me? Does it give me pleasure? . . . He who experiences these impressions strongly, and drives directly at the analysis and discrimination of them, need

23. Sidney et al., *Defence of Poesie*, 25.
24. Sidney et al., *Defence of Poesie*, 23.
25. Beattie, *Essays on Poetry and Music*, 9.
26. Hurd, *Dissertation on the Idea of Universal Poetry*, 28.
27. Hammermeister, *German Aesthetic Tradition*, 3–20.
28. Kant, *Critique of Judgment*, 47.
29. Kant, *Critique of Judgment*, 55.

> not trouble himself with the abstract question what beauty is in itself, or its exact relation to truth or experience—metaphysical questions, as unprofitable as metaphysical questions elsewhere. He may pass them all by as being, answerable or not, of no interest to him.[30]

This position that dismisses truth from the text alienates the readers from what the text purposed in the first place and introduces extreme subjectivism in approaching the text. The reader no longer stands bound to any obligations, but is freed to experience at his will. In another place, Pater expressed his subjective view of literature and stated it in this way:

> At first sight experience seems to bury us under a flood of external objects, pressing upon us with a sharp importunate reality, calling us out of ourselves in a thousand forms of action. But when reflection begins to act upon those objects . . . each object is loosed into a group of impressions—color, odor, texture—in the mind of the observer . . . Every one of those impressions is the impression of the individual in his isolation, each mind keeping as a solitary prisoner its own dream of a world.[31]

I. A. Richards, asking the critical question of what is the value of arts, made the criticism that the aesthetic approach's serious defect is its avoidance of the consideration of value. He said, "The fact that some of the experiences to which the arts give rise are valuable and take the form they do because of their value is not irrelevant."[32] When the experience with the text is reduced only to the impressions of color, odor, and texture, or only to what is sensually beautiful—with the result that it presents its world as independent, complete, and autonomous detached from reality—then the communicative purpose of the text is lost. Pragmatic theory originally concerned art as a means of achieving other purpose, but the theory gradually came to embrace pleasure as its chief end. In like manner, dismissing the truth of Scripture and focusing on how it pleases leads the reader to a dangerous priority of personal experience.

---

30. Pater, *Studies in the History of the Renaissance*, viii.
31. Pater, *Studies in the History of the Renaissance*, 208–9.
32. Richards, *Principles of Literary Criticism*, 11.

Expressive Theory

Expressive theory pays attention to how the authors expressed their personalities in the text. According to Abrams, expressive theory defines poetry as "the overflow, utterance, or projection of the thought and feelings of the poet."[33] Hazard Adams noted that, throughout history, very little attention was on the author's individuality "as something to be conveyed by a literary work," and "there was hardly, if any, interest in the idea that writers had personalities to express."[34]

William Wordsworth (1770–850), in his Preface to the second edition of *Lyrical Ballads*, emphasized the individuality of the poet in the creation of poetry. He said:

> He is a man speaking to men: a man, it is true, endowed with more lively sensibility, more enthusiasm and tenderness, who has a greater knowledge of human nature, and a more comprehensive soul, than are supposed to be common among mankind; a man pleased with his own passions and volitions, and who rejoices more than other men in the spirit of life that is in him; delighting to contemplate similar volitions and passions as manifested in the goings-on of the universe, and habitually impelled to create them where he does not find them.[35]

Mimetic theory focuses on the external world as the source of poetic activities. Wordsworth, however, brought the attention to the man who is the center of his poetic creativity. He is "endowed with more lively sensibility" and has greater understanding of humanity. He delights in seeing the world with the same passion that stirs his heart, and as such, he is impelled to create the same where he does not find them. With Wordsworth, the importance is not on the external reality, but on the internal contemplative power that gives importance to it. The poet, therefore, is not as calculative of the aesthetic effects on the audience as the pragmatic theory holds; but he is rather spontaneous with powerful feelings, comparable to Longinus's view of sublimity. The emphasis, therefore, centers on the sincerity of the writer, and with him, literature began to be regarded as a window into the heart and soul of the writer.[36]

---

33. Abrams, *Mirror and the Lamp*, 22.
34. Adams, *Critical Theory*, 2.
35. Wordsworth and Coleridge, *Lyrical Ballads*, xxviii.
36. Adams, *Critical Theory*, 23.

This observation of Wordsworth signaled a shift in English criticism from mimetic and pragmatic theories to expressive theory.[37] John Stuart Mill took Wordsworth's view of poetry and developed it into a full-scale Romanticism. He stated that poetry is "the expression of uttering forth of feeling."[38] According to Mill, the interest of a poet is not in the exact representation of the truth, but in painting the truth with imageries, as the observation excites in him certain feelings. He argued that human emotions must paint the truth: "If the human emotion be not painted with the most scrupulous truth, the poetry is bad poetry, i.e. is not poetry at all, but a failure."[39]

Mill placed so much emphasis on poet's expression of personality that the audience disappeared from his view. He said poetry is a "soliloquy" speaking "itself to itself in moments of solitude," and that the audience simply *overhears* what the poet expresses to himself.[40] The poet should have no consciousness of the audience at all, and in such absence of concerns for the audience the poet expresses well. Just as an actor would act poorly if he is overly conscious of the audience, the poet expresses himself best when he excludes from his work "every vestige of such lookings-forth into the outward and everyday world."[41] The purpose of literature, according to Mill, was expressing oneself, regardless of the accuracy of the representation or the effectiveness for the audience. In this way, romanticism truly broke away from the concerns of literary criticism in the history of the Western world.

Although Mill's view is perhaps too radical, the expressive theory of literature in general rightly emphasized the role of the writer in the act of communication. Through deep meditations and reflections, the language of John truly soars into the heights of heaven and pulsates with powerful feelings that are divinely inspired. Wordsworth's observation about the nature of poetry opens a window into the meditative style of John. He said:

> For our continued influxes of feeling are modified and directed by our thoughts, which are indeed the representatives of all our past feelings; and, as by contemplating the relation of these general representatives to each other, we discover what is really

---

37. Abrams, *Mirror and the Lamp*, 22.
38. Gibbs, *Early Essays by John Stuart Mill*, 208.
39. Gibbs, *Early Essays by John Stuart Mill*, 207.
40. Gibbs, *Early Essays by John Stuart Mill*, 208–9.
41. Gibbs, *Early Essays by John Stuart Mill*, 209.

important to men, so, by the repetition and continence of this act, our feelings will be connected with important subjects, till at length . . . we shall describe objects, and utter sentiments, of such a nature, and in such connection with each other, that the understanding of the reader . . . must necessarily be in some degree enlightened, and his affections ameliorated.[42]

The Gospel of John is not a mere representation of historical truth; it is colored by the author's inspired heart. In that sense, it is an "impassioned truth."[43]

One the other hand, it is foreign to the scriptural concept that it is "the feeling . . . [which] gives importance to the action and situation, and not the action and situation to the feeling."[44] Scriptural truths moved the apostle to write, and not his ingenuity. John is not speaking "soliloquy;" he is thoroughly intentional and pragmatic in his representation of truths. The Gospel of John is the product of a divinely inspired mind, and inspiration guarantees its historical veracity and persuasiveness.

Objective Theory

Kant's treatment of beauty as "disinterested" of any purpose inevitably gave way to an objective theory of literature. Objective theory sees literary work as serving no other ends, but as a "self-sufficient entity constituted by its parts in their internal relations, and sets out to judge it solely by criteria intrinsic to its own mode of being."[45] Samuel Taylor Coleridge (1772–1834), a towering figure in literary criticism, reflected on Kant's idea of beauty and said, "The sense of beauty subsists in simultaneous intuition of the relation of parts, each to each, and of all to a whole: exciting an immediate and absolute complacency, without intervention, therefore, of any interest, sensual or intellectual."[46]

Coleridge believed that beauty comes from the unity of its parts, or from "multeity in unity."[47] Readers perceive beauty when the object is

---

42. Wordsworth, *Lyrical Ballads*, xi–xii.
43. Gibbs, *Early Essays by John Stuart Mill*, 207.
44. Wordsworth, *Lyrical Ballads*, xiv.
45. Abrams, *Mirror and the Lamp*, 26. According to Abrams, such an approach was already present in Aristotle's view of tragedy, but emerged as an all-inclusive approach in the late eighteenth and early nineteenth centuries.
46. Coleridge, "Essays on the Principles of Genial Criticism," 378.
47. Coleridge, "Essays on the Principles of Genial Criticism," 372.

harmonious in the relation of its parts. The objectivist view of literature amplified this emphasis on the holistic approach to literature. Coleridge also believed that beauty comes when there is no interference of "any interest, sensual or intellectual."[48] He argued this point with the analogy of pure crystal. He said that "the crystal is lost in the light, which yet it contains, embodies, and gives a shape to."[49] Just as Kant argued, Coleridge believed what is beautiful must not be affected by any interest. In this way, the objective theory does not regard meaning as related to any external interests, whether they are ideas, authors, or readers. The text creates meaning only as its parts interrelate with each other.

T. S. Eliot (1888–1965) reacted against the prevalent Romantic idea of literature in his day. Contrary to Wordsworth and Mill, he rejected emotionalism and spontaneity as the highest components in literature. He contended that a great poet is one who has the critical ability to funnel all available elements through his mind. The importance is not on the intensity of the emotion, but the "intensity of artistic process" of the mind.[50]

With this emphasis on the rational activity of the mind, Eliot argued that a literary work is not "individual" to the writer, contrary to the romantic view. He criticized the tendency of his day to praise a poet on account of his individuality. He said, "No poet, no artist of any art, has his complete meaning alone. His significance, his appreciation is the appreciation of his relation to the dead poets and artists."[51] In this way, therefore, Eliot pointed out that art is only a compendium of the past, and the poet stands in the tradition of the "dead poets."

The end of poetry, he argued, is itself and does not exist apart from itself; it is "autotelic."[52] It is this autonomous view of literature that anticipated Russian Formalism and American New Criticism. With this concept of literature, René Wellek and Austin Warren, in a popular textbook on literary theory, stated that the attention on the author is "quite mistaken," and that the meaning of a work of art "is not exhausted by, or even equivalent to, its intention."[53] William K. Wimsatt and Monroe C. Beardsley in "The Intentional Fallacy" similarly attacked authorial intent,

---

48. Coleridge, "Essays on the Principles of Genial Criticism," 377.
49. Coleridge, "Essays on the Principles of Genial Criticism," 377.
50. Eliot, "Tradition and the Individual Talent," 8.
51. Eliot, "Tradition and the Individual Talent," 4.
52. Eliot, "Function of Criticism," 19.
53. Wellek and Warren, *Theory of Literature*, 42.

and said that "the design or intention of the author is neither available nor desirable as a standard for judging the success of a work of literary art."[54] In this way, literary scholars began to view literature as an art form, and divorced it from anything external.

In biblical exegesis, however, readers must approach the Scripture as a communication, and not as an art form. The text is the foundation of communication where the author anticipates the audience and the audience comes to experience the world of the author. Therefore, one cannot detach the author from the text he created. The author, reader, text, and the referred world are all important elements in the creation and the communication of the message. Scripture cannot stand "autotelic" as other literature, because behind the text stands the ultimate Author who desires to communicate with the readers through the medium of the text about the unseen spiritual realities. Literary critics in history highlighted various aspects of communication in literature, and it is still important to maintain a balance in one's approach to the text. Many of the modern literary theories however lack this balance, and the discussion now turns to that subject.

Modern Literary Theories

The second sphere of contextualization for the literary art of John's Gospel is modern literary theories. This discussion is more significant than the previous one due to its immediate application to the Johannine study in what is overwhelmingly diverse choice.[55] Biblical scholars since the Enlightenment have focused their attention on historical-critical inquiries. With the rise of rationalism, scholars carried rigorous scientific investigations to discover the authors behind the texts in order to find their relationships with the texts. Source criticism asked questions about the kind of sources writers might have used. Form criticism asked questions about the oral period and the specific life situation of the communities supposedly responsible for certain forms of the text. Redaction criticism argued for author's role as the editor of his sources.

Biblical scholarship generally regards the biblical text as representing reality. In a way, historical criticism was an endeavor to reconstruct the reality through the text. In searching through the text, historical

---

54. Wimsatt and Beardsley, "Intentional Fallacy," 468.
55. Aichele and Bible and Culture Collective, *Postmodern Bible*.

critic's task was to discover the original situation and possibly the original form of the text. However, in its search for reality through the origins of the text, historical criticism failed to grasp reality by radical denials of the text itself. Norman R. Peterson stated the situation:

> In its quest for the earliest and best evidence for events referred to in biblical narrative, historical criticism defaulted on its own first principle, which holds that a text is first and foremost evidence for the time of writing. Redaction criticism sought to remedy this situation and in its failure showed that literary issues are bound up with the first principle: The text itself must be comprehended in its own terms before we can ask of what it is evidence, whether in relation to the time of writing or in relation to the events referred to in it.[56]

These preoccupations with composition theories, however, gradually began to give way in the last quarter of the twentieth century to methods that approach the text as literary whole. Both conservative and liberal scholarship welcomed this radical turn (although not without caution), and applauded it as a paradigm shift.[57] Concerning this change, John D. Crossman declared that "we are now into a situation analogous to the period in which the historical-critical vision first erupted into biblical studies. In other words, a second revolution is upon us."[58] Multiple methodologies represent this shift but the common facet that unites all under this movement is the *synchronic* reading of the text. Historical criticism approached the text diachronically with attention to the development of the text over time, but literary scholars who espoused this new approach had no such interest.

The impetus for this shift came in part from a distrust in historical criticism to provide meaningful aid in understanding the text. While scholars dissected the text microscopically to search for answers behind the text, the text itself became neglected. This autopsy of the text, or "excavative"[59] campaign for the text, failed to render meaningful asssitance to interpretation. Concerning historical criticism, Sternberg remarked that "rarely has there been such a futile expense of spirit in

---

56. Peterson, *Literary Criticism for New Testament Critics*, 20.

57. Culler, *Structuralist Poetics*, 99; Fishbane, "Recent Work on Biblical Narrative," 99; and Ryken, "Bible as Literature," 3–15. Weima, "Literary Criticism," 150.

58. Crossan, "'Ruth amid the Alien Corn,'" 199.

59. Alter, *Art of Biblical Narrative*, 14; cf. 15, 56; see also Alter, *World of Biblical Literature*, 133.

a noble cause; rarely have so many worked so long and so hard with so little to show for their trouble. Not even the widely accepted constructs of geneticism, like the Deuteronomist, lead an existence other than speculative."[60] The time was ripe to welcome holistic approach to the biblical text, and what mattered now was the reading strategy. It is a positive change that the emphasis is now shifted more or less to 'how to read the Bible,' and its fruit is seen in such publications as the *How to Read* Series by Tremper Longman III[61] and the *Reading the Bible as Literature* Series by Leland Ryken.[62]

However, as it will show below, the cross-disciplinary application of modern literary theories on Scripture was not without problem. The paradigm has shifted from history to literature,[63] suggesting implementations of multiple methodologies, but what remained unchanged, as it seems, is the doubt regarding the authority of the text. The older methodologies questioned it on the ground of textual disruption, and the new ones underrate it by justifying all kinds of reading constructs.

With greater precisions, Scripture is put under critical paradigms. Certain exciting vistas are gained and new possibilities are opened up; but as one follows down the trail, incongruities, as demonstrated below, vex the traveler. The "literary guide" often confuses and misleads the inquiring; so perhaps, what Richards described of literary theories as early as 1930 still rings true today: "The modern student, surveying the field and noting the simplicity of the task [of literary criticism] attempted and the fragments of work achieved, may reasonably wonder what has been and is amiss."[64]

Scripture is a type of literature, and it welcomes literary examination. Men wrote the Bible so that people would read, understand, enjoy, and learn. However, it is not on the same plane as other literatures because Scripture testifies that God is the ultimately responsible author for its production (2 Tim 3:16). This is a fact that no other literature can

---

60. Sternberg, *Poetics*, 13.

61. Longman, *How to Read Genesis*; Longman, *How to Read Exodus*; Longman, *How to Read the Psalms*; Longman, *How to Read Proverbs*; Walton and Longman, *How to Read Job*; and Longman, *How to Read Daniel*.

62. Ryken, *How Bible Stories Work*; Ryken, *Short Sentences Long Remembered*; Ryken, *Sweeter than Honey*; Ryken, *Jesus the Hero*; Ryken, *Symbols and Reality*; Ryken, *Letters of Grace and Beauty*.

63. Thiselton, *Thiselton on Hermeneutics*, 610.

64. Richards, "Chaos of Critical Theories," 5.

claim, and much more weight should be given to this consideration. Just as Northrop Frye remarked, the Bible "is as literary as it can well be without actually being literature."[65] For this reason, one must evaluate contemporary literary approaches according to their methodological validities.

Rhetorical Criticism

Rhetorical criticism is the study of examining how the text achieves its persuasive goal, and, for this reason, it falls under the category of pragmatic theory. Rhetoric signifies an art of communication in the classical sense. Rhetoric as an art probably originated sometime during the fifth century BC, but Aristotle in the fourth century BC fully developed it as a system.[66] He defined rhetoric as "the faculty of discovering the possible means of persuasion in reference to any subject whatever,"[67] and said that there are three means of persuasion: *ethos*, the character of the speaker; *pathos*, the emotional state of the hearer; and *logos*, the argument itself.

Rhetorical criticism in the modern era, however, encompasses a broader scope. In his 1969 presidential address to the Soceity of Biblical Literature (and published afterward as "Form Criticism and Beyond"), James Muilenburg called for scholars to go beyond the the form criticism. While recognizing the substantial gains made through the study of literary types, he warned against too exclusive employment of form-critical methods because "there are other features in the literary compositions which lie beyond the province of the *Gattungsforscher*."[68] Countering the opinion that Hebrew writers paid no attention to literary considerations, he said the Old Testament is a literature of a very high quality, and therefore, "a responsible and proper articulation of the words in their linguistic paterns and in their precise formulations will reveal to us the texture and fabric of the writer's thought, not only what it is that he thinks, but as

---

65. Frye, *Great Code*, 62.

66. Cf. Cole, *Origins of Rhetoric in Ancient Greece*, 2. For ancient theories of rhetoric, see Benson and Prosser, *Readings in Classical Rhetoric*; and Kennedy, *Art of Persuasion in Greece*.

67. Aristotle, *Rhet.*, 1355b.

68. Muilenburg, "Form Criticism and Beyond," 6.

he thinks it."[69] Therefore, he saw the benefits of doing stylistic studies in the Old Testament and labled such as the "rhetorical criticism." He said:

> What I am interested in, above all, is in understanding the nature of Hebrew literary composition, in exhibiting the structural patterns that are employed for the fashioning of a literary unit, whether in poetry or in prose, and in discerning the many and various devices by which the predications are formulated and ordered into a unified whole. Such an enterprise I should describe as rhetoric and the methodology as rhetorical criticism.[70]

The task of the rhetorical critic, then, is to define the limits of literary units, identify formal rhetorical devices, and to grasp the writer's intent and meaning.

Such study of the literary convention of the writer was well within the classical rhetorical system. Rhetoric was not a unified system in antiquity, and rather than being an art of communication exclusively, as Phyllis Trible pointed out, Isocrates and the Sophists studied rhetoric as an art of composition also and Quintilian and the church fathers approached rhetoric in the same manner.[71]

In the New Testament, a classic rhetoric scholar George Kennedy brought the insights of Greco-Roman rhetoric to the interpretation of the New Testament. His aim was to provide an additional tool of interpretation to complement the historical criticisms, and because rhetoric is the art of persuasion, Kennedy saw its validity for the interpretation of the New Testament. In his *New Testament Interpretation through Rhetorical Criticism* (1984), he argued that since the writers of the New Testament had a message to convey and sought to persuade the audience, "as such they are rhetorical, and their methods can be studied by the discipline of rhetoric."[72] The evangelists and Paul must have been familiar with the rhetorical conventions of the time, if not studied them formally. Rhetoric may be colored by the traditions and conventions of the society, but, Kennedy argued, it is a universal phenomenon that reveal the basic workings of human heart. Therefore, what Aristotle described was not just Greek rhetoric, but the "universal facet of human communication," and the categories he identified are "intended to exhaust the possibilities, though the

---

69. Muilenburg, "Form Criticism and Beyond," 7.
70. Muilenburg, "Form Criticism and Beyond," 8.
71. Trible, *Rhetorical Criticism*, 32.
72. Kennedy, *New Testament Interpretation*, 3.

examples of them which he gives are drawn from the specific practice of a Greek city state."[73]

Because Greek rhetoric captured the universal facet of human communication, Kenney believed that

> It is perfectly possible to utilize the categories of Aristotelian rhetoric to study speech in China, India, Africa, and elsewhere in the world, cultures much more different from the Greek than was that of Palestine in the time of the Roman empire. What is unique about Greek rhetoric, and what makes it useful for criticism, is the degree to which it was conceptualized. The Greeks gave name to rhetorical techniques, many of which are found all over the world. What we mean by classical rhetorical theory is this structured system which describes the universal phenomenon of rhetoric in Greek terms . . . Though the Jews of the pre-Christian era seem never to have conceptualized rhetoric to any significant degree, the importance of speech among them is everywhere evident in the Old Testament, and undoubtedly they learned its techniques by imitation. In understanding how their rhetoric worked we have little choice but to employ the concepts and terms of the Greeks."[74]

Particularly important for Kennedy's work was the identification of three species of rhetoric: judicial, deliberative, and epideictic: "The species is judicial when the author is seeking to persuade the audience to make a judgment about events ocurring in the past; it is deliberative when he seeks to persuade them to take some action in the future; it is epideictic when he seeks to persaude them to hold or reaffirm some point of view in the present, as when he celebrates or denounces some person or some quality."[75] He applied the theory to the Pauline epistles and tested it on the other sections of the Gospels as well.

The New Testament scholar Ben Witherington III saw rhetoric as "the art of persuasion used from the time of Aristotle onwards through and beyond the NT era," and argued for its applicability in the New Testament because of its oral culture.[76] He showed that there are five structural elements in Greek rhetoric: (1) The *exordium* begins the discourse preparing the audience; (2) The *narratio* explains the nature of the disputed

---

73. Kennedy, *New Testament Interpretation*, 10.

74. Kennedy, *New Testament Interpretation*, 10–11.

75. Kennedy, *New Testament Interpretation*, 19.

76. Witherington, *New Testament Rhetoric*, ix, 1–9.

matter or the facts that are relevant to the discussion; (3) The *propositio* is the thesis statement that usually follows the *narratio*; (4) The *probatio* enumerates the arguments for the proposition; and (5) the *peroratio* sums up or amplifies some major argument and makes the final appeal.[77] He then argued that the writers of the New Testament were aware of the Greek rhetoric and applied it to Mark, Luke, Acts, and the Pauline and the General epistles.

In the area of the Fourth Gospel, C. Clifton Black discussed the rhetorical grandeur of John in chapters 14–17 and made observations of how his style—especially amplification, repetition, and variation—resembles what Greek rhetoricians used and taught.[78] Bruce W. Longenecker examined the transition markers as key rhetorical components—which Quintilian and Lucian highly praised—and observed their presence and significance in John.[79] Frank Thielman explained perplexing features of John's Gospel, such as its grammar and seeming disarrangements, as rhetorical elements present in the lofty and mysterious religious discourses of the Greco-Roman world.[80] Tom Thatcher said that John's narrative style is according to the rhetorical "mnemotechnique" of Cicero, Quintilian, and *Ad Herennium*.[81] In addition to these works, others have variously applied the principles of classic rhetoric to the Gospel of John.[82]

Although rhetorical criticism made significant contributions to the studies of New Testament epistles,[83] it did not leave a lasting impact upon the study of the Gospels. Black observed this situation and said, "In the twenty-four years since publication of *New Testament Interpretation through Rhetorical Criticism*, astonishingly few interpreters of the gospels have followed the markers laid down by Kennedy."[84] Then he shared an insight as to why rhetorical criticism is methodologically inadequate:

77. Witherington, *New Testament Rhetoric*, 16.
78. Black, "'Words That You Gave,'" 220–39.
79. Longenecker, *Rhetoric at the Boundaries*.
80. Thielman, "Style of the Fourth Gospel," 169–83.
81. Thatcher, "John's Memory Theater," 487–505.
82. George, *Reading the Tapestry*; Stube, *Graeco-Roman Rhetorical Reading*.
83. Cf. Watson, *Rhetoric of the New Testament*.
84. Black, "Kennedy and the Gospels," 68. Since this observation, however, a few more monographs brought rhetorical criticism to the Fourth Gospel: Myers, *Characterizing Jesus*; Parsenios, *Rhetoric and Drama*; Wright, *Rhetoric and Theology*. For a general introduction to rhetorical criticism of the New Testament, see: Black, *Rhetoric of the Gospel*, 2–21.

"The gospels are complex amalgams of many different genres... that resist uniform analysis."[85]

Contrary to Kenney's opinion that Greek rhetoric systematized the universal facet of communication, Carol S. Lipson and Roberta A. Binkley argued that the Aristotelian system does not represent all the rhetorical systems preceding it. They said:

> Some of these early cultures themselves thrived for 2,500 years or longer prior to the Greeks. It's difficult to believe that these cultures could have sustained their longevity and power without well-honed understandings of how to communicate... If we begin the discussion of rhetorical history with the Greeks, we lose much of our ability to see the early rhetorics, and especially to *see* the early history of rhetoric as culturally situated and embedded.[86]

Kenney saw that the classic rhetoric encaptured all the communication art of all cultures, but it is difficult to accept this to be the case. It is not difficult to show that much is lost during the transition from one culture to the other, and each has its own particularities.[87] While Kennedy made a lasting contribution for the study of New Testament letters and speeches, the narrative devices of the Gospels cannot be fully exhausted by the Aristotelian rhetorical system. What Kenney himself recognized is perhaps a useful guide in searching for the proper background for John's literary style: "If rhetorical criticism is to be valid, it must be practiced with some awareness of the traditions of Jewish speech, of which chiasmus is one, and if it is to be useful it must embrace more than style... The ultimate goal of rhetorical analysis, briefly put, is the discovery of the author's intent and of how that is transmitted through a text to an audience."[88]

Narrative Criticism

Narrative criticism in biblical studies is a text-oriented approach to Scripture, originating in the methodological considerations of Russian

---

85. Black, "Kennedy and the Gospels," 70. This observation agrees with Attridge's statement that the Fourth Gospel is "genre bending." Attridge, "Genre Bending in the Fourth Gospel," 18.

86. Lipson and Binkley, *Rhetoric Before and Beyond the Greeks*, 3.

87. Especially see the discussions of the Neo-Assyrian, ancient Egyptian, Chinese, biblical, and alternative Greek rhetorics in Lipson and Binkley, *Rhetoric Before and Beyond the Greeks*, 65–196.

88. Kennedy, *New Testament Interpretation*, 12.

Formalism and American New Criticism. Narrative criticism, a term coined by David Rhoads, concerned the investigation of the "formal features of narrative in the texts of the gospels, features which include aspects of the story-world of the narrative and the rhetorical techniques employed to tell the story."[89] The basic assumption of this approach is the integrity of the text as a unified whole. Rhoads stated that the Gospels are "of remarkably whole cloth: the narrator maintains a unifying point of view; the standards of judgment are uniform; the plot is coherent; the characters are introduced and developed with consistency; stylistic patterns persist through the story; and there is satisfying overall rhetorical effect."[90] In narrative criticism, biblical scholars appropriate various storytelling techniques of the novelists.[91]

Narrative critics observe three elements of communication in the story—the storyteller, the story, and the audience; however, they take a radically different approach to these elements.[92] The most distinctive element of narrative criticism is its view of author and reader. Narrative critics make the distinction among the real author, implied author, and narrator, and among the real reader, implied reader, and narratee. The real author is the historical person who is responsible for the composition; the implied author is the version of the author the text projects, and the narrator is the voice through which the implied author tells the story.[93] Narrative critics then make these distinctions on the readers similarly: the real reader is the historical original audience, the implied reader is what the text itself envisions and constructs as the reader, and the narratee is the discrete person the narrator addresses directly.[94] In narrative criticism, the real author and real reader are unimportant, because they stand outside the text. Because the readers perceive only a "version" of the author, the projected image of the author by the narrator "may not

---

89. Rhoads, "Narrative Criticism and the Gospel of Mark," 411–12.

90. Rhoads, "Jesus and the Syrophoenician Woman in Mark," 343.

91. For a full discussion of these techniques, see Booth, *Rhetoric of Fiction*; Chatman, *Story and Discourse*.

92. For the relationship of these different elements in a story, see Culpepper, *Anatomy*, 6.

93. Booth, *Rhetoric of Fiction*, 67–73.

94. Staley, *Print's First Kiss*, 30–37. Jeffrey Lloyd Staley focused on the implied reader in interpreting the Fourth Gospel.

conform to the identity of the real author at all."[95] With such a view on the real author and real reader, historical references become unnecessary.

Culpepper's *Anatomy of the Fourth Gospel: A Study in Literary Design* was enormously important in Johannine studies.[96] Applying the theoretical model of Seymour Chatman in *Story and Discourse: Narrative Structure in Fiction and Film* (1980), he succeeded in tilting the scale in favor of seeing the Gospel as a literary whole. Rather than inquiring into the speculative history of the text, Culpepper effectively argued to approach the text as a closed system of meaning. His narrative approach to the Gospel—especially his observations on the point of view, narrative time, plot, characterizations, and authorial comments—opened up exciting possibilities in understanding the Gospel's message. Tom Thatcher observed that

> the most enduring contribution of *Anatomy of the Fourth Gospel* rose from the point where the book diverged most sharply from the mainstream of its day: the thesis that John's story is *inherently meaningful*, regardless of its sources, composition history, or historical value. At a time when scholars were deeply absorbed in speculations about literary sources, the Johannine community, and the number of revisions leading up to the present text, Culpepper boldly declared that a close reading of the Gospel of John as a unified narrative could produce striking new insights.[97]

It must be pointed out, however, that the strength of Culpepper's narrative criticism became its serious weakness. While applying the rhetoric of fiction into biblical studies has certainly brought new insights into how narratives work, this methodology seriously undermined the referential function of the text as pointing to reality. Culpupper was aware of this danger of treating the gospel as a fiction, but rather than addressing the issue, he argued that "Scripture must be studied with the same methods

---

95. Booth, *Rhetoric of Fiction*, 70–71; Culpepper, *Anatomy*, 6.

96. Before Culpepper, Birger Olsson was reluctant to concentrate on the external situations of the text in the interpretation of the Fourth Gospel. Instead, he sought to discover the internal (textual) criteria for interpretation through his text-linguistic analysis applied to John 2:1–11 and 4:1–42. He identified different statement units in the text and analyzed them in terms of terminal features, spatial features, logical features, roles of participants, informative flow, point of view, etc. Olsson, *Structure and Meaning*.

97. Thatcher, "Anatomies of the Fourth Gospel," 1.

that are applied to the study of 'secular' literature."[98] According to him, the importance of the text lies in the fact that it reveals something about the real world of the reader and not the reality of the world of the text. He contended that the "text is therefore a mirror in which readers can 'see' the world in which they live. Its meaning . . . lies on this side of the text, between the reader and the text."[99]

Anthony Thiselton addressed this hermeneutical issue: "Holy Spirit communicates a life-changing word from 'Beyond.' The word of Scripture is . . . no merely passive 'mirror' of prior or private prejudices."[100] Kevin J. Vanhoozer criticized the postmodern move to see "texts" as simply mirrors when he said: "Truth is no longer the deliverance of the priest who handles revelation, nor of the teacher who has mastered reason; truth is rather the creation of the artist. The world is a picnic to which the interpreter brings the meaning. Language is the means humans use creatively to colonize a meaningless world."[101] When the text is perceived as a mirror without a reality behind it, it only becomes "an echo chamber in which we see ourselves and hear our own voices."[102]

Murray Krieger also recognized this problematic tendency inherent in the New Criticism and proposed that the text sould be seen as a "set of mirrors that miraculously becomes a window again after all."[103] The language must not be a sign or a substance exclusive of each other, but both at the same time, because "word and World . . . are one."[104] Readers should never separate the word and the world, for the word represents the world, and the world is the substance of the word.

Because of following the narratology of fiction, Culpepper, for example, over-complicated the issue of authorship. According to him, the Beloved Disciple is the narrator's "idealized characterization of an

---

98. Culpepper, *Anatomy*, 10. Culpepper, however, showed that the concern of literary criticism is not historicity: "Our effort to set aside interest in the Johannine community or the historical Jesus should not be interpreted as a denial of any historical core or matrix of the gospel. Once the effort has been made to understand the narrative character of the gospels, some rapprochement with the traditional, historical issues will be necessary." Culpepper, *Anatomy*, 11.

99. Culpepper, *Anatomy*, 5.

100. Thiselton, *Thiselton on Hermeneutics*, 627.

101. Vanhoozer, *Meaning in This Text?*, 21.

102. Vanhoozer, *Meaning in This Text?*, 24.

103. Krieger, *Window to Criticism*, 3.

104. Krieger, *Window to Criticism*, 6.

historical figure" and the narrator at the end "finally identifies, or better, characterizes the implied author as the Beloved Disciple."[105] Following Wayne Booth, he argued that the implied author is the literary image of the artist: "This implied author is always distinct from the 'real man'—whatever we may take him to be—who creates a superior version of himself, a 'second self,' as he creates his work."[106] His consideration of the eyewitness theme of John as a narrative technique has the danger of distorting the truth claim of Gospel. Petri Merenlahti humorously criticized this approach: "If the author is brought to court for trial because of the commitments and beliefs represented by the narrator, we (or at least most of us) would say this is due to a severe misconception concerning the relationship between fiction and reality."[107]

Narrative criticism rightly emphasized the need to read the Gospel as a unified story, and its insight was particularly fruitful in the area of character studies in recent years.[108] The methodology, however, is in a difficult position to be compatible with the truth claims of the Gospel. Fiction, after all, happens in the imaginative creation of an writer in a fictive world, but Scripture is an authoritative testimony to reality grounded in the reality of this world. The interpretative methodology therefore cannot be the same. Recognizing the "anachronistic tendency of novelizing the gospels," Stibbe said, "I choose instead to assess NT narrative against its natural background, which is primarily OT narrative, and secondarily those Greek narrative forms whose presence can be clearly felt."[109] Just as Merenlahti pointed out, fiction is "a game of make believe,"[110] but Scripture, on the other hand, has a "spatiotemporal (as well as a thematic) continuity" with its referred world.[111] What Han W. Frei observed in his 1974 monograph *The Eclipse of Biblical Narrative* is still applicable today:

> Western Christian reading of the Bible before the rise of historical criticism in the eighteenth century was usually strongly

---

105. Culpepper, *Anatomy*, 47.

106. Culpepper, *Anatomy*, 47; The quotation is of Booth. Booth, *Rhetoric of Fiction*, 151.

107. Merenlahti, *Poetics for the Gospels?*, 10–11.

108. Many excellent studies came out recently on John's character and characterization; particularly, see: Bennema, *Encountering Jesus*; Hunt et al., *Character Studies in the Fourth Gospel*; Skinner, *Characters and Characterization*.

109. Stibbe, *John as Storyteller*, 22–23.

110. Merenlahti, *Poetics for the Gospels?*, 10.

111. Sternberg, *Poetics*, 159.

realisitic, i.e. at once literal and historical, and not only doctrinal or edifying. The words and sentences meant what they said, and because they did so they accurately described real events and real truths that were rightly put only in those terms and no others.[112]

Structuralist Criticism

Structuralist criticism is not a single interpretative methodology, but rather has its foundation on various theoretical and philosophical concepts that emphasize relationships of individual elements.[113] Ferdinand de Saussure (1857–1913), who is known as the father of structuralism, pioneered the structural approach in linguistics. In his posthumously published *Course in General Linguistics*, he investigated the nature of language. He conceptualized that the linguistic sign consists of "signifier" and "signified,"[114] and carefully distinguished signified as the mental concept and the signifier as its verbal sound-image. The "sign," then, is what results from the *relationship* of the signified and the signifier. He saw that the linguistic sign, or the relationship between the signified and signifier, is *arbitrary* because the signifier has no natural connection with the signified.

From this observation of signified and signifier, de Saussure further stated that a language system operates on a differential relationship: differences of the signified and the differences of the signifier. A word exists because of the meaning other words do not carry, and what other words do not relationally define the word. By a system of contrast, words obtain meaning in language. He recognized therefore: "A language is a system of which all the parts can and must be considered as synchronically interdependent."[115]

It is these assumptions about language that gave rise to structuralism. Roman Jakobson (1896–1982), who helped to found the Russian Formalism and Prague School of Linguistics, said:

---

112. Frei, *Eclipse of Biblical Narrative*, 1.

113. Cf. Patte, *Structural Exegesis for New Testament Critics*, 2; Polzin, *Biblical Structuralism*; and Malbon, "Structuralism, Hermeneutics, and Contextual Meaning," 209–10. For major facets of structuralism as methodology, see Stancil, "Structuralism and New Testament Studies," 41–59; and Jacobson, "Structuralists and the Bible," 146–64.

114. Saussure, *Course in General Linguistics*, 67–78.

115. Saussure, *Course in General Linguistics*, 86.

> Were we to comprise the leading idea of present-day science in its most various manifestations, we could hardly find a more appropriate designation than *structuralism*. Any set of phenomena examined by contemporary science is treated not as a mechanical agglomeration but as a structural whole, and the basic task is to reveal the inner . . . laws of this system. What appears to be the focus of scientific preoccupations is no longer the outer stimulus, but the internal premises of the development; now the mechanical conception of processes yields to the question of their function.[116]

Just as in the grammar of a language, Jakobson argued that the text works as a "structural whole" without any need for "outer stimulus."

Claude Lévi-Strauss took these remarkable concepts and applied them to the field of anthropology.[117] In the analysis of myths, he said that the Saussarean linguistic model is applicable, since myth was also language for him. As he opposed the diachronic (historical) readings of the myths, he argued that the meaning of myths comes by examining the relationships of units in the myths. In his analysis of the relationships of internal elements in Oedipus, he set an example of structural criticism in literature. Just as one reads a musical score both horizontally and vertically in order to achieve harmony, he demonstrated a way to arrive at a meaning through a holistic reading of the text that excludes any external references.

Russian folklorist Vladimir Propp also brought a significant contribution to structural studies in his *Morphology of the Folktale* in 1928 (Russian). In his study of Russian fairy tales, he observed that the characters in these stories have constant functions, or types of action, and that these functions have uniform sequences.[118] He argued that all these functions boil down to only thirty-one types, and said that the actions of all tales in all people groups fall within these thirty one types. Through the formulation of this scheme, Propp paved the way for scholars, such as A. J. Greimas, Roland Barthes, Claude Bremond, and Tzevatan Todorov, to carry out structural analysis of biblical narratives.[119]

In spite of its theoretical attractiveness, however, there are only a few structural studies of the Fourth Gospel. In *Structural Exegesis for New*

---

116. Jakobson, "Romantic Panslavism—New Slavic Studies," 711.

117. Lévi-Strauss, *Structural Anthropology*.

118. Propp, *Morphology of the Folktale*, 19–22.

119. McKnight, "Structure and Meaning in Biblical Narratives," 5. For the development of structuralism in biblical studies, see McKnight, *Meaning in Texts*.

Testament Critics, Daniel Patte applied structuralist methodology in the analysis of John 3:1–21 and 4:4–42.[120] In this study, he argued that oppositions of actions and characters in the narrative reveal the author's conviction. As he identified these convictions, he developed systems of convictions concerning Jesus, believers, and religious leaders. In comparing and contrasting these systems, he was able to "perceive clearly the pattern that characterizes John's faith."[121] John D. Crossan carried out a structuralist analysis on John 6. He recognized John 6 as a unit, and made observations of how time, space, narrative, and discourse are interrelated in the production of meaning. From his painstaking analysis, he observed that the passage is "characterized by layers of text whose successive levels dominate and absorb the previous ones."[122]

Structural analysis has the merit of trying to find meaning beneath the text in the relationships of individual elements. It is true that the reading process involves taking together the individual parts and making sense of the elements in a holistic way. However, this methodology is too complex to have a lasting impact on biblical studies. Biblical writers clearly did not have a structuralist mindset, and this methodology has the serious flaw of undermining the plain sense of the text.[123] It is highly theoretical; therefore it has limited practical value. Structuralist's emphases on patterns and reduction of text into binary oppositions and predetermined categories have the effect of approaching the text only with predetermined assumptions about the text.[124]

Reader-Response Criticism

Reader-response criticism, which refers to a variety of approaches that focus on the "reader," "response," or "reading process," rose primarily as a reaction against the New Criticism's autonomous view of the text.[125] The major facet of these various reader-response criticisms is

120. Patte, *Structural Exegesis*, 9–72, 79–98.

121. Patte, *Structural Exegesis*, 61.

122. Crossan, "Written," 16.

123. Greenwood, *Structuralism and the Biblical Text*, 118; Cf. Keegan, *Interpreting the Bible*.

124. Poythress argued: "In the end, structuralist exegesis is likely to catch in its net only what the net has been previously designed to catch." Poythress, "Structuralism and Biblical Studies," 231.

125. For these various approaches, see Tompkins, *Reader-Response Criticism*. It is,

the destruction of the objectivity of the text.[126] Reader-response critics variously recognize that the readers play a central role in the communicative process. The deconstructionism of Jacques Derrida, although it is a movement with its own dynamics, is a kind of reader-response theory.[127] Deconstructionism denies that there is a fixed meaning in the text and welcomes a variety of readings.

Norman Holland's psychoanalytical approach exemplifies the philosophy of the reader-response criticism. He regarded the reading process mainly as a function of identity and said that, in reading, the readers respond to the text in ways that their fears and expectations are realized and recreated in the text. Just as readers of *Hamlet* respond differently, readers identify the text with different identity themes. He stated that in reading, "all of us, as we read, use the literary work to symbolize and finally to replicate ourselves."[128]

Stanley Fish addressed the issue of subjectivism raised by reader-response criticism as he moved the objectivity of interpretation from the text to the interpretive community. Being keenly aware of the subjectivity issue of reader-centered approaches, he solved the problem of subjectivity of individuals by identifying them as extensions of an interpretive community. It is an interesting argument that as long as the individuals are extensions of interpretive communities, their readings are valid. He said that the center of authority may be moved to a specific reader in this way, because his interpretive strategies "proceed not from him but from the interpretive community of which he is a member" because "they are, in effect, community property, and insofar as they at once enable and limit the operations of his consciousness."[129] According to Fish, if one is part of such community, his reading is equally as authoritative as anyone else's.

Furthermore, with this concept of authority, Fish destroyed the distinction between objective and subjective. As long as there is a community that supports a reading of the text, its view is no longer inferior to the objective view, because the distinction disappears. He said, "The

---

however, Culpepper's *Anatomy* that opened the door to reader-focused reading of the text. Thatcher, "Anatomies of the Fourth Gospel," 34.

126. Tompkins, *Reader-Response Criticism*, x.
127. Powell, *Narrative Criticism?*, 17.
128. Holland, "Unity, Identity, Text, Self," 124.
129. Fish, *Text in This Class?*, 14–15. Such understanding of text removes the meaning from the text to subjective "community." Community is only an extension of individuals, and it does not confer authority. Cf. Vanhoozer, *Meaning in This Text?*, 24.

claims of objectivity and subjectivity can no longer be debated because the authorizing agency, the center of interpretive authority, is at once both and neither."[130] In this way, interpretation becomes an act of choosing an "interested" reading and, thus, becomes a political issue.[131]

Wolfgang Iser, on the other hand, proposed a more limited view for readers. He rejected the referential meaning of texts, but emphasized that meaning comes from the interaction of the text and the reader. He stated that the production of meaning "must inevitably be virtual in character, as it cannot be reduced to the reality of the text or to the subjectivity of the reader, and it is from this virtuality that it derives its dynamism."[132] Iser had the highest regard for the *continuing* aesthetic effects of the text upon the readers in the reading process. He rejected searching for an authoritative meaning of a text because when one finds it, it ceases to have aesthetic effects upon the reader. In this regard, he resembles the pragmatic view of Walter Pater.[133] As long as the response can remain aesthetic, he saw the interpretative process as valid and commendable, while the traditional interpretative mode is hopelessly fixed and non-aesthetic, having a killing effect upon the aesthetic reading. Upon examination, his view has a highly theoretical nature. He said: "The theory developed here has not undergone any empirical tests. We are not concerned with proving its validity so much as with helping to devise a framework for mapping out and guiding empirical studies of reader reaction."[134]

In the Gospel of John, there has been a sustained interest in reader-focused readings. The two-volume work *"What is John?"* edited by Fernando F. Segovia contain papers submitted to the Annual Meetings of the Society of Biblical Literature from 1991–1993 (in the first volume) and from 1994–1996 (in the second volume) and it represents very well the multiple reader-response approaches.[135]

---

130. Fish, *Text in This Class?*, 14.
131. Fish, *Text in This Class?*, 16.
132. Iser, *Act of Reading*, 21.
133. Iser, *Act of Reading*, 22. Cf. Pater, *Studies in the History of the Renaissance*, viii.
134. Iser, *Act of Reading*, x.

135. Segovia, *"What Is John?" Volume I: Readers and Readings of the Fourth Gospel*; Segovia, *"What Is John?" Volume II: Literary and Social Readings of the Fourth Gospel*. These two volumes explored the ever-increasing literary approaches to reading John's Gospel (especially from reader's perspective) as well as the theological and social approaches.

In the first volume of *"What is John?"* Craig R. Koester in "The Spectrum of Johannine Readers" argued that since Gospel does not envision the readers to be sharing the same perspective (evidenced at different points of the narrative through information sharing and knowledge assumptions), it presupposes a spectrum of implied readers; and, therefore, he supported different levels of reading engagement. Robert Kysar's article "The Making of Metaphor: Another Reading of John 3:1–15" explored how an imaginary first-time reader would engage with this well-known passage in John and tried to demonstrate what the text presupposed its implied reader to be. Michael W. Newheart attempted a psychoanalytical analysis of the reader's experience of the Gospel in "Toward a Psycho-Literary Reading of the Fourth Gospel." In this essay, Newheart analyzed the reader's emotional response to the Gospel using the categories of Swiss psychiatrist Carl Gustav Jung, and argued that the readers approach the text differently according to their emotional needs. Jeffrey L. Staley in "Reading Myself, Reading the Text: The Johannine Passion Narrative in Postmodern Perspective," shared his personal journey to adulthood, and how it shaped him to embrace openness and plurality. Reader-response criticism offered him a way to read Bible closely and yet differently.[136] In the second volume, Ingrid Rosa Kitzberger also asked how a feminist reading can also be a theological reading without the conflict of interest.[137]

Jeffrey Staley's *The Print's First Kiss: A Rhetorical Investigation of the Implied Reader in the Fourth Gospel* interpreted the Fourth Gospel fully focused on the reader-oriented viewpoint. Staley helpfully pointed out that the implied author pulls the implied reader to his conviction through its concentric structure and the alternating use of narration and direct speech. This strategy has the effect of nurturing the faith of the readers by leading them to have "a second look" at the message.[138] But he also argued that the implied author periodically "victimized" the implied readers because the implied author constantly overthrows and remodels their assumptions and understandings of Jesus; so in an odd theological expression borrowed from novelists, he said that the rhetorical strategy of John 4–21 is "the victimization of the implied reader."[139]

---

136. Segovia, *"John? Volume I,"* 5–106.

137. Kitzberger, "How Can This Be?," 19–41.

138. Staley, *Print's First Kiss*, 70.

139. Staley, *Print's First Kiss*, 95. He defined victimization in this way: "It first presents the reader with the narrative 'facts' in such a way that the reader is induced to commit the character's or narrator's errors, then it forces the reader to recognize his or

Reader-response criticism highlighted the importance of readers and their experiences in the communicative process. It is true that not everyone reads the Gospel in the same way, and highlighting different readers have certainly brought new insights and different applications of the text on different audience. However, the tendency of reader-response criticism to shift the authority from the text (or from the author) to the reader is inherent in the methodology, if not exercised with care. The recent rise of ideological criticism demonstrates this point. Contemporary biblical ideological criticism argues that every reading is ideological and that the task of criticism is the "unmasking biases, injustices, privileges, and other oppressive worldviews or structures that are embedded in biblical texts and that similarly circumscribe the interpretation of biblical texts."[140] Legitimatizing all kinds of reading of Scripture from the argument that every reading is ideological, political, and biased is dangerous to biblical faith. While the author expects the readers to engage, the text must constantly modify and guide their interaction. It is not the reader's reading that creates the meaning; biblical communication sees the reader in the receiving end of divine communication.

Deconstructionist Criticism

Jacques Derrida, a French philosopher and linguist, theorized and propelled deconstructionism through his prolific writing career, especially during the 1970s and 1980s, influencing almost all fronts of disciplines. From Saussure's concept that the meaning of words depends on their difference, Derrida argued that Western philosophy is based on the presence, metaphysics, or the self-present word ("logocentrism").[141] Derrida thus argued against the referential function of language and rejected giving a center to structure.

For Derrida, giving a center to structure, while it necessarily organized structure, delimited the structure and confined the "play" of the structure. He argued that that the "absence of the transcendental signified extends the

---

her misjudgments by supplying or implying the corrective perspective." It is doubtful, however, if the author of the Gospel intentionally misleads the reader.

140. Byron, "Idological Criticism," 3:7. Legitimatizing all kinds of reading of Scripture from the argument that every reading is ideological, polical, and biased is dangerous to biblical faith. For the more discussion, see: Carter, "Ideological Readings of the Fourth Gospel," 203–19.

141. For the theory of deconstructionism, see Culler, *On Deconstruction*.

domain and the play of signification infinitely."¹⁴² In this absence of "transcendental signified," the ability for the play of language expands. Only the system of difference must create the meaning, because "there is nothing outside of the text."¹⁴³ J. Douglas Kneale expressed the concept in this way:

> If language, metaphysics, and consciousness really are structured by difference, then there can be no solid foundation, no fixed point of reference, no authority or certainty, either ontological or interpretive. Everything can be "put in question," that is, viewed as arbitrary, free-floating elements in a closed system of "writing," with the result that previously settled assumptions of stability and coherence, both in words and in things, become radically shaken, even, as a number of critics have claimed, to the point of nihilism.¹⁴⁴

This view of the absence of "the transcendental signified," however, was not unique to Derrida. Friedrich Nietzsche similarly observed one hundred years ago, with his philosophy of the "Death of God," that there is no absolute meaning in life. He said "There are no facts, everything is in flux, incomprehensible, elusive; what is relatively most enduring is—our opinions."¹⁴⁵

Stephen D. Moore demonstrated Derrida's philosophical approach very well. In his analysis of Jesus' discourse on living water in John 4, he exemplified Derrida's "dismantling of binary oppositions of metaphysics,"¹⁴⁶ destroying the distinction between physical/spiritual and earthly/heavenly. Just like Derrida,¹⁴⁷ his language is intentionally vague, playful, subtle, and full of confusion. Blundering of the physical/spiritual dichotomy of the water in Jacob's well and of Jesus' pierced side, he said: "Literality and figurality intermingle in the flow from Jesus' side, each contaminating the other."¹⁴⁸ The desire of Jesus, and the desire of the Samaritan woman are ultimately consumed in the desire of God because

---

142. Derrida, *Writing and Difference*, 280.

143. Derrida, *Grammatology*, 158.

144. Kneale, "Deconstruction," 187.

145. Nietzsche, *Will to Power*, 327. Vanhoozer observed this connection between Derrida and Nietzche. Vanhoozer, *Meaning in This Text?*, 21.

146. Moore, "Impurities in the Living Water," 209.

147. Kneale stated that "Derrida's prose may dazzle, critics say, but it does not enlighten, preferring instead to indulge in jargon, rhetorical games, and overly subtle metaphysical conceits." Kneale, "Deconstruction," 187.

148. Moore, "Impurities in the Living Water," 222.

"God's desire is a black hole that slowly draws the Johannine cosmos into it."[149] In another place, he termed his playful and careless exegesis of Mark's Gospel a "concrete criticism."[150] Deconstructionism attends to a close reading of the text, but in a completely different light. "Each of the other theories," Longman noted, "emphasizes one of the elements of the act of literary communication: author, text, or reader. Deconstruction, on the contrary, questions the grounds of all these approaches."[151]

Because of its philosophical proposition of the absence of the "transcendental signified," deconstructionism rejects anything authoritative, and it is fundamentally at odds with the nature the Scripture. Everything in Scripture points to the transcendent God who exists. Therefore, deconstructionism has no relevance in the literary study of the Scripture.

Summary

In the study of the literary art of the Gospel of John, one must always pay close attention to all four areas of communication as Abrams and Jakobson showed: author, audience, text, and represented reality all play important part in the communication of the message. Different aspects of the text can certainly be appreciated by the discussions of its mimesis, pragmatism, expressiveness, and/or objectivity. But interpreters must constantly wrestle with all these planes without neglecting any one of them.

The story John tells in the Gospel is a beautiful mimesis of the glory of Christ. Its pragmatic purpose leads him to persuade the audience in all sincerity and effectiveness. He expresses a powerful feeling as the divine inspiration stirred and moved his spirit, fusing the elements of the story with impressive effectiveness. Readers should regard the text, perhaps, as a magnificent embodiment of the glory of Christ, exhibiting, and at the same time objectifying, his multifaceted rays of light to anyone who would behold it. Such views on the Gospel of John—with each communicative element serving the ends of the others—should properly contextualize the literary study of the Fourth Gospel.

---

149. Moore, "Impurities in the Living Water," 226.
150. Moore, "Illuminating the Gospels without the Benefit of Color," 257.
151. Longman, "Literary Approaches to Biblical Interpretation," 120.

2

Old Testament Poetics as the Literary Background of John

THE LAST CHAPTER CONTEXTUALIZED the literary art of the Fourth Gospel within the context of critical theories throughout history and the modern literary theories. With that background in mind, the aim of this chapter is to provide the justification for using Old Testament poetics as the literary convention of the Fourth Gospel, which various voices have already pointed out. Poetics is an important element in the interpretation of Scripture. In recognizing the compositional artistry of a text, readers pay attention to the details of the text and how the writer crafted the text to convey the message. Studying the poetics of Scripture, therefore, can provide sensible explanations to difficulties and perceived incongruities of the text.

The literary milieu of the biblical world is certainly different from the modern era. There are, of course, unchanging basic elements of human communication that remain the same, but at the same time it is also true that fine nuances get lost as the message crosses cultural and temporal distance. Biblical interpreters must go back to the original context and see the text as the first audience would have seen it or heard it. For this reason, as interpreters pay attention on the writing style of John, they must direct their attention to the literary conventions familiar to John. In this regard, imposing modern literary theories on Scripture is perhaps analogous to clothing David with Saul's armor (1 Sam 17:38). The following discussions will demonstrate that the Old Testament saturates the Gospel of John in its literary artistry.[1] The Gospel's concepts, imageries, and theology find their home in the Old Testament world and ideas. The Fourth Gospel is thoroughly Jewish at its heart; and for this reason, the reader must discern the style of John as it relates to the Old Testament poetics. The following discussions will demonstrate this idea by showing the Jewishness of the Gospel and the selected testimonies concerning the excellence of Old Testament poetics prior to the rise of higher criticism.

Apostle John as the Author of the Gospel

When one compares the writing style of John with Old Testament literature, the first issue one should address is the authorship of the Gospel. As the previous chapter demonstrated, the author is an important part of the communication process, and one should regard the style of the text as originating from the author. The authorship of the Fourth Gospel is in much debate, and there is no scholarly consensus on this issue. The Gospel of John stands anonymous like the Synoptic Gospels, however, there are strong external and internal evidences that point to John, the son of Zebedee, one of Jesus' twelve disciples (Mark 1:19–20; 3:17; and parr.), as the author of the Gospel.

External Evidences for Apostolic Authorship

The external evidences almost unanimously point to the apostle John as the author of the Gospel. The most important witness comes from Irenaeus, who was the bishop of Lyons in the late second century AD. He identified the apostle John as the beloved disciple who wrote the Gospel and said: "Afterwards, John, the disciple of the Lord, who also had leaned upon His breast, did himself publish a Gospel during his residence at Ephesus in Asia."[2] Polycrates, the bishop of Ephesus (ca. AD 130–96) also considered John as the witness and the beloved disciple of the Lord:

---

1. Intertextuality of the Old Testament and the Gospel of John in terms of the content has been amply explored. Freed, *Old Testament Quotations in the Gospel of John*; Hanson, *Prophetic Gospel*; Menken, *Old Testament Quotations in the Fourth Gospel*; Reim, *Studien zum alttestamentlichen hintergrund*; Schuchard, *Scripture within Scripture*.

2. Irenaeus, *Haer.* 3.1.1.

"John, who was both a witness and a teacher, who reclined upon the bosom of the Lord . . . he sleeps at Ephesus."[3]

From the words of Papias, some argued for two Johns. Eusebius recorded the statement of Papias:

> If, then, any one came, who had been a follower of the elders, I questioned him in regard to the words of the elders—what Andrew or what Peter said, or what was said by Philip, or by Thomas, or by James, or by John, or by Matthew, or by any other of the disciples of the Lord, and what things Aristion and the presbyter John, the disciples of the Lord, say.[4]

From this statement of Papias, Eusebius argued that there were two Johns in Asia, and subsequently many argued that elder John is responsible for the Gospel.[5] Martin Hengel dealt with Johannine authorship in a monograph and concluded that the writer of the Fourth Gospel is elder John and not the son of Zebedee. In his view, it was impossible for a disciple so close to Jesus to have written a Gospel of him in a way that is so radical to the historical Jesus, "as pre-existent and exalted Son of God."[6] Yet he said that John the elder must have been "from Jewish Palestine, possibly from the priestly aristocracy in Jerusalem," died at an "extreme age . . . around 100," and "in some way as a young man he came into close contact with Jesus."[7] While he denied the apostolic authorship of the Gospel, he came so close to admitting it.

Even those who discount the apostolic authorship of the Gospel regard the external evidences undisputable. Schnackenburg affirmed that the external data point to John the son of Zebedee as the author of the Gospel, even with the problematic reference to John the Elder.[8] C. H. Dodd said that these external evidences are "formidable," and said that "of any external evidence to the contrary that could be called cogent I

---

3. Eusebius, *Hist. eccl.* 3.31.3. For other church fathers with this view, see the discussions in Robinson, *Priority of John*, 45–66.

4. Eusebius, *Hist. eccl.* 3.39.4.

5. For example, see Beasley-Murray, *John*, lxviii; Moloney, *Gospel of John*, 8; Smith, *John*, 26–27.

6. Hengel, *Johannine Question*, 130.

7. Hengel, *Johannine Question*, 131. For an argument that the distinction Papias made is not between apostles and second-generation elders, see Carson and Moo, *Introduction to the New Testament*, 234.

8. Schnackenburg, *John*, 1:102.

am not aware."[9] Raymond E. Brown said that there is little evidence to suppose that John the Elder is the author of the Gospel, and believed that both external and internal evidences favor John the son of Zebedee as the author.[10] Because of his belief in a Johannine community, however, he did not equate the author with the actual writer of the Gospel. F. F. Bruce made an important point that although the reference is made to an elder, there is no one in the antiquity who attributed the Gospel to this elder.[11] In the discussion of authorship, however, scholars usually ignore these strong external evidences with arguments from internal evidences.

Internal Evidences for Apostolic Authorship

B. F. Westcott gave the classic expression to the internal evidences for the apostolic authorship of the Fourth Gospel,[12] and various writers subsequently discussed the authorship of the Gospel either in favor of or against it. The internal evidences Westcott put forth are as follows.

First, John was a Jew. Westcott pointed out that the writer was well aware of the contemporary Jewish opinions, and put forth many convincing evidences that the author was a Jew. The writer reflects the strong Messianic expectations of his time (1:21; 4:25; 6:14; 7:40; 12:34), and also the popular Jewish thoughts concerning women (4:27), education (7:15), the Diaspora (7:35), cause of sickness (9:2), the Samaritans (4:9), and the Lawless Gentiles (7:49). The narrative presupposes his intimate knowledge of the Feasts, as well as the high priesthood system.

Second, the writer is a Palestinian Jew of the first century. The writer demonstrates his knowledge of Palestine topography in a way unprecedented (as in the expressions of "Cana of Galilee," "Bethany beyond Jordan," "Aenon near Salim," and "Sychar") which would be impossible after the destruction of the Temple ("pool of Bethesda" being "by the sheep gate," "the pool of Siloam," "the brook Kidron," the Pavement and the raised platform of judgment). He noted: "It is inconceivable that any one, still more a Greek or a Hellenist, writing when the Temple was razed to

---

9. Dodd, *Historical Tradition in the Fourth Gospel*, 2.
10. Brown, *Gospel according to John*, 1:xci–xcii, 1:xcviii.
11. Bruce, *Gospel of John*, 1.
12. Westcott, *Gospel according to St. John*, v–xxviii. See also Abbot et al., *Fourth Gospel*.

the ground, could have spoken of it with the unaffected certainty which appears in the fourth Gospel."[13]

Third, the writer is an eyewitness. His accounts of the persons, time, places, and manner are very specific. The Gospel of John uniquely mentions Nicodemus, Lazarus, Simon the father of Judas Iscariot, and Malchus and gives information that is absent in other Gospels. Exact numbers in the Gospel are also significant: two disciples of John the Baptist (1:35), the six waterpots (2:6), the twenty-five furlongs (6:19), the four soldiers (19:23), the two hundred cubits (21:11). All of these elements strongly favor an eyewitness account.

Fourth, the writer was an apostle. Westcott supported this argument from the fact that he intimately knew the details of the apostles: their calling (1:19–34), their travels (4; 6; 7; 9; 11) and their thoughts (2:11, 17, 22; 4:27; 6:19, 60), their words among themselves (4:3; 16:17; 20:25; 21:3, 5), the words of the Lord (4:31; 9:2; 11:8, 12; 16:29), the place of their retreat (11:54; 18:2, 20:19), and their momentary imperfect understandings (2:21; 11:13; 12:16; 13:28; 20:9; 21:4). He also knew the Lord intimately, as well as His emotions (11:33; 13:21) and thoughts (2:24; 4:1, 6; 6:6, 14, 61, 64; 7:1; 13:1, 3, 4, 11; 16:19; 19:28).

Finally, the writer was none other than the apostle John. The Epilogue attributes the authorship of the Gospel to the disciple whom Jesus loved (21:24). This reference to the disciple appears in the Passion narrative (18:23; 19:26), after Jesus' resurrection (21:7, 20), in connection with Peter (13:24; 20:2), and also simply as "another disciple" (18:15). Westcott argued by way of elimination that he could be no one else than the apostle John.

Regardless of these evidences, scholars deny apostolic authorship of the Gospel, primarily because of their belief in the theory of multiple sources and redactions. Rudolf Bultmann, the most prominent voice for source theories, for instance, argued that there are several sources underlying the Gospel—discourse, signs, passion narrative, and other sources—and said that the evangelist or the "ecclesiastical redactor" redacted these materials and produced the final Gospel.[14] His theory, however, suffered many serious criticisms. The most decisive criticism came from E. Schweizer and E. Ruckstuhl,[15] who demonstrated stylistic

---

13. Westcott, *John*, xiii.

14. For the discussion of Bultmann's methodology, see Smith, *Composition and Order of the Fourth Gospel*, 57–85.

15. Schweizer, *Ego Eimi*; Ruckstuhl, *Die literarische Einheit*.

unity throughout the Gospel. What Bultmann once proposed as stylistic traits of the Evangelist is now shown to exist in his "source" passages as well. It is possible that the writer of the Gospel may have used some sort of sources, but even if he did, he has so thoroughly made them his own that they are impossible to extract.[16] Brown rejected apostolic authorship based on his belief that the Gospel has at least five stages of production.[17] Brown, however, stated that this theory has "many inadequacies and uncertainties" and is a "working hypothesis" to answer the difficult Johannine questions.[18]

Behind the Gospel stands eyewitness accounts of the beloved disciple, and there is an intense debate as to his identity in Johannine scholarship. Rejecting the traditional belief that he is apostle John, some have suggested that he is Lazarus, John Mark, Matthias, the Rich Young Ruler, Paul, Benjamin, a Gentile Christian, a community, or the elder.[19] Because of the disciple's close affinity with Jerusalem and Judaea, Culpepper rejected the traditional identification but preferred an unknown person.[20]

Internal evidences strongly point to John the son of Zebedee as the beloved disciple. In John 13:23, the beloved disciple first appears at the Last Supper reclining at the table with Jesus. Matthew 26:20 (cf. Mark 14:17; Luke 22:14) says on that evening, "Jesus was reclining *at the table* with the twelve disciples;"[21] thus it is very unlikely that he would be anyone other than the twelve. On this night, as he is identified as "one of His disciples, whom Jesus loved," he asked Jesus about the identity of the betrayer. In John 18:15–16, he appears at the court of the high priest with Peter, although he is simply referenced as "another disciple," "that disciple," and "the other disciple." In 19:25–27, he is at the foot of the cross, having followed him through the night, with Jesus' mother and other women, and he is once again "the disciple whom He loved," and he is entrusted with the care of Mary. In 20:1–8, he is again "the other disciple whom Jesus loved," and he ran to the empty tomb with Peter on the resurrection Sunday and he saw and believed. In 21:7, Jesus makes

---

16. D. A. Carson pointed out the weaknesses of Bultmann's source theory. See Carson, *Gospel according to John*, 29–35.

17. Brown, *John*, 1:xxxiv–xxxix.

18. Brown, *John*, 1:xxxix.

19. For the arguments and proponents of these views, see Culpepper, *John*, 72–84.

20. Culpepper, *John*, 72–84.

21. Unless otherwise noted, all quotations of Scripture are taken from the *New American Standard Bible* (NASB).

his post-resurrection appearance to the beloved disciple and Peter, and here the beloved disciple cannot be anyone else than one of "Simon Peter, Thomas called Didymus, and Nathanael of Cana in Galilee, and the *sons of Zebedee*, and two other of His disciples" (John 21:2). It is interesting that scholars prefer one of the unnamed disciples here as the identity of this beloved disciple instead of accepting him to be the son of Zebedee.[22] In 21:20, Peter asked Jesus about the fate of this "disciple whom Jesus loved," and here he is once again identified as the one who had leaned back on his bosom at the Last Supper. Then in 21:24, the author identifies this disciple as the writer of the Gospel: "This is the disciple who is testifying to these things and wrote these things, and we know that his testimony is true."

Both external and internal evidences strongly favor the apostolic authorship of the Gospel. There is no reason to reject that the author is an apostle (1:14; cf. 2:11; 19:35), one of the twelve (13:23; 19:26–27; 20:2–9, 21; 21:24–25), and John, the son of Zebedee (20:2). He is consistently associated with Peter in the Fourth Gospel and elsewhere in the New Testament (13:13–24; 18:15–16; 20:2–9, 21; cf. Luke 22:8; Acts 1:13; 3–4; 8:14–25; Gal. 2:9).[23]

Importance of Authorship

Authorship of the Gospel is an important issue. As discussed in the previous chapter, objective theorists argued that the text is all that matters, and that it stands autonomous of any external factors. This view is not

---

22. Cf. Thatcher, "Beloved Disciple," 86. Thatcher considered it most likely that the believed disciple wrote the Gospel and that he could also be 'The Elder' in 2 and 3 John. Thatcher, "Beloved Disciple," 98.

23. Köstenberger, *John*, 6–8; cf. Carson, *John*, 68–81. With strong traditions and evidences, J. Ramsey Michaels however still favored his identity be to elusive. Michaels, *Gospel of John*, 5–24. Morris's mature judgment is still weighty: "No theory so far put forward is without difficulties. It is a matter of choosing that view which presents us with the fewest. Many recent scholars make telling criticisms of the view that John the apostle was the author. But when we turn to their own views we find little to inspire. The suggested reconstructions are often difficult to follow, sometimes bordering on the bizarre. There is certainly none that is free from serious objection. It is a matter, then, of accepting that solution which best accounts for the facts and which has the fewest difficulties in its way. It is for this reason that I accept the view that John the apostle was the author of this Gospel. I agree that this view does not account for all the evidence. But then neither does any other view known to me. This one seems to account for the facts best." Morris, *John*, 24.

congruent with the scriptural claim of authority. Scripture constantly points to God who exists and speaks to His people in diverse manners through His prophets and now through His Son (Heb 1:1). The fact that Scripture uses the word "testimony" in describing the word of God (2 Kgs 23:3; 1 Chr. 29:19; Ps 19:7, 25:10, 78:56) supports this referential function of the Scripture. The Word of God is a testimony to the reality of God and His eternal kingdom.

The scriptural text has several referential functions. First, it points to the God who speaks. Scripture always bears witness to the God who speaks through the text. The divine "I" fills the Scripture. Second, it points to the circumstances of the real readers, and it convicts and comforts them. Scripture speaks to the readers in order that they would respond to the One who speaks through the text. Third, the scriptural text also points to the speakers themselves, because it is inevitably through their speaking voices and their writing hands that the Word of God is proclaimed to the readers. Many biblical texts stand anonymous, but it is a wholly different matter that someone insists anonymity of the text when the author identified himself indisputably. When Jesus referred to several Old Testament books, instead of quoting titles of those books, He often used the personal names of the writers to make reference to their authorship. Jesus frequently spoke therefore, "Moses said," "David said," or "Isaiah said" (Matt 8:4, 12:3, 15:7, 22:43; 19:8; Mark 7:10; Luke 16:29,31, 20:42). Jesus regarded the authors as equally important as the texts that they produced. For this reason, authors should never be detached from the texts they have written. If one cannot be certain of who is speaking in John 21:24, then the truth of his testimony is seriously in question.

Authorship is also important in comparing the poetics of John with the Old Testament writings. A study in poetics presupposes that there is a writer who intentionally crafted the text in order to communicate the message in the way that he intended. Denying the presence of the author in the text with questions regarding its textual integrity seriously hinders a poetic approach to the Gospel. The presence of the author and textual integrity guarantee that seeming incongruities and perplexities are intentional. As E. D. Hirsch rightly pointed out, validity of interpretation comes from the presence of the author.[24] For this reason, disregarding the importance of the authorship and, at the same time, working on the poetics of the text is self-contradictory and cannot produce fruitful results.

24. Hirsch, *Validity in Interpretation*, 1–6.

Jewishness of the Gospel of John

For a long time, scholars regarded Hellenism as the most significant formative background for much of the New Testament writings, and especially for the Gospel of John.[25] Rudolf Bultmann expressed his belief that Christianity is a syncretistic religion between Hellenism and Judaism, and said that the Fourth Gospel is profoundly influenced by Mandaean Gnostic dualism.[26] C. H. Dodd, while taking a more cautious stance, found striking conceptual parallels for the Gospel in the Egyptian Hermetic texts.[27] Many scholars followed a similar path and saw a Hellenistic philosophical background for much of Johannine ideas.[28]

A decisive turn in the Johannine scholarship came with the discovery of the Dead Sea Scrolls in 1947, and since then, scholars began to see the Gospel of John as profoundly influenced by the Judaism of the first century AD. For example, after his examinations of the Dead Sea Scrolls, Frank M. Cross noted:

> We must look for a *Sitz im Leben* for the development of Johannine tradition . . . Some have suggested that John may be regarded no longer as the latest and most evolved of the Gospels, but the most primitive, and that the formative locus of its tradition was Jerusalem before its destruction . . . The point is that John preserves authentic historical material which first took form in an Aramaic or Hebrew milieu where Essene currents still ran strong.[29]

This conclusion confirms Westcott's earlier opinion that the "teaching of St. John is characteristically Hebraic and not Alexandrine."[30] Kurt Schubert also expressed the view that "one of the most important results of Qumran research has been to prove the Jewish origin of the Gospel of John conclusively."[31]

---

25. Kümmel, *New Testament*, 245–80.

26. Bultmann, *Gospel of John*, 7–9; Bultmann, *Primitive Christianity in Its Contemporary Setting*, 175–79.

27. Dodd, *Interpretation of the Fourth Gospel*, 10–53.

28. Tobin, "Prologue of John and Hellenistic Jewish Speculation," 252–69; Painter, "Christology and the Fourth Gospel," 45–62; Painter, "Christology and the History of the Johannine Community," 460–74.

29. Cross, *Ancient Library of Qumran*, 161–62.

30. Westcott, *John*, xviii.

31. Schubert, *Dead Sea Community*, 152. For a similar conclusion, see: Brown,

Old Testament Poetics as the Literary Background of John 53

Semitisms

The beginning of the twentieth century brought in questions as to the nature of the language of the New Testament. From the newly discovered papyri from the Greco-Roman world, Adolf Deissmann argued decisively that the language of the New Testament is not classical Greek nor a special language of the Holy Spirit, but basically a popular colloquial (κοινή) language of that time.[32] Nonetheless, the quest for the Aramaic origin of the Fourth Gospel also began. A. Schlatter (1902) and C. J. Ball (1909)[33] began the investigation of the Aramaic origin of the Gospel, and C. F. Burney developed the theory fully in his *The Aramaic Origin of the Fourth Gospel* (1922). He argued that the Gospel was originally written in Aramaic and was translated into Greek and said that there are many places where the Aramaic original has been mistranslated.

Ernest Colwell (1931), however, rejected any Aramaism in the Gospel, and showed that the Aramaisms of Burney are also found in Greek expressions.[34] As Colwell pointed out, many of the Semitisms of the Fourth Gospel are present in the common Greek language of that time. J. H. Moulton and W. F. Howard rightly pointed out that Burney has not taken into consideration these common areas.[35] Matthew Black (1954) however took up the debate with the newly discovered text of Palestinian Targum of the Pentateuch and argued once again for Aramaic influence on the Fourth Gospel and Acts.[36]

While the debate continued in favor of or against Aramaisms in the Fourth Gospel, J. Courtenay James argued for the *semitization* of the Greek language itself. He expressed his view this way:

> One reason why so many "Semitisms" seem naturalized in Greek, is that some eastern idioms, in the process of the contact of Semite and Greek, silted through into the κοινή. No doubt some forms of Semitic expression were fundamentally

---

John, 1:lxii–lxiv; Charlesworth, *Literary Setting, Textual Studies*.

32. Deissmann, *Light from the Ancient East*, passim, esp. 69.

33. Schlatter, *Die Sprache und Heimat des vierten Evangelisten*; Ball, "Had the Fourth Gospel an Aramaic Archetype?," 91–93; For a good overview of major participants in the debate, see Brown, "From Burney to Black," 323–39.

34. Colwell, *Greek of the Fourth Gospel*, 130–31.

35. Howard, "Semitisms in the New Testament," 483.

36. Black, *Aramaic Approach to the Gospels and Acts*.

> analogous to forms in Greek. These would easily pass into the latter language, and appear like native constructions.[37]

It is possible that some of the Semitic elements might have found their ways into the Greek language, but whether this accounts for all of the Semitisms in John is questionable.

Although a majority of scholars are not convinced by the Aramaic translation theory, many see Semitism (whether Aramaism or Hebraism) in the Gospel.[38] Lightfoot observed that "the whole casting of the sentences, the whole coloring of the language, is Hebrew."[39] Concerning the language of the New Testament, Nigel Turner made the powerful statement that, "Granted that the Greek of the NT was the living language of the day, as it was both written and spoken, it should also be insisted that it was a language *impregnated* by the Bible, its Semitic idioms and thought-forms."[40] Although the vocabulary of the New Testament is from the common language of that time, he pointed out that Scripture gave them special significance. He said:

> Let us see how the biblical content has changed the whole meaning of the Greek. There is a solid group of very important words on which the usage of the *Koine* can shed little, if any, ray of light. Such words as *brother, parousia, fellowship, eternal, apostle, bishop, presbyter, savior, to preach*, are now Christian technical terms charged with a new significance. No acquaintance with Classical authors will help in the exposition of these words to a Christian congregation. The whole content of meaning comes from the NT itself and the Bible that lies directly behind it—the OT.[41]

Turner, in "The Style of John," pointed out that Chiasms, parataxis, asyndenton, "Casus pendens" (a noun phrase standing outside of the clause), word orders, and infinitive absolutes are some strongly Semitic elements in the Gospel of John.[42] Some of these elements also appear in some Greek expressions, but as a whole, they undoubtedly point to Semitism as

---

37. James, *Language of Palestine and Adjacent Regions*, 70.

38. Schnackenburg, *John*, 1:105–11; Brown, *John*, 1:cxxix–cxxxv; Barrett, *John*, 8–11; Wead, *Literary Devices in John's Gospel*, 12–23. Cf. Wead, *Literary Devices in John's Gospel*.

39. Lightfoot, *Biblical Essays*, 135.

40. Turner, "Language of the New Testament," 660. Italics are added for emphasis.

41. Turner, "Language of the New Testament," 660. Italics in original.

42. Turner, "Style of John," 64–79.

the background of the Gospel. Indeed, the Greek of the Fourth Gospel is a "Jewish Greek, syntactically very simple, dignified but without the flexibility of the secular language," and it "moves within well-defined Semitic limits of style and vocabulary."[43]

Centrality of Hebrew Scripture

Even with the diversity within first century Judaism, the common tenet that held them all was the centrality of Hebrew Scripture,[44] and this is the characteristic feature of the Fourth Gospel. In his article, Jacob J. Enz showed that the whole Gospel may have the pattern of Exodus narrative. Both Moses and Jesus came to his people, but they rejected him initially (Exod 2:11; John 1:11). The sign of the serpent is present early in the ministry (Exod 4:4, 29; John 3:14). People responded to the first signs (Exod 4:30; John 2:11), and there is a concentration of signs in the beginning of the books whose purpose was for the belief in the deliverers (Exod 3:12—13:16; John 2:11—12:37). There is also a motif of unbelief in both books (Exod 14:8; John 12:37-40) and the latter portions of the books are concerned with the Lord's own words (Exod 16-40; John 13-21). There are prayers of intercessions for the people (Exod 32-33; John 17) and the last parts show completion of the works (Exod 40:33; John 19:30).[45]

Merrill C. Tenney has shown that Old Testament quotations and allusions saturate the Fourth Gospel.[46] He pointed out that the Gospel has references to every book of the Pentateuch, as well as Psalms and many of the prophets.[47] He said, "All three divisions of the Old Testament canon, the law, the prophets, and the Psalms, were utilized in interpreting the work of Christ."[48] This is an important observation for finding John's literary home in the the narratives, prophets, and the poetry of the Old Testament. In terms of content, there are many Old Testament typologies connected to Jesus, such as the ladder reaching to heaven (Gen

---

43. Turner, "Style of John," 78.

44. Hamid-Khani, *Revelation and Concealment of Christ*, 136. Hamid-Khani discussed this topic in detail.

45. Enz, "Book of Exodus," 208–15.

46. There are many studies on this subject. See Freed, *Old Testament Quotations*; Schuchard, *Scripture within Scripture*; Morgan, "Fulfillment in the Fourth Gospel," 155–65.

47. Tenney, "Literary Keys to the Fourth Gospel, III," 304.

48. Tenney, "Literary Keys to the Fourth Gospel, III," 304.

28:12; John 1:50–51), the manna given in the wilderness (Exod 16:15; John 6:32–33), and the brazen serpent lifted up for the deliverance of the people (Num 21:5–9; John 3:14; 8:28; 12:32, 34). Readers should also note that important events in the Gospel are organized around the Jewish feasts (2:13, 23; 5:1; 6:4; 7:2; 10:31–39; 11:55).[49]

Anthony T. Hanson made the bold claim that the Fourth Gospel is "the prophetic Gospel," because of the fact that it is "full of [Old Testament] prophecy fulfilled in the life of Jesus."[50] Concurring with A. Loisy, he said that John "regards the Word as the mediator of all revelation in the Old Testament."[51] In his view, Hanson saw the Gospel written as a polemic against the Jews and as an encouragement for Christians; but he also believed that the main purpose was to show that his presentation of Jesus is scripturally justifiable. He said:

> One of the main functions of early Christian prophets was to expound scripture in such a way as to show that it was being fulfilled in the present era. John, we may surely surmise, was considered to be a prophet. He writes therefore a *prophetic* Gospel in which he uses all the resources of scripture interpreted as he understood it in order to present the full significance of Jesus, not only the significance of what he actually said and did and suffered, but also the significance of what scripture said he was to be and to do.[52]

Whether one agrees that this is the main purpose of the Gospel or with the point about the early tradition of Jesus, Hanson has correctly captured the central role of Jewish Scripture in the Gospel of John.

Johannes Beutler proposed a thesis that in John's use of Scripture, his interest was not on how individual passages find fulfillment in Jesus, but rather of how Jesus fulfilled the "Scripture." He said, "The impression conveyed is that John is convinced that scripture as a whole bears witness to Jesus. It is of secondary importance how individual passages of scripture contribute to this conviction."[53] Along with the Judaism of his day, John's writing finds its root in the Hebrew Scripture.

---

49. Tenney, "Literary Keys to the Fourth Gospel, III," 305–7.
50. Hanson, *Prophetic Gospel*, 19.
51. Hanson, *Prophetic Gospel*, 32.
52. Hanson, *Prophetic Gospel*, 342. Italics are added for emphasis.
53. Beutler, "'Use of 'Scripture' in the Gospel of John," 158.

Jewish Hermeneutics

In the Second Temple period, there were hermeneutical diversities within Judaism, and scholars debated which hermeneutical principle John must have followed. Some proposed that John is following Targumic interpretation of Scripture. *Targum* refers to Aramaic translation, paraphrase, and interpretation of Scripture. Birger Olsson, Barnabas Lindars, and Matthew Black believed that the Gospel is close to the Targum in appropriating the teaching materials of Jesus in the Gospel.[54] Bruce Chilton, however, compared the Targumic materials with the Gospels and concluded that the interpretative methodologies of the two are different. He observed that the goal of a Targum is "to provide an understanding of a written text," while the Gospels are "designed to explain the significance of a person."[55] Again, he stated this position: "For this reason, I speak of the two processes as being 'cognate' rather than 'identical,' and of the similarities between the two as 'analogies,' not 'parallels.'"[56] The Evangelist's use of Jesus' teaching materials does not exactly match Targumic use of the Old Testament texts.

Some have argued for Midrashic character of the Fourth Gospel. Renée Bloch said that the major characteristics of rabbinic Midrash are its (1) focus on Scripture; (2) homiletical nature; (3) study of the text; (4) adaptation to present circumstances; (5) using either haggadahic (doctrine and history) or halakahic (law) methods.[57] Observing the symbolism, onomastics, and wordplays in the Gospel, Bloch said that the Gospel has Midrashic tendencies.[58] Roger Le Déaut, however, said that it is difficult to define precisely what Midrash is, because it encompasses texts that are very different in literary forms and contents. He suggested that one should define it broadly as concerning with biblical text and with its adaptation for the benefit of the community.[59] The exposition of Old Testament Scripture for the purpose of applying them in the present context in one way or the other is not particularly Midrash. Richard B.

---

54. Olsson, *Structure and Meaning in the Fourth Gospel*, 282; Lindars, "Traditions behind the Fourth Gospel," 115; Black, *Aramaic Approach*, 151.

55. Chilton, *Targumic Approaches to the Gospels*, 126.

56. Chilton, *Targumic Approaches to the Gospels*, 126.

57. Bloch, "Midrash," 31–34.

58. Bloch, "Midrash," 48. See also Borgen, "Observation on the Midrashic Character of John 6," 234; Borgen, *Bread from Heaven*, passim.

59. Déaut, "Apropos a Definition of Midrash," 274–75, 282.

Hays pointed out that "all readings of Scripture by Jews and Christians always and everywhere are instances of midrash."[60]

Others have observed the parallel elements in Qumran and the Fourth Gospel, and proposed that John follows the Pesharism of the Qumran Community. *Pesher* generally refers to the interpretative method the Qumran community practiced, and *pesherim* refers to the works of these methods. Bruce pointed out that pesher in the Qumran community denoted an interpretation of mystery which only the revelation of God makes known. When these two elements of interpretation and mystery meet together, he said, they discovered the meaning.[61] Bruce said:

> [Qumran commentators] believed that all prophetic scripture was concerned with the fulfillment of God's purpose in the end-time, and that the key to the understanding of this purpose had been granted to their Teacher; but the early Christians believed that Jesus was the very embodiment and fulfillment of God's purpose, the one in whom all the promises of God found their "yes."[62]

Both the Qumran commentators and the New Testament writers knew that they were living in the last days, and they showed the fulfillment of Scripture in their writings.

However, finding the exact parallel of Johannine hermeneutics within certain Jewish interpretation method is not commendable. Philip S. Alexander stated: "The fact that A is similar to B in respect of x hardly established a significant and exclusive relationship between A and B unless it can be shown that A is dissimilar to CDEF etc., with respect to x."[63]

While it would be impossible to locate John's hermeneutics precisely within any of these hermeneutical techniques, it is important that his interpretation of Christ was well within the Jewish interpretation of Scripture. Like the rest of the New Testament writers, John showed that events concerning Christ were the fulfillments of Jewish Scripture. The Old Testament prophets already exemplified this method of interpretation. G. W. H. Lampe said: "The Church's interpretation of the Scriptures was revolutionary as regards its content; but its method was not wholly novel. The idea of promise and fulfillment was familiar to the prophets themselves, and an elementary typology was used by such prophets as

---

60. Hays, *Echoes of Scripture in the Letters of Paul*, 11.
61. Bruce, *Biblical Exegesis in the Qumran Texts*, 8–9.
62. Bruce, *Biblical Exegesis in the Qumran Texts*, 68.
63. Alexander, "Rabbinic Judaism and the New Testament," 246.

Hosea and the Second Isaiah."[64] Cohen remarked that the "characteristic of Palestinian exegesis is the effort to affirm the continuing validity of the biblical prophecies and narratives by discovering contemporary situations through which they were fulfilled."[65] Without difficulty, one sees here that John revealed his very Jewishness in the way he presented Christ.

Contents

There are exclusively Jewish elements in the Gospel. In his detailed commentary on John, Keener dealt with specific elements that are exclusively Jewish. Recognizing the possibility that Gentile Christians could have appropriated these elements through their participation in the faith community, he said that these Jewish issues "would make no sense outside a Jewish context."[66]

It is also important to note here that John's Christology is particularly Jewish. John presents Jesus as the Lamb of God who takes away the sin of the world according to the sacrificial system of the Old Testament. Just as the blood of the Passover lamb exempted Israelites from death on the night of God's judgment upon Egypt (Exod 12), John repeatedly presents Jesus as the Passover Lamb through (1) the Baptist's statement (1:29, 36); (2) references to his several journeys to Jerusalem, specifically during the Passover (John 2, 6); and (3) his death during the Passover (John 18–19). He is the one whom the Levitical sacrificial system of Old the Testament foreshadowed (Lev 1–5).

He is the new manna (6:32, 35), the flowing living water from Ezekiel's Temple (7:37–39; Ezek 47), and the one Siloam pointed to (9:7; Gen 49:10). He is the pierced Person, the water, and the smitten Shepherd in Zechariah (Zech 12:10, 13:7, 14:8). He is greater than Jacob (4:12), greater than Moses (5:46), greater than Abraham (8:53), and greater than all of the prophets (8:53). He is the wisdom of God (1:1–18) and the glory Moses and Isaiah witnessed (1:14; 12:39–41). He is Jacob's ladder that connects heaven and earth (1:47–51) and the Suffering Servant of Isaiah (13:1–11).[67]

---

64. Lampe, "Exposition and Exegesis of Scripture," 158.
65. Cohen, *Maccabees to the Mishnah*, 208.
66. Keener, *John*, 173–75.
67. Keener, *John*, 173–75. Keener observed these points.

Implications

This section of the chapter argued for the Jewishness of the Gospel of John. This argument however does not exclude Gentile readership, nor does it propose that its Jewishness made it unintelligible to them. The apostle Paul says that as Gentile Christians became part of the believing bodies of Christians, God has grafted them into the "rich root of the olive tree" of Israel (Rom 11:17–24). One should, therefore, see the grace of God flowing out to the Gentiles through their participation in the richness of Israel's heritage. As the Gentiles became Christians, these strongly Jewish elements of Scripture must naturally have flowed into their faith through reading and studying the Scripture. One should also note here that, in Scripture, there are aspects of truth that are general enough for all people to grasp without understanding the Jewish heritage. Therefore there is no issue in arguing that the Gospel was particularly susceptible to a Jewish audience.

The implication of this observation of the Jewishness of the Gospel is that the Old Testament most adequately explains the content as well as the form of the Gospel. Even as the Gospel addresses Gentile audience, John is faithful to his Jewish roots without apology. Readers therefore should see this character evident in the way he communicated his message.

Selected Testimonies on the Excellence of the Old Testament Poetics

The remaining section of this chapter focuses on the selected testimonies concerning the poetic excellence of the Old Testament throughout history. These testimonies purposefully come from the time period prior to the rise of higher criticisms in biblical studies, focusing on the Second Temple period, Patristic period, Medieval period, and the Renaissance period. James Kugel's *The Idea of Biblical Poetry* and Adele Berlin's *Biblical Poetry through Medieval Jewish Eyes* have excellent surveys on this area.

The Second Temple Period

Speaking about the upbringing of Moses in the court of Pharaoh, Philo of Alexandria said that Moses was highly educated in Egypt, especially in learning the science of rhythm, harmony, meters, and music from the

Egyptians.[68] According to Kugel, Philo is the first one "known to have described Hebrew writing in the terminology of Greek meters."[69] It was Philo's idea that hymns of Old Testament were composed "in every kind of meter and melody imaginable."[70] Concerning the Song of Moses (Exod 15), he said that its choruses are "most admirable" and "beautiful."[71]

Josephus recognized rhythmic nature of the songs and Psalms in the Old Testament. In the Songs of Moses in Exodus 15 and Deuteronomy 32, Josephus said that Moses composed them in hexameters,[72] and in Psalms, he said that David wrote them in various sorts of meters, some trimesters, and some pentameters.[73] Although Josephus did not discuss them in detail, he obviously saw their poetic nature and sought to describe them according to Greek standards. Josephus also wrote of an interesting account of the conversation that took place between Aristotle and an unnamed Jew. The following account comes from *Against Apion*, and it is the Clearchus's account of the conversation between Aristotle his master and the Jewish man:

> The man was a Jew of Coele-Syria . . . Now this man, who was entertained by a large circle of friends and was on his way down from the interior to the coast, not only spoke Greek, but had the soul of a Greek. During my stay in Asia, he visited the same places as I did, and came to converse with me and some other scholars, to test our learning. But as one who had been intimate with many cultivated persons, it was rather he who imparted to us something of his own.[74]

If this account has any historical veracity, it is interesting how Aristotle mentioned that the unnamed Jew informed them more about the learnings. Although there is no mention of the contents, it is not unlikely that the discussion covered topics such as rhetoric and poetics which were Aristotle's own interest.

---

68. Philo, *Mos.* 1.20–24.
69. Kugel, *Biblical Poetry*, 135.
70. Philo, *Contempl.* 29.
71. Philo, *Agr.* 82.
72. Josephus, *Ant.* 2.346.
73. Josephus, *Ant.* 7.304.
74. Josephus, *Ag. Ap.* 1.180–81 (Josephus, "Against Apion," 235–37).

The Patristic Period

Many church fathers also recognized the excellence of Old Testament poetics and sustained the opinion that Greeks learned their philosophy and psaltery from the Hebrews. This knowledge concerning the opinion comes from Eusebius of Caesarea (ca. 263–339) who quoted Aristobulus, a Jewish philosopher from Alexandria in the second century BC. Aristobulus argued that Hebrew Scripture influenced the Greek Philosophers Pythagoras and Plato. As to the possibility of Plato knowing Hebrew Scripture prior to the translation of Septuagint, Aristobulus said that there were others who translated Hebrew Scripture before the Septuagint. Eusebius put it this way:

> It is evident that Plato closely followed our legislation, and has carefully studied the several precepts contained in it. For others before Demetrius Phalereus, and prior to the supremacy of Alexander and the Persians, have translated both the narrative of the exodus of the Hebrews our fellow countrymen from Egypt, and the fame of all that had happened to them, and the conquest of the land, and the exposition of the whole Law; so that it is manifest that many things have been borrowed by the aforesaid philosopher, for he is very learned: as also Pythagoras transferred many of our precepts and inserted them in his own system of doctrines.[75]

It is not unreasonable to follow Louis H. Feldman who believed that biblical themes were probably known among the Greeks before the translation of Septuagint from the evidence of the Oxyrhynchus papyrus; but he also admitted that there are no fragments of such translations.[76]

Origen (ca. 185–254), in his polemical writing against the anti-Christian work of Celsus, mentioned a Greek philosopher Numenius of Apamea (second century AD) who believed that Pythagoras derived his philosophy from the Jews and introduced it among the Greeks. He said: "It is said . . . that it was from the Jewish people that Pythagoras derived the philosophy which he introduced among the Greeks."[77] It is interesting that, if Eusebius and Origen are correct, these testimonies come from both Jewish and Greek philosophers.

---

75. Eusebius, *Prev. Ev.* 13.12 (Eusebius, *Preparation for the Gospel*, 664). Demetrius Phalereus oversaw the translation of Septuagint under Ptolemy Philadelphus.

76. Feldman, *Judaism and Hellenism Reconsidered*, 64n15.

77. Origen, *Cels.* 1.15.

Clement of Alexandria (ca. 150–215), who acquainted himself with various classical authors, poets, dramatists, historians, and philosophers,[78] defended Christian revelation and spoke of the excellency of the Hebrew Scripture in his exposition of Christian Gnosticism in *Stromateis* (or *Miscellanies*). In this work, he argued that the Greek psaltery came from David: "Further, as an example of music, let us adduce David, playing at once and prophesying, melodiously praising God ... The harmony, therefore, of the Barbarian [Hebrew] psaltery, which exhibited gravity of strain, being the most ancient, most certainly became a model for Terpander, for the Dorian harmony, who sings the praise of Zeus thus."[79] Because the Psalms of David are more ancient than the Greeks, Clement saw that the former became the model for the latter.

Kugel exercised reservation in accepting these claims and noted that the idea originated from the Jewish people. He observed that "it was a Jewish bulwark against the inroads of Hellenization, but one that at the same time helped Jews to accept Greek learning without conceding it priority or even originality."[80] He also pointed out that the motive for continuing this idea among the church fathers was to allow poetry and secular learning to have a place within Christianity.[81]

Even if some claims were clearly too radical[82] and the motive may have been apologetical, the church fathers, nevertheless, clearly noticed sublime nature of scriptural communication. As he studied the Hebrew Scripture, Eusebius recognized its excellent rhetoric and said, "And if anyone were also to study the language itself with critical taste, he would see that, for Barbarians [Hebrews], the writers are excellent dialecticians, not at all inferior to sophists or orators in his own language."[83] Augustine admitted that in appearance, Scripture is "lowly as you approach,"

---

78. Malherbe et al., *Early Church in Its Context*, 6.

79. Clement of Alexandria, *Strom.* 6.11. In another place, Clement quoted Aristobulus saying, "Plato followed the laws given to us, and had manifestly studied all that is said in them," and he also quoted Numenius, "What is Plato, but Moses speaking in Attic Greek?" Clement, *Strom.* 1.22; See also Clement, *Protr.* 6; Justin Martyr, *1 Apol.* 44; and Tertullian, *Apol.* 46.

80. Kugel, *Idea of Biblical Poetry*, 143.

81. Kugel, *Idea of Biblical Poetry*, 145.

82. Ambrose claimed, and Augustine accepted, that Plato made a journey to Egypt when Jeremiah went there and learned from him. Augustine, *Doctr. chr.* 2.28.43. Augustine, however, corrected his view later admitting that it was due to miscalculation of dates. Augustine, *Civ.* 8.11.1.

83. Eusebius, *Prep. Ev.* 11.5.

but it is "sublime as you advance, and veiled in mysteries."[84] Augustine confessed that it was his pride that hid his eyes from recognizing the beauty of Scripture: "I feel when I turned towards those Scriptures, but they appeared to me to be unworthy to be compared with the dignity of Tully [Cicero]; for my inflated pride shunned their style, nor could the sharpness of my wit pierce their inner meaning."[85] In *De doctrina christiana*, (*On Christian Doctrine*), he remarked that the writers of Scripture used forms of expression in greater variety and freedom than the Greeks:

> Moreover, I would have learned men to know that the authors of our Scriptures use all those forms of expression which grammarians call by the Greek name *tropes*, and use them more freely and in greater variety than people who are unacquainted with the Scriptures, and have learnt these figures of speech from other writings, can imagine or believe.[86]

Even if Kugel's reservation is accepted, this observation of Augustine, alone with Eusebius's linguistic observation that the Hebrew writers were "excellent dialecticians," is a testimony to the loftiness of the poetics of the Old Testament.

The Medieval Period

Cassiodorus (ca. 485–ca. 585) spent the first half of his life in public service in Roman Italy but devoted the rest of his life to the church. Around AD 555, Cassiodorus founded a monastery in his estate, and shortly after, he composed his two-volume work, *Institutions of Divine and Secular Learning and On the Soul*.[87] In the first book, he gave a survey of biblical books, suggesting recommended readings from the church fathers (especially Hillary, Ambrose, Jerome, and Augustine). In the second book, he catalogued areas of studies of liberal arts which aid biblical studies, such as mathematics, arithmetic, music, geometry, and astronomy. In this second book, however, he listed and discussed the classical rhetoric for Christians, frequently citing Cicero. It is these principles of rhetoric he laid down in this section which he applied in his commentary of the Psalms, *Explanation of the Psalms*.

84. Augustine, *Conf.* 3.5.9.
85. Augustine, *Conf.* 3.5.9.
86. Augustine, *Doctr. chr.* 3.29.40.
87. Cassiodorus, *Institutions of Divine and Secular Learning*.

In the preface of this commentary, he noted the beauty of the Psalms and said that "divine eloquence" fills them.[88] According to Cassiodorus, the Word of God made use of various features of language:

> [The divine Word] exploits its varieties of language in sundry ways, being clothed in definitions adorned by figures, marked by its special vocabulary, equipped with the conclusions of syllogisms, gleaming with forms of instruction. But it does not appropriate from these a beauty adopted from elsewhere, but rather bestows on them its own high status. For when these techniques shine in the divine Scriptures, they are precise and wholly without fault, but once enmeshed in men's opinions and the emptiest problems, they are disturbed by obscure waves of argument.[89]

Cassiodorus observed that Scripture is beautiful in its poetics. Yet with men's opinions and "emptiest problems," he said these poetics (or "techniques" as he called them) are "disturbed by obscure waves of argument." He also continued the arguments of the church fathers that those who are learned in secular arts transferred the techniques of Scripture to "the collection of arguments which the Greeks calls topics, and to the arts of dialectic and rhetoric."[90]

Judah Halevi (ca. 1075–1141), a contemporary of Moses ibn Ezra, was born in Toledo during the golden age of Jewish culture in Spain. In the eleventh century in Spain, Aristotelian philosophy, Islamic theology, and Karaite sect of Judaism seriously challenged rabbinic Judaism at several fronts.[91] Judah Hallevi wrote *Kitab al Khazari* as a defense of Judaism against these challenges. The work is in the form of a dialogue between the pagan king Khazars and a Jewish rabbi. It is a philosophical and polemical treaty originally written in Arabic after the conversion of Khazars and his people to Judaism.

On the lips of the rabbi, Hallevi used scriptural basis in arguing for the originality of Hebrew wisdom and learning and the subsequent transference of these to others nations. He said:

> What is your opinion of Solomon's accomplishments? Did he not, with the assistance of divine, intellectual, and natural power,

---

88. Cassiodorus, *Explanation of the Psalms*, 37.
89. Cassiodorus, *Explanation of the Psalms*, 37–38.
90. Cassiodorus, *Explanation of the Psalms*, 38.
91. For the circumstances surrounding Judah Hallevi's work, see the introduction of Hartwig Hirschfeld in: Hallevi, *Kitab al Khazari*, 1–34.

converse on all sciences? The inhabitants of the earth traveled to him, in order to carry forth his learning, even as far as India. Now the roots and principles of all sciences were handed down from us first to the Chaldeans, then to the Persians and Medians, then to Greece, and finally to the Romans. On account of the length of this period, and the many disturbing circumstances, it was forgotten that they had originated with the Hebrews, and so they were ascribed to the Greeks and Romans. To Hebrew, however, belongs the first place, both as regards the nature of the languages, and as to fullness of meanings.[92]

On the lack of meter in Hebrew poetry, Hallevi stated that Hebrews have something better than meter for effective communication. In verbal communications, he argued, there are several things that make communication effective—such as facial expressions and raising or lowering of voices. He said, "In the remnant of our language which was created and instituted by God, are implanted subtle elements calculated to promote understanding, and to take the place of the above aids to speech." These are, he continued, "the accents with which the holy text is read."[93] His comment about accents is insightful in showing the artfulness of Hebrew language. He said: "They denote pause and continuation, they separate question from answer, the beginning from the continuation of the speech, haste from hesitation, command from request, on which subject books might be written."[94] Due to the metrical influence of the Greeks, however, Hallevi grieved that the knowledge of accentuation in Hebrew language was lost.

The Renaissance Period

Judah Messer Leon (ca. 1420–ca. 1497) was born in Italy and lived in many of its important cultural centers. Having been well-educated both in Judaism and secular philosophy and medicine, and thus duly called the "Renaissance man," he was actively involved in Jewish communities as a scholar, educator, physician, and Rabbi. In the *Book of the Honeycomb's Flow*, presumably a textbook written for training his students, he paid attention to the rhetoric of the Hebrew Bible. Isaac Rabinowitz said that his book is one of the earliest treaties on the rhetorical criticism of

---

92. Hallevi, *Kitab al Khazari*, 124.
93. Hallevi, *Kitab al Khazari*, 126.
94. Hallevi, *Kitab al Khazari*, 126.

the Hebrew Bible.[95] As a handbook on rhetoric, Leon discussed the Aristotelian rhetoric from biblical examples—including topics like arrangement, deliver, memory, style, three kinds of rhetoric (epideictic, judicial, and deliberative), and figures of speech (metaphor, allegory, simile, pleonasm, ellipsis, irony, euphemism, etc.). What is important about this work is that he sought to demonstrate the popular notion that the science of rhetoric is embedded in and originates from the Hebrew Scripture. In the section on "Memory," Leon stated his view about the Hebrew Scripture in this following way:

> In the days of Prophecy, indeed, in the months of old, when out of Zion, the perfection of beauty, God shined forth, we used to learn and know from the holy Torah all the sciences and truths of reason... What other peoples possessed of these sciences and truths was, by comparison with us, very little, so that the nations which heard the fame of us were wont to say: "Surely this great nation is a wise and understanding people." But after the indwelling Presence of God departed from our midst because of our many iniquities, when Prophecy and insight ceased, and the science of our men of understanding was hid, we were no longer able to derive understanding of all scientific developments and attainments from the Torah's words; this condition, however, persists due to our own falling short, our failure to know the Torah in full perfection. Thus the matter has come to be in reverse; for if, after we have come to know all the sciences, or some part of them, we study the words of the Torah, then the eyes of our understanding open to the fact that the sciences are included in the Torah's words, and we wonder how we could have failed to realize this from the Torah itself to begin with. Such has frequently been our own experience, especially in the science of Rhetoric.[96]

Because of their sinful disobediences, Leon said, the glory of the LORD departed from Israel and the people have lost the ability to know the Scripture in its full perfection and beauty, especially "in the science of Rhetoric." The situation, therefore, was that when they learned the sciences from other cultures, they were rediscovering the beauty of Scripture backwardly. Since God is perfect in beauty and glory and his words are faultless, Leon believed that Scripture is also perfect both in content and form. In another place, he commented again: "Now since the prophets

95. Leon, *Book of the Honeycomb's Flow*, xv–xvi.
96. Leon, *Book of the Honeycomb's Flow*, 143–45.

were highly skilled in rhetoric—as by common consent they are held to be without peer among the orators of the Nations—it follows that all their utterances are pure words . . . refined. It also follows that there is no anomaly at all in their words."[97]

Because of this belief in the faultlessness of Scripture, he was able to find deliberate purposefulness behind matters that seem like scribal or grammatical errors otherwise. Thus he noted, "Strange usage is a figure of diction whereby one or more grammatically irregular words are introduced in order to call attention to, enhance, and elevate the strangeness of the subject matter."[98] This observation is what Longinus concurred long ago as that which produces sublimity.

Leon remarkably tried to show through countless examples how Greek and Latin rhetorical features are already present in the Scripture. He demonstrated amply the idea that Hebrew rhetoric (and poetics for that matter) is comparable and even excels the classical, so that "to compare is like comparing the hyssop . . . in the wall with the cedar that is in Lebanon."[99]

Another Jewish scholar who observed the poetics of Old Testament is Azariah de' Rossi (ca.1511–ca.1577). He was born in Mantua of Italy, and probably received an extensive training in Judaism and secular learning. Because of his advanced scholarship, Jewish communities considered him radical in his lifetime. In his magnum opus *Light of the Eyes*, he used a variety of sources at his disposal with critical eyes—such as rabbinic texts, the church fathers, Aristeas, Philo, Josephus, Greek and Latin sources, apocrypha, pseudepigrapha, and the New Testament. His Jewish contemporaries rejected his work initially, but it became known as a prime example of scholarly work among the Jewish people during the Enlightenment.

After speaking about how Josephus recognized hexameters in Scripture according to Greek poetry, and how Jerome followed the same opinion and saw trimesters and tetrameters in Psalms, he investigated the forms of Hebrew poetry. Concerning Hebrew poetry, he agreed with Judah Hallevi that while the songs in Scripture have structures, they were different than what was current in his time. He said:

> At any rate, we do indeed have reason to believe that all the songs of holy Scripture . . . undoubtedly adhere to an arrangement and

---

97. Leon, *Book of the Honeycomb's Flow*, 559.
98. Leon, *Book of the Honeycomb's Flow*, 569–71.
99. Leon, *Book of the Honeycomb's Flow*, 145.

structure, one with one mode and the other with another, or one in its own right containing different measures. On reciting them, we sense that they have a wonderful special quality even though we cannot fully apprehend their structures. In like manner, we speak, get up, and sit down without knowing which nerves and natural faculties enable us to perform those actions . . . Everything is determined by that which suits the purpose of the subject and the variations which occur in the course of the song are due to the movements of the body and soul.[100]

De' Rossi recognized that the songs in the Scripture follow various rules that correspond to "the purpose of the subject," and that these rules are not easy to discern, just like the movement of body. He said that the verses of Scripture are "superior and more notable than those that depend on syllabic feet."[101] He affirmed once again, "The poems based on rhythm with feet and quantities, numbered according to rules, are not truly congruent with the nature of our language."[102] In this way, de' Rossi recognized the special character of Hebrew poetics in the songs that are different from and superior to the Greeks.

Summary

Both Christian and Jewish writers in history have recognized the special nature of Hebrew Scripture as they read it. Whether one receives or rejects the accounts of Josephus, Eusebius, or Origen concerning the influence of Hebrews upon the Greeks, it is important to note that the Jewish people have always observed special characters of their language and their sacred Scripture. A close study of Scripture always yielded the opinion that it excels other literatures in beauty and wisdom. Just as Augustine confessed, it may be the sinful pride of human hearts that blind their eyes to its glory. So the present situation is that one should learn the secular wisdom and bring it to Scripture to discover its poetics. According to de' Rossi, it could be difficult to define what exactly it is that promotes its loveliness. Probably the poetics of Scripture is much more intricate and artistic than what people recognize, just as a simple walking would be incomparable to the whole movement of body in dancing.

---

100. Rossi, *Light of the Eyes*, 714.
101. Rossi, *Light of the Eyes*, 715.
102. Rossi, *Light of the Eyes*, 719.

This chapter laid down the rationale for using Old Testament poetics as the literary convention of the Gospel of John. It handled the authorship issue in order to guarantee a strong presence of the author behind the poetics of the Gospel. It is no accident that certain features are present in the Gospel. A study in the poetics is not a scholarly endeavor to endow meanings to what otherwise would remain tangled, confused, or unintelligible. It is not giving life to what is dead. Rather, it is a process of recognizing how it has been full of life and active for all these years (Heb 4:12). At the center of the poetics, the author is present with his divine creativity and eloquence. A Jewish apostle of Jesus wrote the Fourth Gospel to a primarily Jewish audience.

Gentiles were by no means out of his sight because John must have envisioned God grafting them into Israel just as Paul recognized (Rom 11:17–24). In order to persuade them, however, he did not forsake his rich Jewish heritage. For this reason, students of the Fourth Gospel must approach it with a full confidence that applying the Old Testament to its style is perfectly in harmony with its nature.

Those who paid close attention to the Old Testament always saw how beautiful and how sweet it is (Ps 19:7–11). Cassiodorus said that features not borrowed from anywhere adorn the Scripture, and it is men's opinions and empty problems that disturbed the understanding of these poetics. Leon observed the situation where Jewish people lost the knowledge of the poetics of the Word of God and that now they had to learn it through other sciences. De' Rossi argued that the songs of Scripture conform to some wonderful arrangement and structure, although it is difficult to define it. His statement that the poetics of Scripture follows the special nature of Hebrew language is insightful for the current study.

In the Gospel of John, it is difficult to define precisely what it is that makes it so powerful and so appealing. However, as readers see it through the lens of Old Testament poetics—of how the writers expressed their thoughts and conveyed the messages—it will become easier for them to dance along with John in the divine rhythm of grace and truth.

3

The Gospel of John in Light of the Poetics of Old Testament Poetry

ONE OF THE REASONS that the Gospel is perplexing in close examination is that it is a *poetic* narrative, if this designation is acceptable. Reading the Gospel of John with the awareness that there are distinctive features of Hebrew poetry embedded within its narrative helps one to understand the peculiar aspects of the Gospel. John's favorite literary strategy is making use of double meanings, and perhaps the same principle applies to the nature of the Gospel. It is a narrative on one level, but at the same time, it has characteristics of poetry and demands a reading with poetic sensitivity. However, comparing the Gospel's narrative art with the devices of Old Testament poetry needs some explanation. Is it legitimate to compare the prosaic style of the Gospel with the techniques of Hebrew poetry? An important issue in this discussion is what distinguishes poetry from prose. What is it that enables a person to say that a text is poetry and not prose?

Investigating the vexing problem of what constituted poetry and prose, James L. Kugel made an important remark that the relationship between poetry and prose is that of a "continuum." His observation comes from the fact that biblical parallelism pervades in non-poetical sections of Scripture, and that the degree of parallelism varies among the poetry. He argued that "poetry" and "prose" are non-biblical terms and making that distinction is therefore foreign to Scripture. What one sees in Scripture is not strict polarization of the texts on either side, but much freedom of its form in between these two poles. For this reason, he stated that much of the Bible lies in the rhetorical "intermediate kingdom."[1] Although some challenged his rejection of the distinction between prose and poetry,[2] his argument against a strict categorization of prose and poetry was indeed groundbreaking. David N. Freedman agreed that between prose and poetry, "the distinction is often quantitative rather than qualitative, and in terms of degree rather than kind."[3] Therefore, with these ideas, one can certainly identify a text as poetical without actually calling it poetry. Kugel stated, "In sum, what is called biblical 'poetry' is a complex of heightening effects used in combinations and intensities that vary widely from composition to composition even within a single 'genre.'"[4]

The following sections in this chapter demonstrate that the heavy presence of parallelism, repetition and variation, terseness, double meaning, and imagery, which make up the language of Old Testament poetry, are characteristic of John.

Parallelism

Hebrew poetry has many distinctive features, but Robert Lowth discovered that parallelism is the major feature of Hebrew poetry. In his *Lectures on the Sacred Poetry of the Hebrews* (1753), Lowth stated the laws of parallelism as the *Parallelismus Membrorum*, or the "parallelism of the members." Observing that sacred hymns in Israel are "alternately sung by opposite choirs," answering and corresponding to each other, he said this is the mode of composition in Hebrew poetry.[5] He noted, "almost every poem possesses a sort of responsive form" and that sentences are in "poetical conformation."[6] When the couplet resound same sentiment in equivalent terms, it was synonymous parallelism. When they express thoughts in contrary terms, it was antithetic parallelism. When two

---

1. Kugel, *Biblical Poetry*, 63–69.

2. Adele Berlin argued that the distinction of poetry and prose is inevitable, because "at a certain point quantitative difference becomes qualitative difference." Berlin, "Reading Biblical Poetry," 2097.

3. Freedman, "Pottery, Poetry, and Prophecy," 6. Cf. Gillingham, *Poems and Psalms of the Hebrew Bible*, 21–43; Petersen and Richards, *Interpreting Hebrew Poetry*, 13; Watson, *Classical Hebrew Poetry*, 44–61.

4. Kugel, *Biblical Poetry*, 94.

5. Lowth, *Lectures on the Sacred Poetry*, 1:253–58.

6. Lowth, *Lectures on the Sacred Poetry*, 1:258–59.

sentences answered another in ways indescribable by the former two, it was synthetic parallelism.[7] For Lowth, the essence of parallelism was the correspondence of lines:

> The correspondence of one verse, or line, with another, I call parallelism. When a proposition is delivered, and a second is subjoined to it, or drawn under it, equivalent, or contrasted with it, in sense; or familiar to it in the form of grammatical construction; these I call parallel lines; and the words or phrases answering one to another in the corresponding lines, parallel terms.[8]

Subsequent scholars, however, saw inadequacies in Lowth's theory of parallelism and modified, expanded, and challenged the view. George B. Gray recognized that two lines in Hebrew poetry do not always correspond exactly as Lowth said, so he introduced an important concept known as "complete parallelism" and "incomplete parallelism."[9] He said that complete parallelism is when all parts in the first line have correspondence in the second (i.e., Isa 21:3). Incomplete parallelism is when some terms in the first line do not have their counterparts in the second line (i.e., Song 2:1). Johann G. von Herder, on the other hand, did define find strict categories of parallelism, but instead sought to capture the broader "spirit of parallelism:"

> Poetry is not addressed to the understanding alone but primarily and chiefly to the feelings . . . So soon as the heart gives way to its emotions, wave follows upon wave, and that is parallelism. The heart is never exhausted, it has forever something new to say. So soon as the first wave has passed away, or broken itself upon the rocks, the second swells again and returns as before. This pulsation of nature, this breathing of emotion, appears in all the language of passion.[10]

With this statement, he expressed a romantic idea of poetry that the "breathing of emotion" is the essence of parallelism.

Several noteworthy studies on parallelism advanced the understanding of Hebrew poetry,[11] but Kugel left the most definitive mark in

---

7. Lowth, *Lectures on the Sacred Poetry*, 1:259–67.
8. Lowth, *Isaiah*, xiv.
9. Gray, *Forms of Hebrew Poetry*, 59.
10. von Herder, *Spirit of Hebrew Poetry*, 1:41.
11. Cf. Berlin, *Dynamics of Biblical Parallelism*; Cross and Freedman, *Studies in Ancient Yahwistic Poetry*; Greenstein, "How Does Parallelism Mean?," 41–70; Jakobson,

the study of biblical poetry when he expressed the idea of biblical poetry as "A is so, and what's more, B."[12] With this concept, he recognized that "B" is seconding "A" in many different ways. G. H. Wilson concurred with this observation: "The close grammatical-structural similarity between lines provides continuity that mphasizes the *parallel* character of the two lines, while the distinctive phraseology of each phrase lifts the phenomenon beyond *mere repetition* and offers the opportunity for expansion or advancement on the original line's meaning."[13] Berlin expressed her view similarly and said, "The first line presents a picture and the second line shines a spotlight on a certain part of it."[14] Alter stated that the dominant pattern in parallelism is "a focusing, heightening, or specification of ideas, images, actions, and themes from one verset to the next."[15]

From what Lowth observed as the correspondence of its members, Hebrew parallelism is now understood as a way of varying, focusing, intensifying, and amplifying one thought with another. Peter A. Boodberg made this poignant statement:

> Parallelism is not merely a stylistic device of formularistic syntactical duplication; it is intended to achieve a result reminiscent of binocular vision, the superimposition of two syntactical images in order to endow them with solidity and depth, the repetition of the pattern having the effect of binding together syntagms that appear at first rather loosely aligned.[16]

This statement that parallelism accomplishes a "binocular vision" that binds apparently loose parts certainly speaks of the heart of the matter. When certain parts of the Fourth Gospel of John are intentionally structured in parallelistic constructions, whether in sentences or in larger units, the intention is seconding (Kugel), expanding/advancing (Wilson), spotlighting (Berlin), focusing/heightening (Alter), or establishing binocular vision (Boodberg) of the original idea to achieve depth and profoundness. In John, the poetic style of the narrative invites the readers to

---

"Grammatical Parallelism and Its Russian Facet," 399–429; O'Conner, *Hebrew Verse Structure*; Pardee, *Ugaritic and Hebrew Poetic Parallelism*.

12. Kugel, *Biblical Poetry*, 1–58.

13. Wilson, *Psalms*, 39. Italics in original.

14. Berlin, "Reading Biblical Poetry," 2099.

15. Alter, *Biblical Literature*, 179. Cf. Fokkelman, *Reading Biblical Poetry*, 24–27, 61–86.

16. Boodberg, "Crypto-Parallelism in Chinese Poetry," 001-540701; Boodberg, "Syntactical Metaplasia in Stereoscopic Parallelism," 017-54121.

The Gospel of John in Light of the Poetics of Old Testament Poetry

understand one part in terms of the other, and parallelism has the effect of luring the readers to deeper contemplation without having the need to resort to highly technical analyses such as of structuralism.

Westcott observed that, in the Gospel of John, the spirit of parallelism "runs through the whole record, both in its general structure and in the structure of its parts."[17] Many commentators have noted the parallelism in the Prologue of the Gospel, and it does not need reiteration here. John probably is setting the tone in the Prologue through which the readers must approach and adjust their expectations for the rest of the Gospel. Bultmann famously isolated "Revelation-speech" source material (*offenbarungsreden*) for the discourses in the Gospel based on its poetic format.[18] Although this delineation of source materials is unwarranted, his arrangement clearly demonstrated the prevalence of parallelism in the discourse sections.

Burney also observed numerous parallelisms in the discourses of Jesus.[19] Following the categories of Lowth, he observed synonymous parallelisms (3:11; 4:35; 6:35, 55; 7:34, 37; 12:26, 31; 13:16; 14:27; 15:26; 20:17, 27), antithetic parallelisms (3:6, 18, 31, 36; 4:13,14, 22; 5:29, 43; 6:27, 32; 7:6; 8:23, 35; 9:39, 41; 10:10; 11:9, 10; 12:8, 24, 25; 14:19; 15:2, 15; 16:33), and synthetic parallelism (8:44). He also saw numerous instances of step-parallelism (6:37; 8:32; 10:11; 11:25; 13:20; 14:2, 3, 21; 15:13, 14; 16:7, 20, 22; 10:26, 27; 18:36) and instances where couplets are followed by explanatory and prose-style comments (3:11, 14, 18, 19, 34; 4:22, 36; 6:32). Burney made an important observation that John agrees with "the diction of the Old Testament writers–Prophets, Psalmist, and Wise men, whose utterances are cast in poetic form, the chief characteristic of which is adherence to certain rules of composition which are defined by the terms parallelism and rhythm."[20] One can also see that the sense of parallelism runs throughout the speeches of John the Baptist as well (i.e., 1:30, 34; 3:30, 31, 32–33, 36).[21]

The highly parallelistic Prologue section should be read with poetic sensitivity. For instance, the staircase parallelism in 1:1–2 is a "structure

---

17. Westcott, *John*, liii.
18. Bultmann, *Gospel of John*, 140n2, 155n1.
19. Burney, *Poetry of Our Lord*, passim.
20. Burney, *Poetry of Our Lord*, 5.
21. Cf. Black, *Aramaic Approach to the Gospels and Acts*, 107–11.

of intensification."[22] As John compounds various thoughts, John forcefully makes the statement that the "Word was God." In verse 4, when he says "In Him was life, and the life was the Light of men," what he says is that "In Him was life," *but what is more*, "the life was the Light of men." In this parallel construction, John is seconding, putting a spotlight on, and intensifying the idea that the life *is* the light of men.

When Jesus said, "I am the bread of life; he who comes to Me will not hunger, and he who believes in Me will never thirst" (John 6:35), the second and the third part both function as an elaboration of what He meant in the first part. "Coming" corresponds to "believing," and "hunger" responds to "thirst." In this structure, each term explains the other. Therefore, the effect of the parallelism in this verse is similar to "A=B+C." What "A" means is explained by "B" and "C" taken together. Seconding hunger with thirst and using them to explain what it means for Jesus to be the bread of life powerfully touch the depth of human existence. Jesus' statement, "For My flesh is true food, and My blood is true drink" (6:55), provides another example of poetic power. As "flesh" and "blood" corresponds to each other, signifying the totality of his earthly life,[23] "true food" and "true drink" also signify together the totality of sustenance. In other words, the life He gave is all that people need for true living. In another example, when Jesus said, "peace I leave with you, My peace I give to you" (14:27), He means "peace I leave with you," *but what is more, it is in fact* "My peace that I give to you." It is not a generic peace that he is promising, but it is instead *his* own peace.

When John said, "He must increase, but I must decrease" (3:30), the force of that statement in light of its parallelism is this: "He must increase," *and not only that*, "I must decrease." In this case, the correspondence of the second line heightens the truth of the first statement. This construction has the implication that "my decreasing" achieves "His increasing," and "His increasing" empowers "my decreasing." Sensitivity to the structure of parallelism makes such insights possible and draws out deeper meanings. When John said, "He who believes in the Son has eternal life, but he who does not obey the Son will not see life, but the wrath of God abides on him" (3:36), he forcefully brings the consequence of unbelief by the addition of the third line. What he means is that "he who does not obey the Son will not see life," *but not only that, even more*

---

22. Alter, *Art of Biblical Poetry*, 75–104.

23. This technique of signifying one complex thought by using two words in parallelism is known as hendiadys. Cf. Watson, *Classical Hebrew Poetry*, 324.

so it means, "the wrath of God abides in him." The seconding brings out a far worse consequence of unbelief: Not only unbelievers will not see life, but the terrible and terrifying wrath of God abides and overshadows them. In these examples, when the conjunctions καί and δέ are present, they do not serve simple connective or disjunctive functions, but bridge more complex relationships of the parallel lines.

Parallelism is also evident in the structure of the Gospel, and some examples will be sufficient to demonstrate the point. For instance, in 1:19–51, John the Baptist's testimonies and the coming of the first disciples are constructed in intricate networks of parallelism. In the below layout, the italicized units are seconding the previous sections and they invite comparison, contrast, adding the element of "A is so, and what's more, B," while supplementing them with new insights and heightening important themes and ideas.

John's Testimony (1:19–34)
John's Testimony (1:35–36)
        Disciples Coming to Jesus (1:37–42)
        Disciples Coming to Jesus (1:43–49)
                Promise of Greater Things (1:50–51)

In 2:1–25, Jesus' self-testimonies are powerfully presented in parallel constructions also. This section records Jesus' first sign in Cana, but it is constructed in a way that it follows closely the promise Jesus made of the greater things. Although the promise seems to be directed in a certain direction (as it is elaborated by Jesus' own explanation in 1:51), nonetheless, the arousing of expectation in "You will see greater things" is closely followed by Jesus' self-testimonies:

Greater things,
    namely Jesus' self-testimony
        through changing water into wine (2:1–12)
Greater things,
    namely Jesus' self-testimony
        through cleansing the temple (2:13–25)

It is not difficult to discern a carefully constructed parallelism running through the whole section of 1:19—4:54 in large units; it speaks of the initial witnesses to Jesus and various responses:

John's Testimony (1:19–51)
> Jesus' Testimony in Cana and the Temple (2:1–25)
> Jesus' Discourse with Nicodemus (3:1–21)

John's Testimony (3:22–36)
> Jesus' Discourse with Samaritan Woman (4:1–45)
> Jesus' Testimony in Cana (4:46–54)

These are only some of the examples, but many sentence-level and macro-level parallelism structures in John invite readers to deeper explorations.[24]

Repetition and Variation

The heart of parallelism is in the repetition and variation of corresponding parts. Commenting of the Lowth's observation of synonymous parallelism, James Muilenburg made an observation concerning the nature of parallelism:

> Parallelism is in reality very seldom precisely synonymous. The parallel line does not simply repeat what has been said, but enriches it, deepens it, transforms it by adding fresh nuances and bringing in new elements, renders it more concrete and vivid and telling . . . It is precisely the combination of what is repeated and what is added that makes of parallelism the artistic form that it is.[25]

In other words, the heart of parallelism is the repetition and variation of words, sentences, and ideas for more effectiveness and forcefulness.

Examples of repetition and variation are endless in the poetry of Old Testament, so only some of them receive attention here. Parallelism of Hebrew poetry involves "many types of linguistic repetition or equivalences."[26] As devices of repetition in Hebrew Poetry, Berlin noted that there are keywords (Pss 121; 137), consecutive lines beginning with

---

24. Study in the structure of John itself is a demanding task, but most studies recognize parallelism/chiasm as the most prominent structuring devices. George Mlakuzhyil provided the most thorough investigation in the structure of the Fourth Gospel. Mlakuzhyil, *Christocentric Literary Structure of the Fourth Gospel*. For the structure of John 1–10, see: Kim, *Sourcebook of the Structures and Styles in John 1–10*. Egil A. Wyller's analysis is still insightful: Wyller, "In Solomon's Porch," 151–67.

25. Muilenburg, "Study in Hebrew Rhetoric," 98.

26. Berlin, "Introduction to Hebrew Poetry," 309.

the same word or phrase (Eccl 3:2–8; Ps 13:2–3), consecutive lines ending with same word or phrase (Isa 40:13–14), the last word or phrase repeating in the beginning of the next line (Ps 96:13), immediate repetition of the same word (Isa 28:10; 40:1; 52:1), refrain (Pss 107:1, 8, 15, 21, 31; 136), inclusio (Pss 8; 103), chiasm (Isa 5:20; 40:30–31), ABAB word patterning (Isa 51:6; 54:7–8), and sound patterning (Isa 1:2; 5:7).[27] As this list shows, there are many ways of repetition and variation in Hebrew poetry.

John Goldingay investigated how the psalmists preferred variations in repetition. While some of the refrains repeat exactly (i.e., Pss 8; 136), in most cases, he observed that the writers preferred variations. Examining Psalms 24, 42–43, 46, 49, 56, 57, 59, 62, 80, Goldingay concluded that the "psalmists were more pleased by a new twist to a familiar line."[28]

Concerning the types of repetition, Watson similarly recognized that there are sound repetition of assonance (Jer 49:1), alliteration (Ps 147:13), rhyme (Isa 33:22), initial repetitions (Prov 30:4), end repetitions (Eccl 1:5), immediate repetition (Lam 4:15), refrains (Amos 1–2; 4:6–11; Pss 80:4, 8, 20), inclusio (Pss 8:2, 10; 101:2, 7; 118:1, 29), keywords ("voice" in Ps 29, "to guard" in Ps 121, and "to say" in Ps 129) and chiasmus (Isa 22:22; Prov 7:21).[29] In these repetition devices, variation is the norm.

The use of synonyms is another case of repetition and variation in Hebrew poetry. Luis Anonso Schökel said that synonymy is a poetic device of semantic repetition where the poet repeats the sense through the use of similar words.[30] Synonyms in poetry carry the writer's thought in similar words as it unfolds within his heart by the contemplation of the object. Schökel stated it this way:

> Instead of amplifying by dividing, subdividing, doubling and duplicating always on more particular levels, the poet takes a totality and expresses it in a sentence. When he has finished he takes the same totality again and expresses it with another series of words which are similar or equivalent . . . He presents a contemplation of the same object which reveals new details, new facts . . . Poetic synonymy is a technique for presenting variety in equality.[31]

27. Berlin, "Introduction to Hebrew Poetry," 309–11.
28. Goldingay, "Repetition and Variation in the Psalms," 151.
29. Watson, *Classical Hebrew Poetry*, 274–99.
30. Schökel, *Manual of Hebrew Poetics*, 64.
31. Schökel, *Manual of Hebrew Poetics*, 71.

Through the use of synonyms, the poet impresses the message repeatedly upon the hearers in ever new ways, each time adding new dimensions toward the goal of wholeness. Such repetitions, Schökel mentioned, happen in various quantities (words, roots, incomplete or complete sentences, etc.), qualities (morphological or syntactical), arrangements (side by side, at the beginning, the end, regularly or irregularly, invertedly, etc.), and functions.[32] It will be interesting to see how John's themes are repeated and variegated throughout the Gospel according to these patterns.

What Tenney perceived as a *symphonic* structure in John agrees with Schökel's insight. John certainly uses a limited set of vocabulary, but he uses them so masterfully in repetition and variation, so that its effect is like listening to a symphony. Tenney said:

> These interwoven themes, fluctuating in emphasis but always progress in development, lead steadily forward to the climax which consummates them simultaneously, and creates the cumulative incentive to faith. This type of structure may be called *symphonic*, from its likeness to the form of a symphony. A symphony is a musical composition having several movements related in subject, but varying in form and execution. It usually begins with a dominant theme, into which variations are introduced at intervals. The variations seem to be developed independently, but as the music is played, they modulate into each other until finally all are brought to a climax. The apparent disunity is really part of a design which is not evident at first, but which appears in the progress of the composition.[33]

Each building block of John's symphony may resist microscopic analysis, but the effect is certainly felt and the powerful impression moves the hearers.

As hinted in Schökel's observation, the reason for repetition and variation in Hebrew poetry is deeply embedded in the thought patterns of the Hebrew people. Muilenburg noted it this way:

> The roots of repetition lie deeply embedded in the language and literature of Israel. An examination of the various modes of reduplication in Hebrew syntax or of the repetition of single words in elemental contexts of unreflected speech will reveal very clearly how the primitive spirit of the language continues to be preserved and lends to it an intensity, a spontaneity and

---

32. Schökel, *Manual of Hebrew Poetics*, 70–71.
33. Tenney, "Literary Keys to the Fourth Gospel," 117–18.

freshness, a directness and immediacy which would be difficult to achieve in any other fashion.[34]

The repetitive pattern in the system of the Hebrew language imprinted its mark on the mode of speech.

Johannes Pedersen observed that the Hebrews had a propensity for totality. He said: "For the Israelite thinking was not the solving of abstract problems. He does not add link to link, nor does he set up major and minor premises from which conclusions are drawn. To him, thinking is to grasp a totality."[35] Pedersen set forth several convincing proofs to show that Hebrews thought in totality. He said that this mindset of totality is apparent when (1) one word expresses different nuances under different circumstances; (2) one word formation of verb, subject, and object expressing the whole idea; (3) an intimate coalescence of two nouns that form one concept in a noun construct; and (4) many prepositions do not show consequences, but rather connections to what happened before.[36] Hebrew people moved forward their thoughts as they repeated old elements in various ways and added new nuances to give fresh dimension to the whole. This propensity for totality is evident in how biblical writers conceived and connected sentences in order to create the whole. Pedersen continued:

> Just as the word-images form new wholes by being united in one sentence, so also the sentences form totalities by being connected with each other, in that they concentrate round the specially emphasized main points . . . The Israelite does not argue by means of conclusions and logical progress. His argumentation consists in showing that one statement associates itself with another, as belonging to its totality.[37]

This "striving after totality and movement"[38] expressed itself in repetition and variation, and through these, the Hebrew poets sought to communicate the whole message.

The Gospel of John demonstrates this characteristic feature of poetry. John achieves the totality of thought by repetition and variation of

---

34. Muilenburg, "Study in Hebrew Rhetoric," 101. Cf. Eitan, "La Repetition de la Racine en Hebreu," 171–86.
35. Pedersen, *Israel*, 1:108.
36. Pedersen, *Israel*, 1:108–16.
37. Pedersen, *Israel*, 1:115.
38. Pedersen, *Israel*, 1:123.

words and ideas. Willem Nicol said that "remarkable repetitions" are typical to John.[39] G. van Belle pointed out that, in contrast to John, "the Synoptics rarely used repetition."[40]

A feature noted frequently is the "inclusio," or the envelope structure. It is a literary device that "opens and closes a passage with the same or similar words."[41] Inclusio occurs, for example, in the mentions of Cana (2:11 and 4:46), changing of water into wine (2:1–11 and 4:46), Capernaum (2:12 and 4:46), and inadequacy of faith based on signs (2:23–25 and 4:45, 48).[42] The final verses of chapter 10 close a giant inclusio structure, with Jesus' ministry beginning and ending with the testimonies of John the Baptist (1:19–34 and 10:40–42).[43] The festival cycle that began in chapter 5 comes to a preliminary closure at the end of chapter 10 with its inclusio, setting the stage for the climatic material of raising Lazarus and its aftermath in chapters 11–12.[44] Brown noted that the mention of "glory" in raising Lazarus in 11:40 forms an inclusio with the Cana miracle in 2:11, bringing the first and the last signs together, and the theme of glory serving "as a transition to the Book of Glory, which is the second half of the Gospel."[45] "Believing" and "seeing" the one who sent "me" in 12:44–45 forms inclusio with "receiving" in 13:20, with the implication that the disciples are now the sent one of Jesus;[46] a message powerfully conveyed in the act of foot-washing. Inclusio appears also in the love commandment (15:12 and 17),[47] "Do not let your heart be troubled" statements (14:1 and 14:27, and possibly also with 16:33).[48] In the resurrection account in chapter 20, Gerald L. Borchert believed that the stories of Mary Magdalene (20:1–2 and 20:11–18) envelop the faith of the beloved disciple who is able to believe without seeing (20:8).[49] The mention of "Simon, son of John" in 20:15 is a inclusio with 1:42,[50]

39. Nicol, Sēmeia in the Fourth Gospel, 24.
40. van Belle, "Repetitions and Variations in Johannine Research," 41.
41. Carson, John, 299.
42. Carson, John, 237.
43. Carson, John, 402.
44. Köstenberger, John, 276.
45. Brown, John, 1:435–36.
46. Borchert, John 12–21, 89.
47. Borchert, John 12–21, 151.
48. Köstenberger, John, 444.
49. Borchert, John 12–21, 289–90, 296.
50. Köstenberger, John, 595.

bringing the whole gospel to a closure or perhaps even signaling a new start at the same time. Andrew T. Lincoln recognized 21:24–25 as forming an inclusio with the Prologue in terms of the notion of witness that was introduced in 1:7, 8, 15.[51] In each of these inclusio structures, John is adding subtle nuances to the whole story, and the inclusio structure is only part of the greater repetition and variation strategy that moves toward totality.

Belle produced an excellent survey of the studies in repetition and variation in the Gospel of John. From the works of E. Schweizer, E. Ruchstuhl, F. M. Braun, H. M. Teeple, and M. É. Boismard, he catalogued repetitions of complete sentences or large groups of words and repetition and variation of single words.[52] The list cannot be duplicated in its entirety, but some of the examples will serve the purpose here. Concerning repetitions of complete sentences or larger group of words, there are: chiasms (1:1; 3:12, 20–21, 31, 32–33; 5:31–32; 6:37, 46; 7:18, 22–23; 8:15–16, 18; 10:4–5, 14–15, 38; 12:35–56; 13:31; 14:1; 15:2, 4; 16:27–28; 18:36), repetition of the initial word at the end of the clause or sentence (6:57; 9:28; 10:4–5; 14:11, 20; 15:9, 10; 7:1, 10, 11, 16, 23), antithesis (1:3; 1:6–7, 20, 48; 3:15, 17, 20; 4:42; 5:19, 24; 8:35, 45; 10:28; 15:5, 6, 7), reference to the previous passage (1:24[1:19], 1:40[1:37], 2:22[1:19]; 3:26[1:19]; 4:2[3:22]; 4:45[2:13–23]; 4:46[2:1–11]; 4:54[[2:1–11]; 6:23[6:1–15]; 7:50[3:1–2; 19:39]; 9:13[9:1–7]; 10:40[1:28]; 11:31[11:29]; 12:1[11:1–44]; 18:9[6:39; 10:28; 17:12]; etc), and reference to the following passages (1:6–8[1:19]; 6:64[13:21–31; 18:1–11]; 6:71[13:21–31; 18:1–11]; 11:2[12:1–8]; 12:4[13:21–31]).[53]

There are also repetitions and variations of single words: repetition of the previous word in place of relative pronoun (15:19), repetition of the command in its execution (1:39; 6:10, 12–13; 9:6–7, 11; 11:39–41; 21:6), casus pendens (1:12; 4:14; 5:36; 6:39; 7:38; 12:49; 15:2; 17:2; 18:11), and prolepsis (4:35; 5:42; 7:27; 9:8, 29; 11:31; 14:17; 16:4).[54] In addition to these examples, Belle's survey of previous researches on this topic adds an impressive support that repetition and variation in John is a very important literary skill that greatly increases its persuasive power.[55]

51. Lincoln, *Gospel according to Saint John*, 524.
52. For the complete discussion, see Belle, "Repetitions and Variations," 35–38.
53. Belle, "Repetitions and Variations," 35–37.
54. Belle, "Repetitions and Variations," 37–38.
55. These observations by Belle agree with what Berlin noted of the devices of repetition in Hebrew poetry. Berline, "Introduction to Hebrew Poetry," 309.

Many writers observed John's use of synonyms in the Gospel. E. A. Abbott pointed out that John uses words with "extraordinary discrimination and subtle shades of meaning,"[56] that the whole Gospel "is pervaded with distinctions of thought, represented by subtle distinctions of word and phrase."[57] H. Maynard studied thirty-two sets of synonyms in John and concluded that "the Evangelist uses his words with a fine regard for their exact meaning."[58] Leon Morris studied variations in the Gospel of John and showed that there are twofold variations, threefold variations, and variations in greater numbers.[59] Observing how the Evangelist varies the word μένω in the opening of chapter 15, Morris said: "One would not have thought it possible to get so many statements so close in meaning but with such constant variation."[60]

Peter S. C. Chang, in his dissertation *Repetitions and Variations in the Gospel of John* (1975), made a significant contribution to this subject. He observed that repetition occurs in "many levels of complexity," and that "in spite of the great number of repetitions in John, exact repetitions are rare."[61] As for the possible reasons for repetitions in John, he listed the following: (1) the inherent nature of language; (2) expression of emotions; (3) meditative mood; (4) aesthetic effect; (5) composition technique; (6) memory aid; and (7) worship.[62] Repetition and variation is not simply a literary technique. Chang's explanation for this phenomenon of repetition and variation in the Gospel of John seems to address the heart of the issue:

> With repetitions, though the sentence goes on, the thought is not being pushed forward, but retained. This happens when the subject is too big, too rich, too beautiful or magnificent. It is worth looking at, worth being looked into; therefore, one slows down to enjoy and to digest. The subject may be also new or overwhelming. One is attempting to grasp and lay hold of it by trying out the same words over and over or by using different words to see which are more suitable. The thought is in the process of formation. One must take time. With God both of these

---

56. Abbott, *Johannine Grammar*, 401.
57. Abbott, *Johannine Vocabulary*, 103.
58. Maynard, *Function of Apparent Synonyms*, 425.
59. Morris, *Studies in the Fourth Gospel*, 293–319.
60. Morris, *Studies in the Fourth Gospel*, 315.
61. Chang, *Repetitions and Variations*, 184.
62. Chang, *Repetitions and Variations*, 29–42.

> factors are at work. He is a great God. There is much to meditate. He is also in a sense utterly foreign. He remains a mystery, never to be fully understood. To concentrate our thought on such an unreachable and ineffable center, one can only circle around it and approach it from different angles.[63]

Because the subject of the gospel of Jesus Christ is so glorious and rich, John expressed his thoughts in various ways, trying to grasp the "totality" (which Schökel and Muilenburg observed above) in ever varying degrees. God is unsearchable, unreachable, and unattainable. Words must be tried in varying nuances again and again until the ineffable center becomes unraveled in its mystery. John's emotion, meditation, worship, and persuasive desires are all wrapped up in his repetition and variation style.

In another place, Chang also voiced his idea of the totality of John's mindset. In encountering the Gospel, he said "one does get the impression that there are many sections which form units, each of which contains essentially the message of the Gospel. In other words, there are many miniature gospels of John within the Gospel of John. This unique phenomenon does not occur in the Synoptics."[64]

John is fond of repetition and variation probably because he has already grasped the gospel in its entirety in his mind from his post-resurrection perspective. As he communicates it, the whole permeates its parts and its parts permeate the whole. Everything he adds brings new color and depth to what he stated before, leading the audience to interact deeper and wider with the message. No better method can achieve this effect than the poetic device of repetition and variation.

Terseness

Terseness is also a major characteristic feature of Hebrew poetry. Kugel observed that terseness is "a form of heightening in biblical style . . . one of the most striking and commonly used."[65] Longman stated that it is "arguably the most distinctive to poetry."[66] Poetry expresses the same thoughts in fewer words. Berlin pointed out this character of terseness

---

63. Chang, *Repetitions and Variations*, 35.
64. Chang, *Repetitions and Variations*, 69.
65. Kugel, *Biblical Poetry*, 87.
66. Longman, "Terseness," 791–94.

in the comparison of the poetic and the prose versions of a same event in Judges 4:19 and 5:25:

> He said to her, "Please give me a little water to drink, for I am thirsty."
> So she opened a bottle of milk and gave him a drink; then she covered him.

> He asked for water, she gave him milk;
> In a magnificent bowl, she brought him curds.[67]

This economy of words heightens the sublimity of the text and gives the impression that "each word is heavily laden with meaning."[68] For this reason, biblical writers carefully chose words that are loaded with meaning and multifunctional.

What promotes the sense of terseness in poetic texts? Freedman showed that the relative infrequency of prose particles—which he identified as the definite article *h*, the relative pronoun *'shr*, and the definite object marker *'t*—marks a poetic text.[69] Francis I. Andersen and A. Dean Forbes carried a statistic analysis of nine hundred chapters of the Old Testament and found that chapters with a score of less than 5% of these particles are wisdom (Proverbs and Job) and lyrical poetry, while those with a score of higher than twenty percent are virtually pure prose.[70] Relative absence of these prose particles could indicate that a text is poetry, and this is what promotes the sense of terseness.

Lack of conjunctions also contributes to terseness. Conjunctions join the lines of text together and make explicit the relationship between them, but their sparing use is a characteristic of Hebrew poetry. As in the example of Psalm 23:1 ("The Lord is my shepherd, I shall not want"), the lack of conjunction leaves the relationship of the two lines unexpressed.[71] This absence of conjunction has the effect of adding conciseness to the statement, but it also invites interpretation and meditation from the readers about its unexpressed relationship. In this way, this paratactic construction strengthens the poet's ability to elevate the effectiveness of

---

67. Berlin, "Introduction to Hebrew Poetry," 303.

68. Berlin, "Reading Biblical Poetry," 2098.

69. Freedman, "Another Look at Biblical Hebrew Poetry," 11; Freedman, "Pottery, Poetry, and Prophecy," 5–26. Cf. Andersen and Forbes, "'Prose Particle' Counts of the Hebrew Bible," 165–83.

70. Andersen and Forbes, "'Prose Particle' Counts of the Hebrew Bible," 166.

71. Longman, "Terseness," 793.

the text. Longman observed, "All in all, terseness, with its often-attendant ambiguity, lends interest to the poem and requires the reader/interpreter to be deeply engaged with the material."[72]

Poets use ellipsis to truncate sentences (especially in parallel lines) and to bind two related phrases closely.[73] Ellipsis is the omitting of corresponding words, usually in the second line of a parallel structure. Isaiah 2:3 illustrates ellipsis: "Come, let us go up to the mountain of the LORD, To the house of the God of Jacob." By way of implication, "let us go" is absent in the second line. Ellipsis occurs also in prose sections as Kugel has shown,[74] but it is predominantly a poetic device.[75] C. L. Miller called this feature "the most elusive feature of biblical poetry" because it "involves words that are not present but whose existence is understood by speakers and hearers."[76] Using parallel construction, the poet effectively deepens the message with fewer words through the use of ellipsis. Psalms 88:6 shows this effect of ellipsis: "You have put me in the lowest pit, in deep and dark places."

A paratactic construction with the simple connective *w* is foundational to what promotes the terseness in Hebrew poetry. A paratactic construction in itself does not promote terseness, but it is through this strategy that parallelism and ellipsis work. In Hebrew, *w* can play many functions in coordinating sentences, including: conjunctive ("and"), conjunctive-sequential ("so that"), disjunctive ("but"), and epexegetical (specifying or clarifying).[77] It is this paratactic construction that brings out the richness of Hebrew poetry.[78]

The use of imagery is another element that promotes the terseness in Hebrew poetry.[79] Although the subject of imagery will be treated separately later, it will suffice to say here that imagery enables poetry to be terse. Imagery can bring many meanings to the text without the writer actually expressing them, especially when rich backgrounds of biblical

---

72. Longman, "Terseness," 794.
73. Longman, "Terseness," 794.
74. Kugel, *Biblical Poetry*, 322.
75. O'Connor, *Hebrew Verse Structure*, 122–29.
76. Miller, "Ellipsis," 156–60.
77. Waltke and O'Connor, *Introduction to Biblical Hebrew Syntax*, 648–54.
78. One should see the studies concerning the multivalent conjunction ו as an element that contributes to the terseness and also to the richness of Hebrew poetry. For example, see Gillingham, *Image, the Depths, and the Surface*, 95–96.
79. Longman, "Terseness," 792.

materials enrich them. In the use of imagery in "The LORD is my shepherd," the readers are "invited to unpack the comparison."[80] These poetic devices of infrequency of prose particles, paratactic constructions, ellipsis, parallelism, and imagery add to the terseness of Hebrew poetry while surprisingly enriching it rather than impoverishing it.

Terseness permeates the whole Gospel of John. Asyndeton, or the absence of the conjunction between sentences, heightens the sense of terseness in the Fourth Gospel. Scholars frequently pointed out the asyndetic nature of Johannine sentences,[81] and Abbott noted that "John abounds in instances of asyndeton of the most varied and unexpected kind."[82]

Alfred Plummer observed that "Greek is so rich in particles that asyndeton is generally remarkable."[83] For instance, in the statements of John the Baptist, Synoptists prefer some conjunctions ("I baptized you in water, *but . . .*" [Mark 1:8]; "I baptized you . . . *but . . .*" [Matt 3:11; Luke 3:16]),[84] but John instead has "I baptize in water; among you stands one . . ." (1:26).[85] In many instances, sentences begin asyndetically (i.e., 1:29, 40, 42, 45; 2:17; 5:15; 10:21; 11:7, 16:19), and clauses are connected asyndetically (i.e., 2:16; 5:8, 39, 45; 6:20, 27; 12:35; 14:1, 27, 31; 15:5; 17:9, 17).[86] In asyndeton, sentences are "not fastened together;"[87] therefore, the overall impression is terse and even forceful. So are these statements: "Do not let your heart be troubled; believe in God, believe also in Me" (14:1), and "I am the vine, you are the branches" (15:5).[88] Black observed that at certain times, "this preponderance of asyndeton gives weight and solemnity to the discourse."[89] In this way, the "asyndetic" manner of inserting

---

80. Longman, "Terseness," 792.

81. Abbott, *Johannine Grammar*, 69–73; Black, *Aramaic Approach*, 55–61; Burney, *Aramaic Origin of the Fourth Gospel*, 49–56; Carson, *John*, 42; Turner, "Style of John," 70. When conjunctions are used, on the other hand, it has the heightening effect. See Köstenberger, *John*, 572n8.

82. Abbott, *Johannine Grammar*, 70.

83. Plummer, *Gospel according to S. John*, 67.

84. Italics are added for emphasis.

85. Plummer, *John*, 70. This is author's translation.

86. For the various usage of asyndeton, see Abbott, *Johannine Grammar*, 69–73.

87. Abbott, *Johannine Grammar*, 70.

88. Peter W. Ensor said, "The Johannine Jesus tends to use parataxis and asyndeton," and identified them in the followings: 3:13, 14; 5:27, 37, 39, 40; 7:28; 8:16, 17, 29; 10:16; 12:47, 50; 14:3, 4, 7, 13, 29, 30; 16:3, 8, 22, 23; 17:5, 11, 19, 22 (Ensor, "Johannine Sayings of Jesus," 17).

89. Black, *Aramaic Approach*, 56.

The Gospel of John in Light of the Poetics of Old Testament Poetry   89

the closing narrative concerning Peter (21:1–25) should not surprise the readers. It suddenly, but forcefully, increases the perplexity, elevates the sublimity, and invites meditation from the audience concerning the meaning of Jesus' appearance to Peter at the end.

Paratactic constructions with the simple *kai* are also characteristic of the Johannine Gospel.[90] John favored this technique over the participles and subordinate clauses. Instead of the "answering . . . said" construction of the Synoptic Gospels (i.e., Matt 3:15), he uses "answered and said" (John 3:3). Burney observed that subordinating constructions of aorist participles and genitive absolutes are far less common in John than the Synoptics.[91] Simple *kai* implicitly expresses more complicated relationships For example, it can express:

1. conditional relationships—*erchesthe kai opsesthe*, "*If you* come, *then* you will see" (1:39); aiteite kai *lēmpsesthe*, "*if you* ask, *then* you will receive" (16:24).

2. temporal relationships—*eti tetramēnos estin kai ho therismos erchetai*, "yet there are four months, *then* the harvest comes" (4:35); *eti chronon mikron meth' humōn eimi kai upagō pros ton pempsanta me*, "Until a short time I am with you, *then* I go to Him who sent me" (7:33).

3. consecutive relationships—*sabbaton estin, kai ouk exestin soi arai ton krabatton sou*, "It is the Sabbath, *therefore* it is not permissible for you to carry your mat" (5:10); *kagō erōtēsō ton patera kai allon paraklēton dōsei humin*, "I will ask the Father, *so that* He will give you another Counselor" (14:16).[92]

Ellipsis also characterizes the Fourth Gospel. Abbott identified two kinds of ellipsis—contextual ellipsis (what is omitted is supplied from the context) and idiomatic ellipsis (what is omitted is due to customary expressions).[93] What he identified as contextual ellipsis demonstrate the poetic terseness of the Gospel. The contexts expect the readers to supply

---

90. Burney, *Aramaic Origin*, 56–63. Barrett called it "the most striking feature of John's style." Barrett, *John*, 7.

91. Burney, *Aramaic Origin*, 56–57. Burney said that the comparative rarity of the genitive absolute is due to parataxis and a temporal clause introduced by ὅτε and ὡς. Burney, *Aramaic Origin*, 57–58.

92. These examples are from Turner, "Style of John," 71. Parataxis is common also in the Gospel of Mark. For the different forms of parataxis, see Moulton and Howard, *Accidence and Word-formation*, 2:420–23. The translations are the author's.

93. Abbott, *Johannine Grammar*, 172–73.

the omitted words, and it has the effect of drawing their engagements. The "I am" statements of Jesus in various contexts maximize this elliptical effect (i.e., 6:20; 9:9; 18:5, 6, 8). The italicized words (in parentheses) in the follow examples are omitted intentionally:

1. *egnō oun ho patēr hoti [en] ekeinē tē hōra en hē eipen autō ho Iēsous*, "So that the father knew that (*it was*) at that hour in which Jesus said to him" (4:53).

2. *aron kai peripatei*, "Pick up (*your pallet*) and walk" (5:12).

3. *all' egō kai ho pempsas me patēr*, "but I and the Father who sent Me (*are judges together*)" (8:16).

4. *kyrie, mē tous podas mou monon alla kai tas cheiras kai tēn kephalēn*, "Lord, (*wash*) not only my feet, but also (*wash*) my hands and my head" (13:9).

5. *meinate en emoi, kagō en humin*, "Abide in me, and I (*will abide*) in you" (15:4).

6. *mē touton alla ton Barabban*, "(*Release*) not this man, but (*release*) Barabbas" (18:40).[94]

David Alan Black also observed numerous elliptical expressions in John 17—such as, "in order that they may know" (17:3), "ask" (17:9, 15, 20, 23), and "we are one" (17:11).[95] As one surveys the words that are omitted, the impression is that they are not omitted only for brevity, but to elevate the importance of these omitted words in the minds of the hearers and the readers.

Double Meaning

Double meaning in the Old Testament comes under the broader concept of wordplay. An important aspect of Hebrew poetry is the sublimity expressed with the economy of words. The writers accomplished this goal through playing with sounds and exploiting various nuances inherent in the words. Laurence Perrin said, "Where the scientist requires and has invented a strictly one-dimensional language in which every word is confined to one denotation, the poet needs a multidimensional language,

---

94. Abbott, *Johannine Grammar*, 173–75. NASB supplies many of these ellipses, but not all of them.

95. Black, "Style and Significance of John 17," 152.

and creates it partly by using a multidimensional vocabulary, in which the dimensions of connotations and sound are added to the dimensions of denotation."[96] Such plays on words are not exclusive to poetry, but their strong presence is indicative of poetic text. In wordplay, biblical writers utilized multiple meanings in the word ("polyvalence") to create intentional ambiguities and to heighten poetic effectiveness through them.

Ambiguity originally meant vagueness or imprecision of expression, but William Empson identified it as a poetic device where a single word can have multiple meanings. Empson noted seven types of ambiguity and showed that ambiguity arises when:

1. A word or a sentence means several things at once.
2. Multiple meanings are resolved into one.
3. Two unrelated ideas are expressed with one word.
4. Two or more meanings of a statement are disagreeing with each other but reveal the complex thought of the author.
5. The author was inconsistent because his ideas were developing through writing.
6. Statements contradict each other but invite interpretation.
7. The author has real contradictions in his mind.[97]

D. G. Firth observed that Old Testament writers created these ambiguities except for the fifth and the seventh type.[98] In the use of ambiguity, readers become perplexed at first because of the presence of multiple meanings in the word, but multiple meanings challenge them to think through the options; so as the result, they engage even deeper with the message of the author.

There are several types of wordplay that utilize multiple meanings.[99] The first type is "paronomasia" (sometimes referred to as homonymy) where the writers make use of words which have equivalent or similar sounds. According to Immanuel M. Casanowicz, its effectiveness lies in the "union of the similarity of sound with dissimilarity of sense."[100] Bibli-

96. Perrine, *Sound and Sense*, 38.
97. Empson, *Seven Types of Ambiguity*, passim.
98. Firth, "Ambiguity," 11–13.
99. There are numerous wordplays on the sound of words, such as alliteration, assonance, rhyme, and onomatopoeia. See Schökel, *Manual of Hebrew Poetics*, 20–29.
100. Casanowicz, *Paronomasia in the Old Testament*, 36.

cal writers use this type of wordplay commonly with place and personal names.¹⁰¹ For example, there is a paronomasia in this verse in Psalms 15:3: *loʾ-ʿasah lereʿehu raʿh*, "he does not do evil to his neighbor."

Sometimes writers play on the root of the words: *tsarei retsin*, "adversaries from Rezin" (Isa 9:11); *maleʾ meʾeleh*, "too strong for this" (Jer 4:12); *qirbam . . . qeber*, "their inward part . . . grave" (Ps 5:10); *wayirekab ʿal-kerub*, "he rode upon a cherub" (Ps 18:10); and *liqhahh bekheleq*, "her persuasions with flattering" (Prov 7:21).¹⁰²

Other times, poets use "polysemy" or the multiple meanings inherent in a word. Sometimes double meaning refers to this type of pun.¹⁰³ The following are some of the words that have two or more meanings: *khlq*, "to be slippery/destroy (Hiphil)" (Prov 28:23); *spl*, "to speak quietly/be abased" (Isa 29:4); *ʾkhbh*, "love/leather" (Hos 11:4; Song 3:10); *linsok massekah*; "to pour out liberation/cast molten images" (Isa 30:1); and *ʾeshshaqka . . . ʾashqka*, "I would kiss you . . . give you to drink" (Song 8:1–2).¹⁰⁴ Daniel J. Estes said that, "Poets are fond of drawing on the complete semantic range of terms as they accomplish their purpose."¹⁰⁵

"Janus parallelism" demonstrates another skillful use of multiple meanings in a word. C. H. Gordon stated that this kind of parallelism "hinges on the use of a single word with two entirely different meanings: one meaning paralleling what precedes, and the other meaning, what follows."¹⁰⁶ Gordon identified this type of parallelism in Song of Songs 2:12:

> The flowers have appeared in the land.
> The time of *zmyr* arrived.
> The voice of the turtledove is heard in our land.

Here *zmyr* has both meanings of "pruning season" and "music." Gordon said, "The poet knew how to exploit the double meaning of *zāmîr*. Retrospectively it parallels the first member of the tristich pertaining to the growth of the soil; proleptically it parallels the final member pertaining to

---

101. Greenstein, "Wordplay, Hebrew," 6:968–71; cf. Guillaume, "Paronomasia in the Old Testament," 282–90.

102. Watson, *Classical Hebrew Poetry*, 240.

103. Watson, *Classical Hebrew Poetry*, 237–38; see Ullmann, *Principles of Semantics*, 188–89.

104. Watson, *Classical Hebrew Poetry*, 241–42. See also Gevirtz, "Of Patriarchs and Puns," 33–54; Grossberg, "Multiple Meaning," 77–86; Chisholm, "Wordplay in the Eighth-century Prophets," 44–52.

105. Estes, "Hermeneutics of Biblical Lyric Poetry," 428.

106. Gordon, "New Directions," 59.

The Gospel of John in Light of the Poetics of Old Testament Poetry 93

song."[107] Janus parallelism typifies the poet's skillful use of words. Finding polysemous parallelism in Akkadian, Sumerian, Hittite, Ugaritic, Arabic, Egyptian, and medieval Egyptian literature, Scott B. Noegel argued that the ancients considered the ability to understand wordplay and polysemy as equivalent to gaining wisdom. He said, "In short, polysemy in particular and perhaps word-play in general is conventional to wisdom literature; to the ancients, recognition of the device was tantamount to the acquisition of wisdom."[108]

Georg Fohrer made important observations on the twofold aspects of Hebrew words and said that Israelites were in the habit of presenting ideas or events from two different perspectives, such as between divine and human, in order that "the idea or event might be understood in its entirety."[109] According to Fohrer, twofold meanings occurs when: (1) basic meaning of the root is applied to its derived words (from the root word "to cover," comes "bed-covering," "clothing," "deck of the ship," "fat on the entrails") (2) a word goes through a semantic development where a word denoting a thing develops into a word denoting a person (i.e., "sending" becomes "messenger"); (3) concrete words also have abstract meanings (i.e., "nose" and "anger"); and (4) view a single event from two aspects of cause and effect to denote wholeness (i.e., the feeling of "shame" and its result of "disgrace," the action involving "sword" and its result "plunder," the noun "cord" and its result of having a measured "portion a land").[110] Double meanings are sometimes the result of semantic development common to languages; but at other times, they are the intentional creation of Hebrew writers to express wholeness in the most succinct way.

One important characteristic of the Johannine Gospel is John's succinct use of the words. His vocabulary is far smaller than that of the Synoptic writers, yet his words are often heavily laden with meanings and utilized in greater economy. John carefully crafted his words and, for this reason, wordplay is an important poetic device for him. The most apparent type of wordplay in the Gospel of John is the double meaning. Terms like "double entendre" or "double intent" sometimes refer to

---

107. Gordon, "New Directions," 59–60. The translation is Gordon's.

108. Noegel, *Janus Parallelism in the Book of Job*, 139. For other scholars who followed the trail of Gordon, see Rendsburg, "Janus Parallelism in Gen 49:26," 291–93; Tsumura, "Janus Parallelism in Nah. 1:8," 109–11; Tsumura, "Janus Parallelism in Hab. III 4," 124–28; Kselman, "Janus Parallelism in Psalm 75:2," 531–32.

109. Fohrer, "Twofold Aspects of Hebrew Words," 95.

110. Fohrer, "Twofold Aspects of Hebrew Words," passim.

double meaning. Hamid-Khani pointed out that this type of wordplay "encapsulates two dimensions of the same thought in a situation where the author does not wish to force an either/or choice."[111]

Some of the noted lexical double meanings in the Gospel are as follows: *katalambanō*, "to comprehend/overcome" (1:5); *airō*, "to take upon oneself/take away" (1:29); *anōthen*, "from above/again" (3:3–8); *didōmi*, "to give/hand over" (3:16); *elegxai*, "to expose/reprove" (3:20); *apeitheō*, "to disbelieve/disobey" (3:36); *misthos*, "wages/reward" (4:36); *parrēsia*, "plainly/publicly" (i.e., 7:13; 10:24); *chōreō*, "to have place/make progress" (8:37); *bastaxō*, "to bear/pilfer" (12:6); *kathairō*, "to prune/cleanse" (15:2); and *krinein*, "to separate/judge/decide/condemn" (i.e., 3:16–19; 7:51; 9:39–41).[112] John makes use of full lexical possibilities of these words to create paradox, suspense, and irony, and thereby invites the hearers and readers into deeper discourse with him.

Double meanings, however, are not confined to lexical area. E. Richard recognized that double meanings are "more extensive, complex, and varied than is usually conceded,"[113] and include double meanings at the conceptual level. He said that the "expressions of double meaning" include ambiguity, misunderstanding, irony, and vague Christological titles.[114] Some of the examples of these conceptual double meanings—where the multiplicity of meaning does not lie in the words but in their references—appear in these terms: *ta idia*, "his own people/place" (1:11); *naos*, "temple/body" (2:19); *typhlos*, "physical blindness/spiritual blindness" (chap. 9); *anistēmi*, "physical rising/eschatological resurrection" (11:23); and *hupagō*, "his death/his going to the Father" (13:33).[115]

---

111. Hamid-Khani, *Revelation and Concealment of Christ*, 47.

112. Hamid-Khani, *Revelation and Concealment*, 48; Hamid-Khani, *Johannine Expressions of Double Meaning*, passim; Richard, "Expressions of Double Meaning," 96–112; Barrett, *John*, 158, 205, 208.

113. Richard, "Expressions of Double Meaning," 97.

114. Richard, "Expressions of Double Meaning," 97–104.

115. For these examples and a fuller treatment, see Hamid-Khani, *Revelation and Concealment*, 52–60. See also: Van der Watt, "Double Entendre in the Gospel according to John," 463–81.

The Gospel of John in Light of the Poetics of Old Testament Poetry 95

Double meanings in the Gospel of John elevate the ambiguity,[116] irony,[117] and misunderstanding.[118] In the past, scholars attributed the origin of these double meanings to the translations, especially from Aramaic, but it is John's skillful use of the language.[119] The use of double meanings in John is a poetic strategy of conveying the sense of wholeness, imparting wisdom to searching minds, and presenting the truth in its entirety to the readers. John invites the readers to step into the chasm created by dual meanings and leads them to grasp the message in its fullness.

Imagery

Along with parallelism and terseness, a heavy reliance on the use of images is the distinguishing mark of poetry. Schökel stated that images are "the glory, perhaps the essence of poetry,"[120] and Ryken said that "poets think and write in images."[121] Images are a favorite mode of expression for poets, because it "bring[s] greater emotional impact" and "can convey multiple connotations, and it adds to the terseness."[122]

Imagery refers to word pictures. Poets draw pictures in the minds of hearers through the use of imagery. In this way, imagery is another term for figurative language that evokes pictures in the hearers' mind.[123] Leland Ryken, James C. Wilhoit and Tremper Longman well expressed the importance of imagery when they said: "Bible is a book that *images* the

---

116. Attridge, "Ambiguous Signs, an Anonymous Character," 267–88; Barrett, *John*, 208; Conway, "Speaking through Ambiguity," 324–41; Fenton, *Gospel of according to John*, 19–20; Schnackenburg, *John*, 1:350; Thatcher, *Jesus the Riddler*.

117. Paul Duke observed, "All ironic communication contains some incongruity or clash of meaning." Duke, *Irony in the Fourth Gospel*, 14. See also: Wright, *Governor and the King*.

118. Richard said, "Ambiguity leading to misunderstanding is by far the best known category of 'expressions of double meaning' in John." Richard, "Expressions of Double Meaning," 97. Culpepper noted, "All of the misunderstandings arise from an ambiguous statement, metaphor, or double-entendre in Jesus' conversations." Culpepper, *Anatomy*, 160. See also: Han, *Use of Misunderstanding in the Fourth Gospel*. Skinner, "Misunderstanding, Christology, and Johannine Characterization," 111–28.

119. Richard, "Expressions of Double Meaning," 105.

120. Schökel, *Manual of Hebrew Poetics*, 95; Berlin, "Introduction to Hebrew Poetry," 311; Berlin, "Reading Biblical Poetry," 2101.

121. Ryken, *How to Read the Bible as Literature*, 90.

122. Lucas, "Poetics, Terminology," 520–25.

123. Watson, *Classical Hebrew Poetry*, 251. See also Strawn, "Imagery," 306–14.

truth as well as stating it in abstract propositions."[124] Images are concrete objects and actions that picture the truths of God. Thomas A. Golding recognized that the purpose of using figurative language is to move from "the known to the unknown, from the familiar to the unfamiliar."[125] Images make unfamiliar terms known through familiar ones. Since the source of images is everyday life, those images have evocative power that bring up associated emotions and feelings, and this is the reason why images are powerful means of conveying the truths of God.

Imagery is a figurative language where one thing stands figuratively for another. Quintilian divided figurative language into two groups: figure of thoughts and figure of schemes, where the former concerns the forms of expression in words and speech, and the latter concerns purposeful changes in meaning from ordinary use of language.[126] Figurative language, or imagery, is a special use of language where the poet says one thing by means of another.[127]

There are several types of figurative language in the Scripture.[128] "Synecdoche," or taking together, is the use of the whole for the part, or the part for the whole. Different body parts can stand for the whole person (Ps 78:61; 1 Kgs 14:12; Isa 23:7; Hab 3:16). "Metonymy," or a change of name, is one thing representing another thing. For example, scepter represents kingly rule (Gen 49:10), a key stands for authority (Isa 22:22), and a sword for war (Ezra 9:7). Simile and metaphor are devices of comparison where the relationship is explicit in the former (Job 20:8) and implicit in the latter (Ps 23:1).

Personification is the use of animate for the inanimate, as "wisdom" in Proverbs 8 and "death" in Hosea 13:14. Allegory is "a story intended by the author to convey a hidden meaning," whereas allegorizing is "to impose on a story hidden meanings which the original author neither intended nor envisaged."[129] George B. Caird considered the story Nathan told David in 2 Samuel 12:1–7 as an allegory.[130] Scripture uses various

---

124. Ryken et al., "Introduction," xiii. Italics in original.

125. Golding, "Imagery of Shepherding in the Bible," 20. See also, Gregory, *Seven Laws of Teaching*, 54; Painter, "Johannine Symbols," 33; and McFague, *Metaphorical Theology*, 15.

126. Quintilian, *Institutio Oratoria*, vol. 3, 353–57.

127. Cf. Watson, *Classical Hebrew Poetry*, 251; Oliver, *Poetry Handbook*, 92.

128. Watson, "Hebrew Poetry," 270–73; Mitchell, "Image," 556–59.

129. Caird, *Language and Imagery of the Bible*, 165.

130. Caird, *Language and Imagery of the Bible*, 165.

ways of figurative language, but the essence is that one thing represents another.[131]

Among these various devices, the most profound use of figurative language is simile and metaphor. In classical usage, simile and metaphor are similar terms where the former makes explicit association of two elements of comparison with words like "as" and "like," while the latter does it implicitly without using those terms. Aristotle defined metaphor as "giving the thing a name that belongs to something else; the transference being either from genus to species, or from species to genus, or from species to species, or on grounds of analogy."[132] In this way, metaphor is a shortened form of simile whose function is to compare a literal object with a metaphorical object, seeing "the similarity in dissimilars."[133] In addition to this comparative role, metaphor also has substitutionary function where a term substitutes a metaphorical concept. In this view, metaphor is that which says one thing but means another.

I. A. Richards, however, argued that the essence of metaphor is not analogy or substitution, but the "interaction" between two terms he called "vehicle" (the literary term) and "tenor" (the metaphorical concept). Recognizing that meaning is a product of its context, he said that metaphor is fundamentally "a borrowing between and intercourse of *thoughts*, a transaction between contexts."[134] In other words, words from two different contexts merge together and produce a meaning through their interactions. Max Black further developed this interaction theory and said that the literal term functions to project a system of "associated implications" ("frame") upon the metaphorical idea ("focus").[135]

Ryken similarly noted that in metaphor, there is a multiplicity of correspondence between the literal and the figurative terms: "When expositors begin to make the transfer of meaning from one sphere to the

---

131. Friedman, "Imagery," 559–66.

132. Aristotle, *Poet.*, 1457b.

133. Aristotle, *Poet.*, 1459a; see also, Aristotle, *Rhet.* 1406b. Coming to a precise definition of metaphor is problematic. Janet M. Soskice expressed the difficulty when she said, "Any one who has grappled with the problem of defining a metaphor will appreciate the pragmatism of those who proceed to discuss it without giving any definition of it at all." Soskice, *Metaphor and Religious Language*, 15; cf. Mitchell, "Image," 556–59.

134. Richards, *Philosophy of Rhetoric*, 94.

135. Black, "More about Metaphor," 28; see also Black, "Metaphor," 273–94; A definition of metaphor is, however, an elusive one. For other theories on metaphor, see, Wallae Martin, "Metaphor," 760–66.

other, they will almost certainly find that the meanings are multiple. To picture God as a father, or to think of God's providence as a fortress, for example, at once invites people to see a multiplicity of correspondences."[136] Through the use of metaphor, the author effectively brings manifold associated ideas into the text without naming them. Max Black succinctly expressed this function of metaphor in this way:

> Why stretch and twist, press and expand, concepts in this way—why try to see A as metaphorically B, when it literally is not B? Well, because we *can* do so, conceptual boundaries not being rigid, but elastic and permeable; and because we often need to do so, the available literal resources of the language being insufficient to express our sense of the rich correspondences, interrelations, and analogies of domains conventionally separated; and because the metaphorical thought and utterance sometimes embody insight expressible in no other fashion.[137]

It is an important insight that metaphor expands the limits of literal language with rich associations and correspondences.

In regard to the Gospel of John, Ruben Zimmermann argued that the writer is self-conscious about the figurative nature of his Gospel. The Gospel does not use terms like parable, metaphor, allegory, symbol, myth, or riddle, but terms such as *paroimia* "figurative language" (10:6; 16:25, 29) and *sēmeion* "signs" (2:11, 23; 3:2; 4:48, 54; 6:2; etc.) "make clear how the Fourth Gospel conceives of imagery."[138] It is important to note that Septuagint translates *mshl* ("proverbs") in Proverbs 1:1 as *paroimia*. In this regard, the Gospel of John has some similarities with the wisdom literature of the Old Testament. Concerning the definition of wisdom literature, Robert Gordis stated, "In its literature, Wisdom seeks to transmit its ideas about man's duty and destiny to readers and pupils. To achieve this objective, one of its principal methods is to call attention to the similarity existing between two objects, activities, situations, or types of character, thus revealing a relationship which the reader had not previously suspected."[139] John's way of calling attention to the "similarity existing between two objects, activities, situations, or types of character" through the use of imagery is certainly similar to wisdom literature. Just

---

136. Ryken, "Bible as Literature, Part 3," 264.
137. Black, "More about Metaphor," 34.
138. Zimmermann, "Imagery in John," 9.
139. Gordis, *Book of God and Man*, 199.

as Proverbs 1:2–6 exhorts the listeners to understand its proverb, figure, and riddles as a way of receiving wisdom, John silently invites the readers to unpack the meanings of the images.

The Gospel of John makes extensive use of imagery, especially through the use of symbolism. In his influential study, Craig R. Koester defined symbol as "an image, an action, or a person that is understood to have transcendent significance," having the function of spanning "the chasm between what is 'from above' and what is 'from below' without collapsing the distinction."[140] Words like water, wine, lamb, temple, bread, light, darkness, and vineyard are important symbols in the Fourth Gospel and have frequently attracted scholarly attentions.[141] As the symbols guide the readers, they must pay attention to discover their "transcendent significance" in these words.

As noted in Koester's definition, symbolism also encompasses actions and persons in the narratives. Although it cannot be discussed here in detail, it will suffice to say that the stories in John have symbolic significance. Dodd already observed that the whole gospel shows an "intricate network of symbolism" and represents "a world in which phenomena—*things* and *events*—are a living and moving image of the eternal . . . a world in which the Word is made flesh."[142] Dodd said that the σημεῖα of Jesus are symbols,[143] and scholars are observing increasingly that Johannine narratives have symbolic significance.[144] Zimmermann noted that the "poetic dimension of the Gospel narratives can be characterized as 'figurative' based on . . . their mimetic function . . . not only the entire Gospel but also individual Johannine narratives can be considered to be 'image text.'"[145]

The third area of imagery in John is metaphor. The most prominent metaphors are the "I am" statements of Jesus (6:35; 8:12; 10:9,10;

---

140. Koester, *Symbolism in the Fourth Gospel*, 4.

141. Zimmermann, "Imagery in John," 20–23; Koester, *Symbolism*, passim; Hamid-Khani, *Revelation and Concealment*, 69; Jones, *Symbol of Water*; Coloe, *God Dwells with Us*; Kerr, *Temple of Jesus' Body*.

142. Dodd, *Interpretation*, 143 (italics are added for emphasis); cf. Painter, "Johannine Symbols," 32.

143. Dodd, *Interpretation*, 141–43.

144. Olsson, *Structure and Meaning*, 114; Schneiders, "History and Symbolism in the Fourth Gospel," 371–76; Lee, *Symbolic Narratives of the Fourth Gospel*, 11–20; *Flesh and Glory*, 9–28; Ng, *Water Symbolism in John*, 7–9.

145. Zimmermann, "Imagery in John," 25.

11:25–26; 14:6; 15:5). In his extensive treatment on the Johannine metaphor, Jan G. Van der Watt stated that through the use of metaphor, John "carries" the reader into the spiritual world.[146] Metaphor invites the reader into its conceptual—more specifically, spiritual—world. It is not, however, an open-ended quest. The author provides the guardrails (the context) to lead the onlookers safely as they see and experience the world. In this way, the author can convey meanings through the framework of the imagery. Van der Watt noted: "In a context the writer employs his ideas/message according to the framework presented by the image. This has the effect that the image becomes more and more specified and determined as the text progresses. The image should therefore be interpreted in the light of the text, just as the text should be interpreted in the light of the image."[147] The metaphors in the Gospel are closely linked together to project a cohesive world, so that, in the Gospel, a "complex network of different metaphors are woven together to form the family imagery."[148]

A strong presence of imagery in the Gospel necessitates cultural sensitivity for the interpretation. To interpret imagery means to have the ability to "decode the text" in light of its cultural context, because when "one moves outside that sphere of consensus, the symbol will no longer communicate as symbol."[149] When metaphor loses its "otherness" and becomes a part of ordinary language, it becomes ineffective and turns into a "dead metaphor."[150] In reading the Fourth Gospel, the readers must approach the Gospel with a sensitivity to the poetic images it draws. In this regard, Ryken's observation is important. He said: "Metaphors are images or pictures first of all. Their impact depends on letting the literal level sink into one's consciousness before carrying over the meaning to a figurative or second level. If this is not done, the whole point of speaking in metaphor evaporates."[151] John Painter rightly observed that the world is "a store-house of symbols which can become vehicles of the revelation."[152] Metaphor is truly a helpful "lens" through which one sees the truths of God. In metaphors, "it is as though the speaker were saying,

---

146. van der Watt, *Family of the King*, 155.
147. van der Watt, *Family of the King*, 139.
148. van der Watt, *Family of the King*, 398.
149. van der Watt, *Family of the King*, 2.
150. Caird, *Language and Imagery of the Bible*, 152.
151. Ryken, "Bible as Literature, Part 3," 263.
152. Painter, "Johannine Symbols," 32.

'Look through this and see what I have seen, something you would never have noticed without the lens!'[153] Instead of paying singular attention to the linguistic aspects, the readers must be ready to see the world the author draws with images and appreciate the metaphorical vehicles to understand the metaphorical tenors correctly.

Summary

John's language and style are peculiar, but as exegetes bring and apply all the available features of the Hebrew poetry to its text, the text begins to make sense in greater degrees and hidden treasures come into light. In fact, when this chosen lens shows everything clearly, the object is no longer strange and no longer blurred; it reveals its inner beauty.

From Kugel's observation of the relationship between poetry and prose as a continuum, this chapter demonstrated that the Fourth Gospel is in the style of Old Testament poetry, even though it is not a poetry technically. As this chapter detailed, there are many excellent studies on how individual devices of parallelism, repetition and variation, terseness, double meaning, and imagery are used in the Fourth Gospel; but instead of reading John through any one particular chosen device, this chapter exhibited how all these poetic techniques are at work in John. There are many seconding (Kugel), spotlighting (Berlin), and intensifying (Alter) structures, and different parts and units fuse together to create a binocular vision (Boodberg). A limited set of vocabulary goes through ever increasing varieties in repetition, and it arrives at a marvelous totality (Chang). Space is created for readers to contemplate and to ponder with terseness and reticence. Peculiar to wisdom literature, double entendre in dual meanings, ambiguities, and ironies marks the pages of John, and then, readers come away swayed by the powerful imageries evoked in their minds as John images the truth.

These observations in the poetic features of the Fourth Gospel are only in one category of literary art of the Old Testament. The next chapter will now show the narrative techniques of the Old Testament that John familiarly used in the writing of his Gospel.

---

153. Caird, *Language and Imagery of the Bible*, 152.

4

The Gospel of John in Light of the Poetics of Old Testament Narrative

In addition to the discussions of the poetics of Old Testament poetry and its application in the Gospel of John, this chapter seeks to illuminate the literary art of John in light of Old Testament narratives. Along with poetry, narratives comprise the bulk of Old Testament literature, and their storytelling conventions provide the best background to understand John's unique narrative style.

Several important publications from notable biblical scholars and cross-disciplinary applications of secular literary theories have propelled studies in the poetics of narratives in recent decades. Cross-disciplinary studies from literary theories have been beneficial to biblical studies especially for the reason that they bring spotlights upon the biblical narratives from previously unattended angles. In a limited sense, Scripture is a literature like any other literature of the world, so it invites literary studies.

The Bible, however, diverges widely from other literatures on many levels. It is uniquely inspired by God and is divinely authoritative. Its unique historical, cultural, and religious situations further particularize it from other texts, so that universalizing scriptural poetics with general literary theories falls short of describing the richness of scriptural style. Although this chapter mentions narrative theories, it shows how the poetics of Old Testament narratives best illuminate the narrative art of the Fourth Gospel. The categories of literary theories will be useful, however, in assisting the identification, organization, and discussion of the poetics of scriptural narratives.

Point of View

The point of view is a fairly modern development in literary theory. Although the ancients had some awareness of it, they did not vigorously utilize it in literature.[1] From the eighteenth century onward, writers began to realize the role of point of view in literature, and only in the last century did literary critics systematize categories of point of view in literature. Abrams defined point of view concisely as "the way a story gets told."[2] Traditionally in modern literary tradition, the point of view relates to the degree of involvement of the narrator in the narrative. A writer can shape the narrative at any involvement level between direct involvement and complete absence in the story. The narrator may or may not choose the position of omniscience in the way he tells the story.

Boris Uspensky recognized that there are five planes in the point of view. He showed that one can analyze point of view from an ideological plane (the narrator's evaluative view), a phraseological plane (the narrator's adaptation of the speech pattern of a character to effect the shift of point of view), a psychological plane (internal or external point of view), a spatial plane (the narrator's spatial orientation), and a temporal plane (the narrator's temporal orientation).[3] Up until Uspensky's time, readers evaluated point of view mainly in terms of the degree of the narrator's involvement in the story, but Uspensky refined the narrator's involvement with psychological, phraseological, and ideological planes of point of view, and added two more dimensions of space and time to the discussion.

Gérard Genette, on the other hand, coined the term "focalization" and categorized the term as: (1) "zero focalization" or "nonfocalized narration" where the narrator speaks omnisciently from outside the story without any character's involvement; (2) "internal focalization" where character or characters convey the narrative perspective; and (3) "external focalization" where the narrative does not give the readers any access to the consciousness of the characters and eliminates the omniscience

---

1. Yamasaki, *Watching a Biblical Narrative*, 6.
2. Abrams, *Glossary of Literary Terms*, 165.
3. Uspensky, *Poetics of Composition*, 8–100.

of the narrator from the story.[4] What has been generally observed in the modern era concerning the literary concept of point of view is that it deals with the person(s) of narration and the degree of knowledge. A narrator may choose freely his narrative mode.[5]

Berlin, however, explained point of view simply as the camera lens through which the narrator captures the scenes to tell the story. As the film director is free to choose the depth and the angle of the lens, a narrator chooses the way of telling the story.[6] In the Old Testament, writers utilize point of view in various ways. Sometimes, they employ multiple viewpoints, and they contrast them, shift them, and converge them in order to convey the message dynamically.

In the story of Joseph's dream (Gen 37), the narrator shows several perspectives at play. Although the story is in the interest of Joseph, the points of view in the chapter are those of Jacob and the brothers.[7] Jacob loved Joseph more that his other sons "because he was the son of his old age" (v. 3), and the brothers hated Joseph and could not speak to him favorably because "*their* father loved him more than all his brothers" (v. 4; italics are added). When Joseph tells his dreams, the focus is not on Joseph, but how the reports affected the brothers and the father (vv. 8–11). Even when the brothers threw Joseph into the pit and sold him to Midianite traders, the story focuses only on the words and deeds of the brothers (vv. 18–31). The story then ends with Jacob's sorrow upon the deceptive report of the brothers concerning Joseph (vv. 32–35).

The play of multiple perspectives in the story shows that the issue is really the conflicting perspectives of the disparate family members. Berlin observed that the chapter "draws a portrait of a family in disharmony—each member with his own view, each working against the others . . . It is a story of a family that, quite literally, found itself."[8]

---

4. Genette, *Narrative Discourse*, 186–88. Cf. Chatman, *Story and Discourse*, 151–57. F. K. Stanzel provided a theoretical concept of "narrative situation" that is unique. His concept of "narrative situation" is that of continuum along three lines of mode (narrator, reflector), person (narrator standing inside or outside of the story, thus identity/non-identity), and perspective (inside, outside). Stanzel, *Theory of Narrative*, 46–60.

5. See also Booth, *Rhetoric of Fiction*, 149–63; Scholes and Kellogg, *Nature of Narrative*, 240–82; Lanser, *Narrative Act*.

6. Berlin, *Poetics and Interpretation*, 44. Cf. Fokkelman, *Reading Biblical Narrative*, 123–55.

7. Berlin, *Poetics and Interpretation*, 48.

8. Berlin, *Poetics and Interpretation*, 51. Jean Louis Ska directed attention several passages (i.e., Exod 3:1–6; 2 Sam 18:24–32; Gen 38) and showed the shifting of

In contrast to multiple perspectives, biblical writers also use singular perspective effectively. In the masterful analysis of the story of Dinah's rape (Gen 34), Sternberg showed that the point of reference is consistently on Jacob and his inaction concerning Dinah's defilement.[9] The writer introduces Dinah in the story as "the daughter of Leah, whom she had borne to *Jacob*" (v. 1; emphasis added). Jacob heard that Shechem defiled Dinah, "*his* daughter," but he stays silent until his sons come back from the field (v. 5; italics added), who explode with indignation upon hearing the news (v. 7). The father of Shechem, who comes to Jacob to act on behalf of his son, stands in stark contrast to what Jacob does for Dinah. Dinah's brothers initiate the negotiation, attack the people deceitfully and rescue her, but the story constantly refers to them as the "sons of Jacob" (vv. 7, 13, 25, 27). In this story, the narrator consistently points to Jacob in all important moments as the head of the household, but shows his inaction. This singular perspective perhaps conveys the message that Jacob's silence is most responsible for the actions of his sons.

Old Testament writers use external or internal perspectives variously. In the story of Abraham sacrificing his son Isaac, the story's perspective is strictly external (Gen 22).[10] The narrator does not provide any details concerning Abraham's inner thoughts, perhaps to show the readers that it is not the feelings but only the obedient act that counts before God. On the other hand, in the story of Joseph's reconciliation with his brothers (Gen 42–45), the narrator probes into the internal thoughts and feelings of the participants. Perhaps the purpose of this strategy is to show that the forgiveness and reconciliation between the offender and the offended deal with the innermost part of a person. The writer had to relate the inner thoughts of the brothers to show how reconciliation came.

The perspectives of the narrators may protrude into the stories. Narrators in the Old Testament rarely make specific references to themselves, with the exceptions of Ezra and Nehemiah, but readers sense the presence of the narrators always.[11] Sometimes, biblical writers speak of their temporal association with the story with phrases like "as it is to this day" (Gen 35:20; Josh 8:28; Judg 18:12; 2 Sam 18:18; 1 Kgs 9:21). They

---

perspectives. Ska, "Fathers Have Told Us," 69–76. Sternberg demonstrated the convergence of perspectives in the story of wooing of Rebekah. Sternberg, *Poetics*, 131–52.

9. Sternberg, *Poetics*, 445–75.

10. Cf. Ska, "Fathers Have Told Us," 72.

11. Bar-Efrat, *Narrative Art in the Bible*, 23–45. Bar-Efrat has an excellent discussion of this topic.

frequently add explanatory remarks (Judg 9:56–57; 2 Sam 16:23; 17:14; 1 Kgs 2:27), moral judgments (1 Kgs 11:6; 13:33; 15:11; 2 Kgs 23:25), and character evaluations (Gen 25:27; Judg 19:22; 1 Sam 9:2).[12]

It is not uncommon, moreover, that narrators adopt the viewpoints of the character. In the story of Ishmael, Ishmael is "the son of Hagar the Egyptian" for Sarah, but he is "his son" for Abraham:

"Now Sarah saw *the son of Hagar the Egyptian*, whom she had borne to Abraham." (Gen 21:9)

"The matter distressed Abraham greatly because of *his son*." (Gen 21:11)[13]

The explanatory remark followed by *ki* could belong to the character or to the narrator in this example: "The men were grieved, and they were very angry, *because (ki)* he had done a disgraceful thing in Israel by lying with Jacob's daughter, for such a thing ought not to be done" (Gen 34:7).[14] This "perspectival tangle"[15] or the "coalescence of two points of view"[16] is the biblical narrator's skillful wielding of his inspired creativity.

A unique feature of the Gospel of John is that the story is almost singularly in the perspective of Jesus.[17] Jesus is the only Person whose internal thoughts and feelings the writer conveys consistently. While the narrator takes glimpses into the thoughts of the characters, his treatment of the characters are usually external. When he gives the internal views of the characters, these views are usually his evaluation of their faith or unbelief. John therefore says that the disciples "believed" in him (2:11), "remembered" what the Scripture said (2:17), "marveled" that he was speaking with a woman (4:27), "did not understand" Jesus' figure of speech (10:6), "thought" that Jesus was speaking of literal sleep (11:13),

---

12. Bar-Efrat, *Narrative Art in the Bible*, 23–45.
13. Bar-Efrat, *Narrative Art in the Bible*, 36. Italics are added for emphasis.
14. Sternberg, *Poetics*, 454. Italics are added for emphasis.
15. Sternberg, *Poetics*, 454.
16. Bar-Efrat, *Narrative Art*, 39.
17. There are some significant monographs written in the perspectives in John. From Stanzel's paradigm of point of view, Derek Tovey proposed that the narrative mode of the Gospel of John lies and oscillates somewhere between the narrator and the reflector-character boundary, because, according to him, sometimes it is the narrator who tells the story, and sometimes it is the beloved disciple. Tovey, *Narrative Art and Act*. James L. Resseguie analyzed the point of view in the Fourth Gospel through the scheme set forth by Uspensky. Resseguie, *Strange Gospel*.

and was "perplexed" to know who was the betrayer (13:22). His brothers did not even "believe" in him (7:5). The Jews were "seeking all the more" to kill Jesus (5:18), they "did not realize" that He was speaking of the Father (8:27), and the Scribes and Pharisees were "testing" Jesus (8:6). The crowd "believed" (7:31), "muttered" (7:32), and "supposed" (11:3). On the other hand, the writer's attention on Jesus' internal thoughts and feelings are more profound: Jesus "loved" (11:5), was "deeply moved" (11:33,38), was "knowing that His hour had come," and "having loved His disciples, He loved them to the end" (13:1–3), "became troubled in spirit" (13:21), and "knowing all things that were coming upon Him, He went forth" (18:4).

The preeminence of Christ in perspectival orientation is evident in the representation of his speeches. John is careful to present the long discourses of Jesus as well as his most intimate prayers to his Father. Through these, the readers become immersed in the person and the perspectives of Jesus. This presence and eminence of long discourses within the narrated events is characteristic of Old Testament narratives. Alter recognized the significance of speech in Old Testament, and said that the "third-person narration is frequently only a bridge between much larger units of direct speech . . . The third-person restatement of what has been said in dialogue directs our attention back to the speakers, to the emphases they choose."[18] This is why, in the Fourth Gospel, the "incidents narrated receive an interpretation of their evangelical significance in the discourse; or, to put it otherwise, the truths enunciated in the discourse are given dramatic expression in the actions described."[19] In words and deeds, Jesus is the focal point. For this reason, even at the moment of betrayal, the point of view is consistently that of Jesus, and not Judas: "Now Judas also, who was betraying Him, knew the place; for Jesus had often met there with *His* disciples" (18:2; italics are added). Everyone and everything are oriented to Jesus. Fostering faith in him is the singular aim of the narrative (20:30–31).

Another unique way John tells the story is that the narrative voice is much stronger than the narratives of the Synoptics, almost lapsing into the narrative voice of the prophetic corpus. In other words, the narrative guidance is much more passionate. Tenney labeled these narrative

---

18. Alter, *Biblical Narrative*, 82.
19. Dodd, *Interpretation*, 384.

comments as "footnotes" and identified fifty-nine of them in ten categories.[20] He showed that there are footnotes of translation (1:38, 41–42; 4:25; 9:7; 19:13, 17; 20:16, 24), time and place (6:23; 7:2; 8:20; 9:14; 10:22–23; 11:30; 19:31, 42; 21:8), customs (2:9; 4:9), reference to the writer himself (1:4; 13:23–27; 19:35; 21:23, 24), recollections of the disciples (1:14, 16; 2:22; 10:6; 12:16; 13:28; 20:8, 9), explanations of circumstances (2:9; 6:23; 7:5, 39; 12:6; 20:30–31; 21:19), enumeration of signs and resurrection appearances (2:11; 20:18, 19, 26), identification of people (7:50; 11:21; 18:10, 14, 40; 19:39), Jesus' knowledge (6:6, 64; 13:11), and theological notes (3:16–21, 31–36; 12:37–43).[21] The pervasiveness of John's narrative footnotes and the extensiveness of his theological notes show that John, by all means, wanted his audience to *understand* the message clearly and to *persuade* them to faith in Jesus Christ. In this way, the Fourth Gospel is full of the fingerprints of John and the designation, *impassioned* narrative, captures its spirit.

John artfully uses space to modulate the engagement of the readers. The terms like "here" and "there" show how John uses space in the narrative. In the Gospel of John, "there" or "from there" (*ekei* or *ekeithen*) occurs twenty-four times, and the narrator uses most of them for his storytelling. This usage clearly shows that the author narrated from outside the story (2:1, 6, 12; 3:22, 23; 4:6, 40, 43; 5:5; 6:3, 22, 24; 10:40, 42; 11: 31, 54; 12:2, 9; 18:2, 3; 19:42; exceptions are 11:8, 15; 12:26). "Here" or "from here" (*hōde, enteuthen,* or *enthade*) appears thirteen times (2:16; 4:15, 16; 6:9, 25; 7:3; 11:21, 32; 14:31; 18:36; 19:18; 20:27), but different characters and Jesus speak most of them as part of their speeches. In 19:18, however, the narrator uses a unique spatial orientation feature in describing the location of Jesus on the cross. While the Synoptists describe the location of the robbers as being "on the right and on the left" from Jesus (Matt 27:38; Mark 15:27; Luke 23:33), clearly in the spatial orientation of outside, John intentionally narrates the story from within the cross of Jesus by specifying the location of the robbers as "from here and from here," (*enteuthen kai enteuthen,* John 19:18).[22] This is certainly an awkward

---

20. Tenney, "Footnotes of John's Gospel," 349–64.

21. Tenney, "Footnotes of John's Gospel," passim. Cf. O'Rourke, "Asides in the Gospel of John," 210–19; Thatcher, "New Look at Asides in the Fourth Gospel," 427–39.

22. *Enteuthen* pertains to "extension from a source near the speaker, *from here.*" Danker et al., "ἐντεῦθεν," 339. Johannes P. Louw and Eugene A. Nida defined this word as "extension from a source, with the point of reference near the speaker—'from here.'" Louw and Nida, "84.9 ἔνθεν; ἐντεῦθεν," 1:720; Compare also the related word

construction and the Synoptists' descriptions are more natural, but John's usage shows his theological purpose. From this point on until the moment of his death, John invites the readers to observe everything that happens from the spatial orientation of Jesus on the cross.

From the inter-disciplinary studies of linguistics, scholars recognized verbal aspects as playing an important role in the viewpoint of the story.[23] The perfective aspect often expressed by aorist indicative brings external viewpoint of an event as in a summary, and the imperfective aspect often expressed by present and imperfect indicatives brings internal viewpoint describing action as it unfolds.[24] Buist M. Fanning defined aspect in this way: "The action can be viewed from a reference-point *within* the action, without reference to the beginning or end-point of the action, but with a focus instead on its internal structure or make-up. Or the action can be viewed from a vantage-point *outside* the action, with focus on the whole action from beginning to end, but without reference to its internal structure."[25] In line with this definition, Constantine R. Campbell argued that indicative verbs semantically encode not only aspect but also spatial value of remoteness or promixity.[26] These insights from linguistics have a great bearing in understanding narratives and they come under what is known as discourse analysis. It will be dealt again in the discussion of plot below,[27] but it is worth noting here that narrative techniques

---

enthen in this example: "between us and you there is a great chasm fixed, so that those who wish to come over from here (*enthen*) to you will not be able" (Luke 16:26).

23. Stanley E. Porter and Buist M. Fanning's works were groundbreaking in the verbal aspect studies in the New Testament. Porter, *Verbal Aspect in the Greek of the New Testament*; Fanning, *Verbal Aspect in New Testament Greek*. Porter believed that indicative verbs are purely aspectual while Fanning believed that they also have tense as semantic value.

24. In addition to perfective and imperfective aspects, there is a debate whether there is the stative aspect which Porter argued. Campbell, *Advances in the Study of Greek*, 130.

25. Fanning, *Verbal Aspect in New Testament Greek*, 27.

26. Campbell, *Basics of Verbal Aspect in Biblical Greek*, 129–30.

27. Discourse analysis enriched the understanding of biblical narratives from previously unattended angles with linguistic sensitivities. Prominence, foregrounding and backgrounding techniques, and highlighting devices are now recognized as important aspects of narratives. Levinsohn, *Discourse Features of New Testament Greek*; Porter, "Discourse Analysis and New Testament Studies"; Porter, "Prominence: An Overview"; Runge, *Discourse Grammar of the Greek New Testament*. For full bibliography on discourse analysis in the New Testament, see: Campbell, *Advances in the Study of Greek*, 227–43.

using verbal aspects and prominence devices are also inherent in the Hebrew language,[28] and the narratives of the Gospels are fruitful field of investigation with discourse analysis.

Character and Characterization

There are several ways literary critics describe characters in narratives.[29] Most prominently, E. M. Forster distinguished between "flat" and "round" characters.[30] He said that flat characters are "types" and "caricatures" whose representation is around a single idea or quality, and the round characters are those who have more of these qualities and show multiple character traits. Flat characters do not undergo changes and are not complicated, so the readers understand and remember them easily. Round characters, on the other hand, are more complex and show depths of human life. Sometimes, instead of flat and round distinctions, some critics use "dynamic" and "static" categories where the first type of character is developed throughout the story while the second is not.[31] Still others recognized that there are "heroes" (central figures), "foils" (whose role is only for the main characters), "agents" (who exist for the plot), and "walk-ons" (who are merely the backgrounds).[32]

Scholes and Kellogg's description of the difference between Greek and Hebraic characters are well noted:

> The heroes of the Old Testament were in a process of becoming, whereas the heroes of Greek narrative were in a state of being. Process in Greek narrative was confined to the action of a plot. And even so, the action exemplified unchanging, universal laws; while the agents of the action, the characters, became as the plot unfolded only more and more consistent ethical types.

---

28. One may wish to compare and contrast the application of discourse analysis in the New Testament and Old Testament narratives. For Old Testament, see: Noonan, *Advances in the Study of Biblical Hebrew and Aramaic*; and Patton and Putnam, *Basics of Hebrew Discourse*. Consult the bibliography in Noonan, *Advances*, 281–324.

29. Cf. Wellek and Warren, *Theory of Literature*, 226–28; Scholes and Kellogg, *Nature of Narrative*, 160–206; Chatman, *Story and Discourse*, 108–38.

30. Forster, *Aspects of the Novel*, 65–75, 103–4.

31. Arp, *Perrin's Story and Structure*, 79–80.

32. Scholes and Kellogg, *Nature of Narrative*, 164; Frye, *Anatomy of Criticism: Four Essays*, 39–43, 171–77; Chatman, *Story and Discourse*, 119–34; Harvey, *Character and the Novel*, 63.

> Abraham, Jacob, David, and Samson, on the other hand, are men whose personal development is the focus of interest.[33]

Following the lead of Scholes and Kellogg, Culpepper observed the similarity between the characterization of John and of the Old Testament in some of the characters of John. He said,

> In John, the character of Jesus is static; it does not change. He only emerges more clearly as what he was from the beginning. Some of the minor characters, the Samaritan woman and the blind man in particular, undergo a significant change. To some extent, therefore, the Gospel of John draws from both Greek and Hebrew models of character development, but most of its characters appear to represent particular ethical types.[34]

Although Culpepper did not follow through this observation, his suggestion certainly hinted at the validity of a comparative study of John and Old Testament's characterization.[35]

A unique feature of biblical characterization is its "reticence."[36] Scripture does not give detailed description of characters as in other literatures, and it sometimes appears to be deficient of literary finesse. Auerbach noted that biblical characterization is scarce, yet it communicates the message so effectively. Alter asked the question: "How does the Bible manage to evoke such a sense of depth and complexity in its representation of character with what would seem to such sparse, even rudimentary means?"[37] When Saul asked the medium of Endor, "What is his form?" concerning the spirit she conjured up, the description is only that he is "an old man . . . wrapped with a robe" (1 Sam 28:14).[38] Scripture does not give concrete physical descriptions, as if "the prohibition on graven images has been extended to literary images."[39] What God said to Samuel is probably true of biblical characterization: "Do not look at his appearance

---

33. Scholes and Kellogg, *Nature of Narrative*, 169; Cf. Staley, "Stumbling in the Dark," 55; Culpepper, *Anatomy*, 103.

34. Culpepper, *Anatomy*, 103.

35. Applying the insights of Alter, Berlin, Sternberg, and Bar-Efrat, Staley explored this "Hebraic model" of characterization in John 5 and 9. Staley, "Stumbling in the Dark," 55–80. Cf. Fokkelman, *Reading Biblical Narrative*, 55–72.

36. Alter, *Biblical Narrative*, 143.

37. Alter, *Biblical Narrative*, 143.

38. This is of course the statement of the medium; but it is all that the narrator chooses to convey as well. cf. Berlin, *Poetics and Interpretation*, 35.

39. Berlin, *Poetics and Interpretation*, 34–35.

or at the height of his stature, because I have rejected him; for God sees not as man sees, for man looks at the outward appearance, but the LORD looks at the heart" (1 Sam 16:7).

How does the Scripture see characters then? From the narrator's description of David in 1 Samuel 16:18, Sternberg observed five elements that make up biblical characterization:

1. Physical feature ("a handsome man")
2. Social feature ("a son of Jesse the Bethlehemite")
3. Particularizing feature ("skillful musician")
4. Moral feature ("the LORD is with him")
5. Psychological feature ("a mighty man of valor, a warrior, one prudent in speech")[40]

He observed that biblical characterization that utilizes all or most of these features are "far more prevalent in biblical history than is usually thought."[41] In other words, biblical narrators are able to describe characters amply with these descriptions.

The reason for this type of characterization probably originates from the plot-centeredness of biblical narratives. Outi Lehtipuu, in regard to the Gospels, said: "In general, there are at least two overall categories of narrative: plot-centered (apsychological) and character-centered (psychological) narrative. The Gospels no doubt belong to the former group, because the whole conception of psychological characters is quite recent."[42] When biblical narrators describe characters, it serves the plot purpose. However they choose to describe the characters, the descriptions serve the plot later in the narrative. Sternberg called this an "art of proleptic epithet."[43] Such examples include: the serpent was "crafty" (Gen 3:1); Noah was "righteous" (Gen 6:9); Esau was "hairy" (Gen 25:25); Isaac's eyes were "dim" (Gen 27:1); Ehud was "a left-handed man" and

---

40. Sternberg, *Poetics*, 326. Berlin noted: "The purpose of character description in the Bible is not to enable the reader to visualize the character, but to enable him to situate the character in terms of his place in society, his own particular situation, and his outstanding traits—in other words, to tell what kind of a person he is" (Berlin, *Poetics and Interpretation*, 36).

41. Sternberg, *Poetics*, 326.

42. Lehtipuu, "Characterization and Persuasion," 79. Cf. Chatman, *Story and Discourse*, 113.

43. Sternberg, *Poetics*, 328.

Eglon was "a very fat man" (Judg 3:15–17); Abigail was "beautiful" and Nabal was "harsh and evil" (1 Sam 25:3); Asahel was "swift-footed" (2 Sam 2:18); and Naaman was a leper (2 Kgs 5:1).[44] In the story of Ehud (and in other stories as well), what the readers anticipate through proleptic description of his character becomes reality in the story, showing how those anticipated elements find fulfillment in the actual event. In this regard, Sternberg made the following observation:

> Between the figuring forth of prospection and the gap-filling of retrospection, there extends a range of mixed dynamics, characterized by an active *two-way* traffic along the reading sequence ... The initial epithets generate some fairly determinate expectations, which the sequel so resolves or ramifies as to shape afresh our understanding of the entire causal chain.[45]

As one sees characters in this light, he begins to understand the biblical way of naming characters. Naming has important ramifications. It endows persons with individuality, identity, distinction, and significance.[46] Depriving characters of names could mean the opposite—or at least that the character's identity is not important.[47] In the Book of Ruth, after a short introduction, the narrator begins the narrative indicating the names of these people: "The name of the man was Elimelech, and the name of his wife, Naomi; and the names of his two sons were Mahlon and Chilion, Ephrathites of Bethlehem in Judah" (1:2). Except Naomi, these people do not have any roles in the story, yet their names provide a significant context to understand the story.[48] When the identification is not necessary—or even undesired—however, a character remains nameless, although he/she may be a significant character. In First Kings 13, the narrator tells the story of a man of God coming to Jeroboam and prophesying against the altar in Bethel. Interestingly, the writer devotes the whole chapter to him, but the man of God remains nameless. The identification of his name is undesired, but the fact that he is a man of

---

44. Sternberg, *Poetics*, 328–41.
45. Sternberg, *Poetics*, 336.
46. Resseguie, "Narrative-Critical Approach to the Fourth Gospel," 12–13.
47. The story of rich man and Lazarus shows this contrast (Luke 16:19–31).
48. Elimelech means "My God is King;" Naomi, "to be pleasant;" Mahlon, with an uncertainty, "to be sick;" and Chilion, "to be finished." The names Elimelech and Naomi probably reflect the spiritual heritage they received (at least in their naming), but the names Mahlon and Chilion show spiritual and/or physical destitution they were in at the time of their births. cf. Block, *Judges, Ruth*, 624–25.

God is. In biblical narratives, naming and namelessness are not arbitrary, but have a clear purpose.

In addition to names, narrators often refer to characters in terms of personal relationships Berlin said that "the use of these relationship terms is an important sign of significant relationships within the story."[49] In the story of David's flight in Second Samuel 15–19, he is "David" to his devoted friend Hushai (2 Sam 15:33, 37), "the king" to Mephibosheth's servant Ziba (16:2). He is again "David" to the contemptuous Shimei who curses him (16:6, 11, 13), but "the king" to Shimei when David returns back to Jerusalem (19:17, 18, 19).[50]

It is important to observe that both Old Testament and New Testament writers embed theological purpose in characterization. Hebrews 11, probably the most extensive character study of Old Testament characters in the New Testament, shows that the purpose of Old Testament characters or characterization is to reveal their faith in the Lord. An important function of characters in the Old Testament is to illustrate some aspects of their faith, and the writer of Hebrews shows repeatedly what these characters were able to accomplish "by faith" (cf. Rom 4:23–24).

Secondly, in addition to revealing the element of faith, Old Testament characters also serve to show the sinfulness of human hearts. In speaking about the Exodus generation in First Corinthians 10:1–5, especially of how they did not enter the Promised Land, Paul says that these things happened as examples: "Now these things happened as examples for us, so that we would not crave evil things as they also craved" (v. 6; cf. v. 11). The purpose of Old Testament characters and their characterization is to show how sin entered into the world and affected human race. For this reason, biblical writers are not interested in physical descriptions, but in the description of their hearts and their inward thoughts. Inward thoughts and direct speeches, therefore, take prominence in biblical characterizations.

Thirdly, Old Testament characters have the function of revealing the character and the work of God. God, who is unseen and unknown, reveals himself to the world mainly through his dealings with—and in his words to—the characters of the Old Testament. So, the writer of the Hebrews testifies: "God, after He spoke long ago to the fathers in the prophets in many portions and in many ways" (Heb 1:1). The lives of the Old Testament

---

49. Berlin, *Poetics and Interpretation*, 59.

50. Berlin, *Poetics and Interpretation*, 39–40. This strategy is also in the story of Bathsheba (Bar-Efrat, *Narrative Art in the Bible*, 37–39) and Judah and Tamar (Berlin, *Poetics and Interpretation*, 60–61).

people clearly demonstrate God's manifold mercies and faithfulness, so that the New Testament believers frequently referred to God as the "God of Abraham, Isaac, and Jacob" or simply as the "God of our fathers" (Matt 22:32; Acts 5:30, 32; 22:14; 24:14). The revelation of God belonged to the "fathers," or to the characters of the Old Testament narratives.

Moreover, the Old Testament characters also revealed the redemptive work of God in their lives. While the characters themselves may not have known this fact, God used them in achieving his salvific purpose (Matt 1:1–17). Scripture speaks of Ruth, not just because her faithfulness is exemplary, but because she became the great grandmother of David (Ruth 4:18–22) through whom Christ came. So are the stories of Judah fathering Perez and Zerah by Tamar (Gen 38), and Rahab hiding the spies and being delivered in the conquest (Josh 2:1–14; 6:15–25).

For these reasons, the Old Testament precedents must illuminate the method of characterization in the Fourth Gospel. John speaks of characters in the Gospel in order to show their favorable responses of faith or their negative responses of rejection to Jesus. Culpepper recognized this function of the characters:

> They are in effect the prism which breaks up the pure light of Jesus' remote epiphany into colors the reader can see. In John's narrative world the individuality of all the characters except Jesus is determined by their encounter with Jesus. The characters represent a continuum of responses to Jesus which exemplify misunderstandings the reader may share and responses one might make the depiction of Jesus in the gospel. The characters are, therefore, particular sorts of choosers. Given the pervasive dualism of the Fourth Gospel, the choice is either/or. All situations are reduced to two clear-cut alternatives, and all the characters eventually make their choice. So must the reader. The evangelist, who stands entrenched within one perspective, uses all the powers at his disposal to coax the reader to his side.[51]

The characters in the Fourth Gospel demonstrate the compassion and righteousness of Jesus in his dealings with them, and they exemplify the kind of responses people have toward Jesus.[52] The characters are representative figures[53] of faith and unbelief. Their interactions with Jesus are

---

51. Culpepper, *Anatomy*, 104.

52. Culpepper, "Weave of the Tapestry," 18.

53. Collins, "Representative Figures of the Fourth Gospel," 26–46; Collins, "Representative Figures of the Fourth Gospel, Part II," 118–32 (reprinted as Collins,

revelatory themselves of the nature of Jesus, and their faith (or lack of faith) encourages positive response of faith to Jesus from the readers' part. In this light, the trilateral interactions of loving God, inner-workings of depraved human hearts, and the exercise of saving faith are what typify the characters in the Fourth Gospel.

As far as the character studies in the Gospel of John are concerned, the characters are not full-fledged characters as in modern novels, so there are limitations in this undertaking; but Cornelis Bennema recently argued that the characters in John are more complex than usually thought and that there is a degree of characterization from agent to type to personality to individuality.[54] James L. Resseguie also helpfully pointed out that "changes in characters elaborate and develop a narrative's meaning," and that "since character and plot a are intricately bound, a change or development in a character often provides a clue to the direction and meaning of the plot and theme."[55] The developing characters have significant functions in the development of the plot in John.

It is important to note that the function of the Prologue of the Gospel is similar to the proleptic epithetic descriptions of the Old Testament. Just as it was normal for biblical narrators to create reader's expectations concerning the characters through epithetic descriptions, thus foreshadowing the full play-out of these initial descriptions, John creates the frame in the beginning through which the reader should understand the following narratives. Francis J. Moloney said that "the prologue is the 'telling' while the narrative is the 'showing'" of who Jesus is.[56] This function of the Prologue was the author's way of ensuring the reader's correct understanding of Jesus and His works.

The writer consistently presents John the Baptist's function as the witness for Christ. This presentation as a witness is what the Prologue emphasizes (John 1:6–8, 15) and what his following speeches consistently portray (1:19–36; 3:22–36). The writer keeps the reference to his other ministries at minimum (3:23–24).[57]

"Representative Figures," 1–45).

54. Bennema, *Encountering Jesus*; cf. Bennema, "Comprehensive Approach to Understanding Character," 36–58. There are too many literatures in characterizations in John to be listed here. For bibliography, see: Skinner, "Introduction," xvii–xxxii.

55. Resseguie, "Narrative-Critical Approach," 11.

56. Moloney, *Belief in the Word*, 24.

57. Talbert pointed out five places that mention John the Baptist (1:1–18; 1:19—2:11; 3:22—4:3; 5:31–47; 10:40–42), and he said, "The dominant description of the

Nicodemus receives a full description: he is "a man of the Pharisees, named Nicodemus, a ruler of the Jews" (3:1). Obviously, his character is an important one, and the descriptions are significant. In Scripture, "overspecification" carries an important function, because the information it provides "reiterates thematic information about the entity or provides some elaboration about them that exceeds the minimum needed to 'pick them out of a lineup.'"[58] As the epithetic descriptions of characters in the Old Testament had significant plot functions, overspecification has an important function in the narrative. Runge observed that "Epithets can also be used to (re-)establish a thematic relation of a participant to the discourse (e.g. *Isaac, his son*), anchoring them in a specific way."[59] The descriptions of Nicodemus have the important function of anchoring him in the themes of the narrative in specific ways.[60]

In the case of the woman who encounters Jesus in chapter 4, readers immediately notice that the chapter gives more description of the place than the identity of the woman. The place of the encounter is specified as "a city of Samaria, called Sychar, near the parcel of ground that Jacob gave to his son Joseph . . . Jacob's well" (4:5–6). In Nicodemus' case, Nicodemus as a Jewish person is overly specified, but in case of this woman, it is the place that receives that focus. In this lengthy description, it is as if the writer is saying, "Jesus is at Jacob's well now; by the way, that is in *Samaria*!" In light of all the enmity and hostility between the two people groups of Jews and Samaritans, the woman's identity as a "Samaritan" woman was probably more important than any other description, and even more than her own name.[61]

Baptist from start to finish is: John is the ideal witness to Jesus, Christ's best man, friend of the bridegroom" (Cf. Talbert, *Reading John*, 108–9).

58. Runge, *Discourse Grammar*, 317.

59. Runge, "Pragmatic Effects," 87.

60. A profound study in all the characters in the Fourth Gospel has been done recently. Hunt et al., *Character Studies in the Fourth Gospel*. Because of the limitation of this study, refer to the volume for extensive discussions on the characters in John.

61. Jews and Samaritans were age-old enemies to each other. When the exile returned to the land of Judah, Samaritans bitterly opposed their rebuilding of the temple (Ezra 4:7–23). When Coponius was the procurator of Judea (AD 6–9), some Samaritans secretly entered the Temple and committed a horrible sacrilege of throwing human bones in the porticoes and the sanctuary (Josephus, *Antiquities* 18:29–30). In AD 51, in the Samaritan village of Ginae, which was not too far from Jacob's Well, Samaritans murdered a Jewish pilgrim traveling from Galilee to Jerusalem. The Roman governor refused to get involved and this event triggered the crowd of the Passover Feast to rush to Ginea and massacre all its inhabitants and burn down the whole

Many characters (i.e. the royal official, the paralyzed man, the woman caught in adultery, the man born blind, etc.) purposefully remain anonymous in the Gospel of John.[62] The Gospel is, after all, the story of Jesus who came to be the Savior of the world, and the anonymity of other characters contributes to this overall message in special ways.

In contrast to anonymity, it is Jesus who receives many names in the Gospel of John. Just in the first chapter, He is the "Word" (1:1,14), "Lamb of God" (1:29,36), "Son of God" (1:34), "Rabbi" (1:38), "Messiah" (1:41), "the King of Israel" (1:49), and "Son of Man" (1:51).[63] John endows him with manifold names. He is the most significant Person with honor and worth in the Fourth Gospel.[64]

Plot

Plot in literature concerns the organization or the sequence of the events.[65] Abrams defined it as "the structure of its actions, as these are ordered and rendered toward achieving particular emotional and artistic effects."[66] Aristotle gave the classic definition of plot as the "combination of the incidents of the story" and said that it is the most important element in a story.[67] Yairah Amit's analysis of Old Testament narratives is helpful in understanding what plot does. She said:

---

village (Josephus, *Jewish Wars* 2:232–46; *Antiquities* 20:118–36; Tacitus, *Annals* 12:54). This event became a turning point in the Jewish relationship with Rome which eventually led to their fall in AD 70. Rhoads, *Israel in Revolution*, 72; cf. Ford, *My Enemy Is My Guest*, 84–86. When John wrote his Gospel, this event and its location must have brought every raw emotion in his Jewish audience.

62. Such namelessness amid ample significations (as in the paralyzed man in chap. 4) does not mean inferior storytelling. Readers must grapple with the meaning of such facelessness in its context. Some minor characters are nameless because their identity is insignificance (such as the headwaiter, servants, and the bridegroom in chap. 2).

63. Talbert, *Reading John*, 86. In addition to these, Jesus has many other titles or names in John, such as the "Bread of Life" (6:35), "Light of the World" (8:12), "Vine" (15:1), "Way," "Truth," "Life" (14:6), "Resurrection and Life" (11:25).

64. Steve Booth counted the number of occurrences of all the names in John and observed that, "The most striking observation made ... is that there are more occurrences of 'Jesus' in the Fourth Gospel (245) than all the other proper names put together (204)." Booth, *Selected Peak Marking Features*, 53.

65. Scholes and Kellogg, *Nature of Narrative*, 207; Chatman, *Story and Discourse*, 62–95; Abrams, *Glossary of Literary Terms*, 139–42.

66. Abrams, *Glossary of Literary Terms*, 127.

67. Aristotle, *Poet.*, 1450a.

> The plot is the selection and organization of events in a particular order of time; it is a purposeful structure built around the conflict between the personae, or it may be the internal conflict of one character. The author, who has a purpose in mind, selects a series of events out of countless possibilities and decides how to organize them, what comes after what. The author may organize them in chronological order or may deviate from it and anticipate later events, or introduce at some late stage in the sequence developments that were, chronologically speaking, earlier.[68]

Plot is the way the writer organizes the events of a story for specific purposes in mind, and there are several such structural schemes in the Old Testament.

The classic definition of plot, or the "pediment structure" as Amit termed it, recognizes change as the most important element in story. It has three stages: "complication," "crisis," and "unraveling," in addition to its opening and the ending.[69] In the story of the Tower of Babel (Gen 11:1–9), the opening shows that all people had one language. The story goes through the complication stage when the people started to build the tower in defiance of God's will (v. 4), and it reaches its crisis when God sees the tower and says that nothing will be impossible for them if they are left alone (v. 6). The story unravels, then, as the Lord comes down and scatters the language of the people (vv. 7–8), and arrives at a new situation when the languages of the earth are now confounded, and the people are all scattered abroad (v. 9).[70] Because such a story finds its peak at the climax, pediment structure is often in symmetry with its parts corresponding to each other.

There are also narratives in the Old Testament with a scenic structure. Scenic structure is a way of examining a story "first in terms of the transitions of time, place, and character, and also in terms of distinguishing between 'telling' and 'showing.'"[71] In the scenic plot structure, the writer composes episodes in different scenes with changes of time, place, and characters. In the story of Ahab taking the field of Naboth, the narrator arranged the scenes with locations as the principal organizing element; so there are five scenes of the vineyard (1 Kgs 21:2–3), the palace

---

68. Amit, *Reading Biblical Narrative*, 47. Cf. Fokkelman, *Reading Biblical Narrative*, 73–96.
69. Amit, *Reading Biblical Narrative*, 73–96.
70. Amit, *Reading Biblical Narrative*, 48.
71. Amit, *Reading Biblical Narrative*, 49.

(vv. 4–10), the city where the condemnation takes place (vv. 11–14), the palace (vv. 15–16), and the vineyard (vv. 17–27).[72]

In scenic structure, narrative voice indicates the change of scenes. A narrator may "tell" the whole story in his own voice (i.e. Judg 3:7–11), or "show" the story indirectly, but more dramatically and vividly, through the actions and speeches of the participants (i.e. Judg 16:1–3).[73] A change of narrative voice can also indicate important transitions of scenes, or sub-scenes, or by the transition from "telling" to "showing." For instance, in Joshua 7:26 the narrative explanation signals a change of unit in the flow of the story: "They raised over him a great heap of stones that stands to this day, and the LORD turned from the fierceness of His anger. Therefore the name of that place has been called the valley of Achor to this day."[74]

Old Testament narratives may also have "three-and-four numeric structure." This method of structuring is "often used to convey confrontation and persuasion and for effecting a change of attitude. It entails four events sharing a common denominator, the last of which entails a change in position; in other words, after three ineffective occurrences, there is an effective fourth."[75] This persuasive or confrontational structure is numerous in the Old Testament. In the parable of Jotham, when the trees went out to appoint a king over them their initial three attempts over the olive tree, the fig tree, and the vine were unsuccessful, but the fourth one to the bramble was successful (Judg 9:7–15). In the story of Samson and Delilah, Delilah's first three attempts were unsuccessful, but she succeeds in the fourth one (Judg 16:4–21). In the disasters Job experienced, it is because of the fourth one that Job becomes completely broken (Job 1:13–22).[76] In Proverbs 30:15–33, the writer uses three-and-four persuasive structure effectively, with the fourth element bringing the punch.

---

72. Amit, *Reading Biblical Narrative*, 56.
73. Amit, *Reading Biblical Narrative*, 50.
74. Walsh, *Style and Structure*, 119, 125.
75. Amit, *Reading Biblical Narrative*, 62.
76. Amit provided these examples in Amit, *Reading Biblical Narrative*, 62–64.

"There are three things that will not be satisfied, four that will not say, 'Enough.'" (v. 15)

"There are three things which are too wonderful for me, Four which I do not understand." (v. 18)

"Under three things the earth quakes, And under four, it cannot bear up." (v. 21)

"There are three things which are stately in *their* march, Even four which are stately when they walk." (v. 29)

In all of these instances, the punch comes with the fourth item.

The writer of Job may have used three-and-four structure in the confrontational speeches of Job and his friends. Job and his three friends argue against each other in three cycles and the speech of Elihu and then the speech of the LORD replace the fourth cycle.

First Cycle

	Eliphaz	Job	Chs. 4–7
	Bildad	Job	Chs. 8–10
	Zophar	Job	Chs. 11–14

Second Cycle

	Eliphaz	Job	Chs. 15–17
	Bildad	Job	Chs. 18–19
	Zophar	Job	Chs. 20–21

Third Cycle

	Eliphaz	Job	Chs. 22–24
	Bildad	Job	Chs. 25–26
		Job	Chs. 27–31

Fourth Cycle

	Elihu		Chs. 32–37
	The LORD	*Job	Chs. 38–42 (*Job speaks in 42:1–6)

The writer introduces Elihu's speech rather extensively in the beginning of the fourth cycle in 32:1–3. He says:

> Then these three men ceased answering Job, because he was righteous in his own eyes. But the anger of Elihu . . . burned;

against Job his anger burned because he justified himself before God. And his anger burned against his three friends because they had found no answer, and yet had condemned Job . . . And when Elihu saw that there was no answer in the mouth of the three men his anger burned.

In contrast to Job's three friends, Elihu's speech then is reported with a greater force in this forth cycle. But most importantly, it is the LORD who has the final words in the last part of the fourth cycle: "Then the LORD answered Job out of the whirlwind and said" (38:1). In this way, the writer of Job uses the confrontational three-and-four structure most effectively to show the words of the LORD as most authoritative and decisive.

Sometimes, this three-and-four structure is modified to "six-and-seven structure" in the Old Testament. From the quotation of Yair Zakovitch, Isaac Kalimi said that "Numerical patterns are whole numbers used in a literary unit to structure a 'pattern in which the number of component parts is X + 1, with the final component being the decisive one.'"[77] Kalimi recognized in the six-and-seven pattern, that the seventh part is the decisive one. He argued that this structure is apparent in the way the Chronicler regards David as the seventh son of Jesse in First Chronicles 2:13–15, whereas in First Samuel 17:12–14, David is the eighth son.[78] He noted that the "postbiblical Jewish sages and artists were already sensitive to this," and many recognized that "all sevenths are always favored . . . the seventh son is favored, and it is said: 'David—the seventh.'"[79] The following examples also show six-and-seven persuasive structure:

"From six troubles He will deliver you, even in seven evil will not touch you." (Job 5:19)

"There are six things which the LORD hates, yes, seven which are an abomination to Him." (Prov 6:16)

---

77. Kalimi, *Reshaping of Ancient Israelite History*, 362. The work of Yair Zakovitch was not available to the present writer. Zakovitch, *Pattern of the Numerical Sequence Three-Four*.

78. Kalimi, *Reshaping*, 362–68. Contrary to Kalimi, a simple explanation could be that a son died so that David is the seventh in 1 Chr 2:13–15. Bergen, *1, 2 Samuel*, 190–91.

79. Kalimi, *Reshaping*, 367.

These examples show that the three-and-four and six-and-seven numeric structures were important persuasive and confrontational methods in the Old Testament.

The last area of discussion in the Old Testament narrative plot is the unique structure of repetition and parallelism. Storytelling is a universal phenomenon. However, as Jerome T. Walsh observed, "individual *stories* are inexorably particular," because they are "the product of a particular time ... culture ... [and] language."[80] Hebrew narratives, and their episodes and scenes, have a unique structure of parallelism. Repetitions and symmetrical patterns are the most prominent compositional techniques in the Hebrew narratives.[81] Therefore, when constituent parts do not synchronize in prominently parallelistic structure, it heightens the rhetorical effectiveness. Walsh noted: "Hebrew narrative will sometimes violate an otherwise symmetrical pattern with an insertion, deletion, or other disturbance of the patterned regularity. The clearer the fundamental symmetry and the more obtrusive the disturbance, the more the asymmetrical element draws a reader's attention."[82]

Walsh also demonstrated that varying forms of symmetry organize Old Testament narratives. Some narratives are in:

1. Complete reverse symmetry
2. Forward symmetry (corresponding units occur in the same order)
3. Partial symmetry (only some units correspond, i.e. inclusio structure)
4. Multiple symmetry (the corresponding pattern is complex)
5. Asymmetry with deviating units.[83]

In other words, in Old Testament narratives, repetitions in varying forms and degrees join and give meaning to the subunits.[84]

In the Gospel of John, some writers observed a pediment structure with a climax where its corresponding parts mirror and contrast each other. Egil A. Wyller argued that the whole Gospel has a concentric structure and

80. Walsh, *Style and Structure*, 1.
81. Walsh, *Style and Structure*, 1–7.
82. Walsh, *Style and Structure*, 8.
83. Walsh, *Style and Structure*, passim. Walsh's examples show that Old Testament narrators freely adapted the spirit of parallelism as an organizing principle of the narratives.
84. Walsh, *Style and Structure*, 145.

that 10:22–38 is the center of the work, forming the "structural summit" of the Gospel and a "change of fate" place in the dramatic development.[85] The chiastic structure he set forth was: Prologue (1:1–18), introduction (1:19–51), first act (chaps 2–4), second act (chaps 5–7), third act (chaps 8–12), fourth act (chaps 13–17), fifth act (chaps 18–20), conclusion (21:1–23), and Epilogue (21:24–25).[86] As his analysis indicates, the pediment and scenic structure are correlated to each other in the Gospel of John.

Wyller made some interesting analyses on the correspondence of these acts. First, he said that the approximate length of each part corresponds to its opposite pair, except for the Prologue and the Epilogue. Second, the narratorial "we" in the Prologue (1:14) finds its match in the Epilogue (21:24). Third, the one-on-one calling in the "introduction" (1:19–53) corresponds with the one-on-one sending in the "conclusion" (21:1–23), where Peter, Nicodemus, and the unnamed disciple are reciprocated. Fourth, the first act (chaps 2–4) and the fifth act (chaps 18–20) correspond thematically in some degree.[87] Fifth, the second act (chaps 5–7) and the fourth act (chaps 13–17) agree in that in the second act, Jesus comes into sharp conflicts with his own people and he withdraws from them; but in the fourth act, Jesus abides with his disciples who received him and understood him. Sixth, the third act, which forms the center of the Gospel, begins with the *pericope adulterae*, whose theme is the light of the world, and ends with the same theme of light (12:46).[88] Following his lead, Gunnar Østenstad proposed that "the Evangelist has composed the Fourth Gospel concentrically in seven main sections, symmetrically oriented around chs. 8:12—12:50."[89]

In light of the Old Testament precedent, whether one fully follows Wyller-Østenstad's scheme or not, the symmetrical arrangement of the plot—and the "insertion, deletion, or other disturbance of the patterned regularity"[90]—has a highly functional role in the Gospel of John. The Gospel invites the readers to compare and contrast the constituent parts, especially in light of its numerous repetitions and chiasms of different sorts, in order to derive a deeper significance of each section.

---

85. Wyller, "In Solomon's Porch," 153.
86. Wyller, "In Solomon's Porch," 157.
87. Some of his associations are subjective at this point.
88. Wyller, "In Solomon's Porch," 159–62.
89. Østenstad, "Structure of the Fourth Gospel?," 35.
90. Walsh, *Style & Structure*, 8.

The Gospel of John in Light of the Poetics of Old Testament Narrative   125

Finally, one can test the three-and-four persuasive/confrontational plot structure of Old Testament narratives on the Fourth Gospel with fruitful results. The opening chapter of the Gospel provides three personal testimonies of John the Baptist (1:19–28; 29–34; 35–36), where temporal and/or spatial indications signal the transitions of the scenes. Different episodes come after his three testimonies, but his fourth testimony decisively brings his witnesses to a close (3:22–36). In the story of calling his disciples, John mentions four disciples,[91] where the most decisive Messianic revelation comes with the fourth disciple, Nathanael. In Jesus' discourse with the Samaritan Woman in chapter 4, the persuasive dialogue follows a three-and-four and six-and-seven structures. In the discourse, the most significant points of persuasion come in the fourth and seventh exchanges. The following layout of the passage presents the dialogue in a shortened form to see the structure:

Jesus: "Give me a drink." (v. 7)
Woman: "How is it that you, a Jew . . . ?" (v. 9)

Jesus: "If you knew the gift of God . . ." (v. 10)
Woman: "Sir, you have nothing to draw with." (v. 11–12)

Jesus: "Everyone who drinks of this water will thirst again." (vv. 13–14)
Woman: "Sir, give me this water." (v. 15)

Jesus: "Go, call your husband." (v. 16)
Woman: "I have no husband." (v. 17)

Jesus: "You have said correctly." (vv. 17–18)
Woman: "Sir, I perceive you are a prophet." (vv. 19–20)

Jesus: "Woman, believe me, an hour is coming." (vv. 21–24)
Woman: "I know that Messiah is coming." (v. 25)

Jesus: "I am He." (v. 26)
Woman: Leaves the water bucket and runs to the city. (v. 28)

---

91. One may group Andrew and the other disciple as one (1:37–39), because John gives prominence to Andrew only.

Jesus makes the most important request to the woman, "Go, call your husband" in the fourth verbal exchange, to open up her sinfulness (or hurtful) past. The most decisive statement of persuasion, then, comes in the seventh place—which is also the fourth place from the central statement—"I am He." At this statement, the woman drops the bucket and runs into the city.[92]

John arranged many episodes in four scenes where the fourth scene carries significant weight in the context. In chapter 4, the episode has four scenes.

1. Jesus and the Samaritan woman (vv. 7–26)
2. The woman and Samaritans (vv. 28–30)
3. Jesus and the disciples (vv. 27, 31–38)
4. Jesus and the Samaritans (vv. 39–42)

In chapter 5, the episode has four scenes.

1. Jesus and the paralyzed man (vv. 5–9)
2. The Jews and the paralyzed man (vv. 10–13)
3. Jesus and the paralyzed man (v. 14)
4. The paralyzed man and the Jews (v. 15)

In chapter 6, there are four scenes.

1. Jesus and the disciples' response to the lack of bread (vv. 5–14)
2. Jesus and the disciples on the Sea (vv. 15–21)
3. Jesus and the crowd (vv. 22–66)
4. Jesus and the disciples (vv. 67–71)

---

92. In the fourth exchange of dialogue in the Bread of Life discourse in 6:26–66, Jesus reveals, "I am the bread of life" (v. 35) and the attitude of the crowd changes negatively toward Jesus at this point (vv. 41–42). After the seventh speech of Jesus, many of his disciples leave him permanently (v. 66). In the discourse between Jesus with the Jews who believed in him (8:31–59), Jesus and the Jews have seven exchanges of dialogue, and it is in the seventh dialogue that Jesus makes the Messianic claim, "Before Abraham was born, I am," and it is at this statement, that the Jews pick up the stones to stone him (vv. 58–59). In this way, the persuasive and confrontational speeches render valuable insights as readers analyze them according to the three-and-four or the six-and-seven narrative structures. However, not all discourses have this arrangement (i.e., the healing of the blind man in chap. 9).

The Gospel of John in Light of the Poetics of Old Testament Narrative

Analyzing the plot structure of the Fourth Gospel is a difficult task. No one scheme can do justice to the Gospel's complexity.[93] However, as one applies the narrative plot structures of the Old Testament in reading the Gospel, John's frame of mind becomes more apparent and readers gain insights into the effectiveness of his persuasion.

Gaps and Ambiguities

Due to the nature of literature itself, there are abundant informational omissions in stories. A story cannot communicate everything that there is to know, and the narrator must inevitably select what he will and will not tell. Gaps, in this present discussion, however, do not deal with these inevitable omissions in a storytelling, but rather concern the intentional leaving out of details which readers expect.[94] Sternberg made an important distinction between these two types of informational omission in a story, calling the former "blanks" and the latter "gaps." Recognizing "blanks" as irrelevant and "gaps" as relevant to the story, he said: "To

---

93. For example, Mlakuzhyil identified twenty-four different structural schemes of John which scholars proposed. He identified the following according to different criteria used: (1) geographical-chronological structure; (2) chronological-liturgical structure; (3) numerical-symbolical structure; (4) literary-chronological structure; (5) typological structure; (6) theological-typological-symbolical structure; (7) liturgical-symbolical-typological structure; (3) liturgical-symbolical-sign structure; (9) chiastic structure; (10) chiastic-symbolic structure; (11) symmetrical-concentric structure; (12) rhythmical-symmetrical structure; (13) centric-symmetrical structure; (14) narrative structure; (15) narrative-discourse structure; (16) dramatic-chronological-geographical structure; (17) dramatic-episodic structure; (18) revelatory structure; (19) revelatory-dramatic structure; (20) revelatory-response structure; (21) revelatory-narrative structure; (22) revelatory-eclectic structure; (23) literary-thematic structure; and (24) journey-structure. He also identified three categories of about thirty criteria that may be used to arrive at an objective structure in John's Gospel. They are (1) literary criteria—introduction, conclusions, inclusions, characteristic vocabulary, geographical and chronological indications, liturgical feasts, transitions, bridge-passages, hook-words, techniques of repetition of the same terms or formulae or type-scene or similar sayings or discourses of Jesus, change of literary genres such as narrative, dialogue, discourse; (2) dramatic techniques—introduction of dramatis personae, change of dramatis personae or scenes, techniques of diptych-scenes or alternating scenes or seven scenes, techniques of double-stage action or stage-duality or vanishing characters, sequence of action-dialogue-discourse, dramatic development of the plot and dramatic pattern; and (3) structural patterns—parallelism, chiasmus, concentric structure, and spiral structure. Mlakuzhyil, *Christocentric Literary Structure*, 17–85, 87–135.

94. Genette, *Narrative Discourse*, 52; Chatman, *Story and Discourse*, 30.

make sense is to make distinctions between what was omitted for the sake of interest and what was omitted for lack of interest: between what I called, for short gaps and blanks. Only the former demand closure, while the latter may be disregarded without loss, indeed must be disregarded to keep the narrative in focus."[95] Readers, therefore, must distinguish between intentional and unintentional gaps.

Scripture has many informational blanks. For instance, narrators do not see the need to tell how tall Adam and Eve were, how big the Garden of Eden was, or how many animals came into Noah's ark. Such information is simply irrelevant to the story. There are, however, relevant informational gaps that the readers must fill in as part of the reading process. Sternberg noted the importance of such gap fillings: "This gap-filling ranges from simple linkages of elements, which the reader performs automatically, to intricate networks that are figured out consciously, laboriously, hesitantly, and with constant modifications in the light of additional information disclosed in later stages of the reading."[96] The meaning of Abraham's silence in obeying God's command to sacrifice his son would be an example of a gap, and the writer is expecting the readers to make sense of it (Gen 22:1–2).

However, there should be cautions in bringing closures on the gaps, as it is not always easy to distinguish between these two types of informational absence. It is possible that they could "over-read" irrelevant blanks as gaps with subjective readings.[97] The rabbinical assertion that Uriah divorced Bathsheba prior to going to war[98] obviously is a contradiction to what Nathan says in 2 Samuel 12:1–9. Any gap-fillings must be cautious and the text should guide the practice.

There should be a proper view of the gap-filling also. Walsh contended that with the gap-filling, the reader is involved with the text in "creation of the story." He said that gap-filling "permit[s] different readers to realize a story in different ways. In other words, the narrator supplies the reader with the *potential* for many variant stories; it is ultimately the

---

95. Sternberg, *Poetics*, 236.

96. Sternberg, *Poetics*, 186.

97. Its opposite case of reading too little of the meaningful "gaps" is less dangerous, because more explicit and less ambiguous statements can compensate such "under-readings." For the discussion of "over-reading" and "under-reading," see Sternberg, *Poetics*, 50.

98. Neusner, *Tractate Shabbat*, 239. Sternberg made this reference in Sternberg, *Poetics*, 188.

reader who determines which of those variants to actualize."⁹⁹ However, one must be cautious, for this view of gap-filling has the potential of misleading the readers to shape the story in a way that the writer did not intend. As Sonek has noted, readers are not "totally free to create out of gaps everything they can possibly imagine . . . It is very often the case that the text imposes very strict limitations upon the reader."¹⁰⁰ That is why Sternberg called Bible as foolproof when he said, "By foolproof composition I mean that the Bible is difficult to read, easy to underread and overread and even misread, but virtually impossible to, so to speak, counterread."¹⁰¹ For this reason, the question of whether Uriah had the knowledge of David's deed, or whether David had the knowledge of Uriah's knowledge, remains in the unknowable domain. The text does not guide the readers in closing this gap.¹⁰²

Iser's contention that gaps are more important than what the writer explicitly states is another example where one can take gaps and ambiguities to the extreme. He stated his view this way:

> What is missing from the apparently trivial scenes, the gaps arising out of the dialogue—this is what stimulates the reader into filling the blanks with projections. He is drawn into the events and made to supply what is meant from what is not said. What *is* said only appears to take on significance as a reference to what is not said; it is the implications and not the statements that give shape and weight to the meaning.¹⁰³

According to Iser, what the writer says is only secondary to, and acquires meaning from, what he does not say. This position is clearly a radical view of communication.

Gaps and the resulting ambiguities can happen in various places. Sternberg said that a "gap is a lack of information about the world—an event, motive, causal link, character trait, plot structure, law of probability—contrived by a temporal displacement."¹⁰⁴ Walsh said that gaps

---

99. Walsh, *Old Testament Narrative*, 65–66.

100. Sonek, *Truth, Beauty, and Goodness*, 222.

101. Sternberg, *Poetics*, 50.

102. Sternberg's extensive discussion on this point assumes that the reader must make sense of this gap.

103. Iser, *Act of Reading*, 168.

104. Sternberg, *Poetics*, 235.

happen in regard to fact, motivation, and continuity.[105] The narrator may withhold factual data (such as in Nathan's reference to David's oath-making for Solomon's installation as the next king in 1 Kings 1:13). The narrator may hide the motivation of characters from the readers (such as when Bathsheba asked Solomon to give Abishag to Adonijah in First Kings 2:13–18). The narrator may leave out details concerning a logical connection between passages. First Kings 10:1–13 tells the story of how the Queen of Sheba came to Solomon, observed all his riches and wisdom, and gave gifts to him (vv. 1–10). In verse 13, Solomon gives gifts to Sheba in return. However, in between these exchanges, there is a story of Hiram bringing precious things to Solomon (vv. 11–12), and the narrator does not specify the relationship between these two story lines.[106]

In the analysis of Ehud's story (Judg 3:12–30), Amit observed the presence of gaps in the transitions of the scenes. She observed that there is no information between the scenes of preparing the dagger and presenting the tribute, and that the writer does not show how Ehud came into the palace. In the tribute and the killing scenes there is nothing to show how Ehud managed to get into the cool upper chamber, and between the killing and escape, the narrator does not tell how Ehud locked the door, and how he had enough time to rally the army and attack the Moabites before they came to them.[107] In regard to these informational gaps, she said:

> When we examine these transitions we find that there are many gaps in the story, particularly in the passage from unit to unit. This gives the reader a feeling of being dropped from one unit into the heart of another, having skipped over the intervening stages. A series of such cumulative drops creates a significant effect—it suggests that someone has taken care of the intervening stages, put the events in motion, and orchestrated their timing. In this way, the many-gapped scene structure of this story underlines the central role the author has assigned to God: God creates the circumstances, and God makes the tactics succeed.[108]

In other words, biblical writers show in these informational gaps how the sovereign God intervenes in the course of history.

105. These biblical examples are from Walsh, *Old Testament Narrative*, 66.

106. This paratactic arrangement of stories is what readers encounter frequently in the Fourth Gospel.

107. Amit, *Reading Biblical Narrative*, 61.

108. Amit, *Reading Biblical Narrative*, 61.

There are numerous gaps in the Gospel of John.[109] The author's paratactic storytelling style leaves the reader to struggle with the relationships of statements and episodes. As an example, John does not justify his abrupt mention of John the Baptist in the Prologue, nor the presence of the second conclusion of the Gospel in chapter 21.

Nicodemus' coming to Jesus by night opens a gap for the reader. He came to Jesus and admitted that they acknowledged him as a teacher from God; but as to his real intention, the writer does not relate. Readers can only guess his true motivation from his words. Unlike the story of the Samaritan Woman, the narrator does not communicate to the readers how the encounter resolved at the end of the discourse. The story rather ends with a long discourse of Jesus.[110] In this way, the narrator leaves the conclusion of the story, of how Nicodemus responded to Jesus on that night, ambiguous.

The healed man's action of reporting back to the Jewish authority that the healer was Jesus (chap. 5) remains as a gap to the reader. Why did he report back to the authority concerning Jesus? Did he have a negative attitude toward Jesus, or was his action simply naïve? What kind of response did he have toward Jesus? The writer does not choose to answer these important questions which could have relieved the tension. Why does John leave the man's response shrouded in mystery, while he communicates the responses of other characters in different occasions? One should note here that the author strategically placed the ambiguous response of the healed man between the positive initial responses of early witnesses and the hostile responses that follow afterward. A comparison of this story with the story of the blind man in chapter 9 shows that the ambiguity is intentional. In this way, the healed man in chapter 5 serves as a transition between the two types of responses to Jesus.

In light of the Old Testament precedent, these gaps enable complex characterization of important characters in John. The paratactic relationship of the light and the witness in the Prologue may subtly point to the light and sun relationship in Genesis 1. Just as the creation of the sun in the fourth day serves the purpose of embodying and bearing testimony to the light which God created on the first day, John's role was to give

---

109. Robert Fowlers observed the function of gaps in the Gospel of Mark and said that the "paratactic-episodic" narrative style is "full of gaps and places of indeterminacy," and this invites the readers to make sense of the text actively through "prospection and retrospection." Fowler, *Let the Reader Understand*, 134.

110. John 3:16–21 could be a narrative comment of the writer.

testimony to the true light who is Jesus. The Prologue's strong allusion to the creation account in Genesis makes such connection possible, but John left the association to the readers for them to discover. In the closing of the Gospel, John is intentionally bringing a double closure, doubly visiting the closing themes, one in terms of the story of the Gospel and another in terms of the important disciple of the Gospel, Simon Peter. John, however, leaves the rationale and the relationship open for the readers' meditation, perhaps because one cannot easily grasp or hastily arrive at a proper conclusion of the Gospel.

Nicodemus is one of the principal characters in the Gospel. His identity as a Pharisee and a ruler of the Jews and his undisclosed progress toward Jesus present an important message that John desired to communicate to the readers. Nicodemus is full of obscurity, because John purposefully veils from the readers all his inner struggles and reasoning. There is a silence concerning Nicodemus's initial response and his motives for the subsequent actions (7:50; 19:39). Only through his actions, the readers must fathom his internal thoughts. Perhaps in this intentional vagueness, John is powerful persuading Jews who are inwardly struggling to identify themselves boldly with the actions of Nicodemus. In this way, the gaps are not simply indeterminacies, but an effective way of deepening readers' response and inviting them to have faith in the Lord Jesus.[111]

Narrative Time

In addition to point of view, characters and characterization, plot, and gaps and ambiguities, biblical narrators effectively use time in telling stories. Narrative time is an important element in story-telling.[112] In real life,

---

111. Insights from discourse analysis also render interesting light on how plots develop, especially through observations in the verbal aspects. Discourse analysis recognizes that the story is told through the mainline and offline strands. Aorist indicative normally carries the mainline story in skeletal structure. Imperfect and pluperfect indicatives usually indicate offline materials which provide the supplemental information that describes or fills out the mainline action. Direct or indirect discourse relates speeches as they happen or as a report, and they are indicated by present and perfect indicatives. Historical present also carries the mainline story and is a prominence marker. As readers are informed by the Old Testament's plot development techniques, they should also pay close attention on the verbal aspects. Cf. Campbell, *Verbal Aspect*, 239–41.

112. Ricoeur, *Time and Narrative*, 52–90; Genette, *Narrative Discourse*, 33–85; Chatman, *Story and Discourse*, 62–84; Rimmon-Kenan, *Narrative Fiction*, 43–58;

time flows in a linear fashion, and one event leads to the next in an uninterrupted and consequential way. In narratives, however, the narrator has the flexibility to modify and modulate the usual flow of time of the narrative world in order to tell the story. He has the freedom to choose what he will represent in which order he chooses.

The first way that the narrator uses time is the modulation of the speed of the narration in relation to the narrated story time. Narration time is the time it takes for the narrator to tell the story in words, sentences, or paragraphs, and the narrated time is the time of the world of the narrative. How the narrator relates these two time aspects in the narrative determines the speed of the narration and reveals the purpose of the narrator. Bar-Efrat observed that: "Since the decision as to what to include and what to omit, what to convey rapidly and on what to dwell at length, is closely bound up with the importance of the various subjects, the character of time as it is shaped within the narrative will be of great value in any attempt to analyze and interpret the narrative."[113]

Summaries represent a rapid method of storytelling, where the narrator only highlights important points and gives a sweeping overview of the event. On the other hand, reports of dialogues and lengthy monologues show the story almost in real time. The effect is that the readers experience the events almost contemporaneously with the characters. A narrator may stop the narrated time all together and describe a scene carefully or explain situations and terms, or he may jump through a large span of time in few words. Bar-Efrat said, "Time stops in two situations: a. when interpretations, explanations, conclusions or evaluations are given by the narrator; b. when depictions are given within the narrative."[114] The writer may represent the narrated time anywhere in the continuum.

The Old Testament writer manages narrative time in various ways. He may indicate a large span of time by narrative comments, such as in this case: "Now the time that the sons of Israel lived in Egypt was four hundred and thirty years" (Exod 12:40). The narrator may give summary accounts of a period as in this case: "Leah conceived and bore a son and named him Reuben" (Gen 29:32). The writer may report conversations and synchronize the narrative pace to real time (cf. Gen 3; 1 Sam 9:1—10:16; 2 Sam 14:4–20). Narrative time may become much slower

---

Culpepper, *Anatomy*, 63–70; Reinhartz, "Jesus as Prophet," 3–16.

113. Bar-Efrat, *Narrative Art*, 142–43.

114. Bar-Efrat, *Narrative Art*, 146.

than real time or even halt in physical descriptions or in narrative interpretations. The narrator almost stops the narrated time in his physical description of Absalom:

> Now in all Israel was no one as handsome as Absalom, so highly praised, from the sole of his foot to the crown of his head there was no defect in him. When he cut the hair of his head (and it was at the end of every year that he cut it, for it was heavy on him so he cut it), he weighted the hair of his head at 200 shekels by the king's weight. (2 Sam 14:25–26)[115]

Another way the narrator modifies time in biblical narratives is through the order of events. Usually, a biblical writer tells stories in chronological fashion, but he may disrupt the order to emphasize points, interpret incidents, or correlate thematic events. He may narrate past events in the present as a way of flashback, or insert a future incident as a way of foreshadowing. The narrator may also break the flow of time of an event and resume later, arrange the story atemporally, make use of overlap, interweave two developments together, or may even show no signs of relation through simple paratactic placements.[116]

There are many flashbacks in the Old Testament, such as in Genesis 20:18: "For the LORD had closed fast all the wombs of the household of Abimelech because of Sarah, Abraham's wife." There are also foreshadows, as in 2 Samuel 17:14: "Then Absalom and all the men of Israel said, 'The counsel of Hushai the Archite is better than the counsel of Ahithophel.' For the LORD had ordained to thwart the good counsel of Ahithophel, so that the LORD might bring calamity on Absalom."

The writer may interrupt the time sequence and then resume after reports of some other event, as in this example of Second Samuel 17:24–28:

> *Then David came to Mahanaim.* And Absalom crossed the Jordan, he and all the men of Israel with him. Absalom set Amasa over the army in place of Joab. Now Amasa was the son of a man whose name was Ithra the Israelite, who went in to Abigail the daughter of Nahash, sister of Zeruiah, Joab's mother. And Israel and Absalom camped in the land of Gilead. *Now when David*

---

115. These biblical examples are in Bar-Efrat, *Narrative Art*, 51, 141–65.
116. Ska, *"Our Fathers Have Told Us,"* 8.

> had come to Mahanaim, Shobi . . . Machir . . . and Barzillai . . . brought beds . . . wheat . . . and cheese from the herd.[117]

In this example, the story of Absalom and his company interrupts the story of David's arrival at Mahanaim. In this layout of the events, the narrator juxtaposed two parties at the same time in order to convey the tension. Second Samuel 14:24–28 shows another such example:

> However the king said, "Let him turn to his own house, and let him not see my face." So Absalom turned to his own house and did not see the king's face. Now in all Israel was no one as handsome as Absalom, so highly praised; from the sole of his foot to the crown of his head there was no defect in him. When he cut the hair of his head (and it was at the end of every year that he cut it, for it was heavy on him so he cut it), he weighed the hair of his head at 200 shekels by the king's weight. To Absalom there were born three sons, and one daughter whose name was Tamar; she was a woman of beautiful appearance. *Now Absalom lived two full years in Jerusalem, and did not see the king's face.*[118]

It is customary for biblical narrators to interrupt the flow of time, digress into related matters, and resume the original topic.

Time does not necessarily flow in a linear fashion in biblical narratives. First Kings 1:5–7 illustrates this point:

> Now Adonijah the son of Haggith exalted himself, saying, "I will be king." So he prepared for himself chariots and horsemen with fifty men to run before him. His father had never crossed him at any time by asking, "Why have you done so?" And he was also a very handsome man, and he was born after Absalom. He had conferred with Joab the son of Zeruiah and with Abiathar the priest; and following Adonijah they helped him.

In this example, readers observe that the narrated events are "dischronologized"—a proper chronological order would be of his birth, his father's way of upbringing him, his ambition to be the king, his aids,

---

117. Italics are added for emphasis.

118. For these two examples, see Conroy, *Absalom Absalom!*, 54, 110n57. Cf. Ska, "Our Fathers Have Told Us," 9. In the case of the second example, Conroy said that "the presence of the non-temporal material of vv. 25–27 between v. 24 and v. 28 serves to fill out this interval of time, to suggest its length, and so to make Absalom's subsequent actions (vv. 28–32) more understandable" (Conroy, *Absalom*, 110). Italics are added for emphasis.

and his preparation.[119] Organizing the material in this way enables the narrator to emphasize Adonijah's ambition and his subsequent actions.

In the Gospel of John, the narrator modulated the narrative speed. The writer begins with a reference to an unknown span of time in eternity past (1:1–2), moves quickly to the creation (v. 3), to the time of John the Baptist (vv. 6–8), and to the time of Jesus' incarnation (vv. 9–14). There are numerous dialogues and monologues that synchronize the narration time with the narrated time (i.e., 1:19–51; 3:1–21), but there are summary statements that cover longer periods of time (i.e., 2:23–25; 4:40, 45; 12:37–43; 21:25).[120]

There are also numerous intentional anachronisms that point to a time outside of human history, to the historical time outside the narrative, and to the time within the narrative.[121] Most notable are the proleptic references of Jesus' hour (i.e., 2:4; 4:21, 23; 5:25, 28; 7:30; 8:20; 12:23, 27; 13:1), of his death and resurrection (2:22; 7:39; 12:16), and of Judas's betrayal (6:71; 12:4). Douglas Estes correctly recognized that alleged flaws of "the 'transitions,' 'sequences,' and 'movements,' are strongly *temporal* in nature."[122] In other words, theories of displacement which flourished in the past are proposed solutions to the peculiar temporal aspects of the Gospel.[123]

John's use of the historical present in the Fourth Gospel shows his artful way of engaging the readers. Just as Hebrew verb tenses have a foregrounding and backgrounding function in the Old Testament narratives,[124] the historical present tense has a significant place in John's narrative poetics.[125] The usual mode of narration is the past tense, but when the

---

119. Martin, "'Dischronologized' Narrative," 184.

120. For a fuller discussion on the narrative tempo of the Gospel, see Estes, *Temporal Mechanics of the Fourth Gospel*, 192–99.

121. For an extensive list of different types of anachronisms in the Gospel of John, see Estes, *Temporal Mechanics*, 182. Cf. Culpepper, *Anatomy*, 51–76.

122. Estes, *Temporal Mechanics*, 132.

123. Cf. Hoare, *Original Order and Chapters*; and Bernard, *Critical and Exegetical Commentary*, 1:xvi–xxvi.

124. Alviero Niccacci said that verb tenses have different functions in narratives and discourses. He said that *wayyiqtol* form continue the main story line in the narrative while *weqatal* form presents the background materials. Niccacci, *Syntax of the Verb*, 20; cf. Niccacci, "Analysis of Biblical Narrative," 176–77.

125. Matthew has 39 historical presents, Mark has 151, Luke has 12, and John has 167. There are clusters of historical presents in John especially in chapters 1, 4, 13, 20, 21—all of which are significant places. Campbell, *Advances*, 138–39. See Hawkins, *Horae Synopticae*, 143–49; O'Rourke, "Historic Present in the Gospel of John," 585–90;

writer tells the story in the present tense, this choice has the function of arresting the reader's attention. This technique has the power to bring the readers into the middle of the story, letting them experience the story as if it were happening in the present time. Stanley E. Porter observed that the shifting of verbal tenses has the effect of marking boundaries in a discourse.[126] Stephen H. Levinsohn argued that historical present is a prominence marker. He said:

> The primary motivation for using the historical present . . . is to *highlight* and that, particularly in Mark and John, what is highlighted by the HP [Historical Present] is not so much the speech or act to which it refers but the event(s) that follow. In other words, like other devices employed for highlighting, the HP usually occurs *prior* to the event or group of events that are of particular significance.[127]

According to these observations of Porter and Levinsohn, one sees that the historical presents in the non-speech materials in the Gospel of John have the function of indicating prominence of the following materials.

The historical present introduces significant persons into an existing scene in the following examples:

"Then, when they had rowed about three or four miles, they *see* (*theōrousin*) Jesus walking on the sea and drawing near to the boat." (John 6:19)

"There *comes* (*erchetai*) a woman of Samaria to draw water." (4:7)

"The scribes and the Pharisees *bring* (*agousin*) a woman caught in adultery." (8:3)[128]

The historical present also has the function of bringing a character into a significant location.

Campbell, *Verbal Aspect*, 66–68; Fanning, *Verbal Aspect in the Greek New Testament*, 231–34; Buth, "Mark's Use of the Historical Present," 7–13; Boos, "Historical Present in John's Gospel," 17–24.

126. Porter, *Idioms of Greek New Testament*, 301.

127. Levinsohn, *Discourse Features*, 200.

128. Levinsohn, *Discourse Features*, 209. Other examples Levinsohn gave are: 1:15, 29, 41, 43, 45; 2:9; 5:14; 9:13; 12:22; 13:6; 13:26; 18:3; 20:1, 2, 6, 12, 14, 18, 26; 21:20. In these and following examples, NASB substituted historical presents with past tenses.

"So He *comes* (*erchetai*) to a city of Samaria called Sychar." (4:5)

"So Jesus, again begin deeply moved . . . *comes* (*erchetai*) to the tomb." (11:38)

"Then they *lead* (*agousin*) Jesus from Caiaphas into the Praetorium." (18:28)[129]

The writer uses historical presents also to introduce speech materials, and they function to highlight the speeches.

"He *says* (*legei*) to them, 'Come, and you will see.'" (1:39)

"Jesus *says* (*legei*) to her, "Give Me a drink." (4:7)

"So Jesus *says* (*legei*) to them, "My time is not yet here." (7:6)

In this sense, the highlighted speeches come to the foreground while other materials function as the background.

Concerning the use of imperfect, aorist, and present tense in the narrative, Yamasaki made an observation that there is a "degree of immediacy" in Greek tenses:

> At the bottom, producing the least degree of immediacy, is the imperfect tense, with a move to the aorist tense marking an increase in immediacy, but a move to the present tense signaling an even more acute sense of immediacy. This hierarchy can be used to monitor how the narrator is drawing the audience in or pushing the audience back while proceeding through the narration of an event.[130]

In other words, in the narrative voice of the writer, imperfect tenses indicate background materials, aorist tenses carry the story, and the historical presents highlight significance.

In John chapter 1, Yamasaki observed that the present tense verb *legei* introduces the statement "Behold the Lamb of God" (v. 36), but the subsequent actions of John's disciples are in aorist tenses, *ēkousan* and *ēkolouthēsan* (v. 37). When Jesus sees these disciples, He *says* (*legei*) to them, "What do you seek?" but the disciples *said* (*eipan*) to Him, "Rabbi, where are you staying?" (v. 38). Jesus *says* (*legei*) to them "Come and see,"

---

129. Levinsohn, *Discourse Features*, 210.
130. Yamasaki, *Watching a Biblical Narrative*, 167.

but the disciples' subsequent actions of going (*ēlthan*), seeing (*eidan*), and staying (*emeinan*) are in aorist tenses (v. 39). When the story, however, provides background information ("it was about the tenth hour" [v. 39], and "one of the two . . . was Andrew" [v. 40]), imperfect *ēn* indicates the information.[131] However, present tense verbs *heuriskei* and *legei* report Andrew's finding of Peter and speaking to him (v. 41).[132]

The trial scene of Jesus before Pilate (18:28—19:16) also demonstrates the effectiveness of the historical presents in engaging the readers into the story. The scene opens with historical presents: the Jews leading (*agousin*) Jesus into the Praetorium (v. 28) and with Pilate speaking (*phēsin*) to the Jews concerning Jesus (v. 29). At once, John draws the readers into the present time of the story. To be more precise, the writer is indicating with the historical presents how Jesus enters a new significant location, and how another important character comes into the scene.

After this introduction of the scene, aorist verbs introduce the subsequent dialogues between Pilate and the Jews: "*apekrithēsan . . . eipan . . . eipan . . . eipon*" (vv. 30–32). When Pilate begins the interrogation of Jesus, aorist verbs introduce his actions and the verbal exchanges with Jesus: "*eisēlthen . . . ho Pilatos kai ephōnēsen . . . kai eipen . . . apekrithē Iēsous . . . apekrithē ho Pilatos . . . apekrithē Iēsous . . . eipen oun autō ho Pilatos*" (vv. 33–37). However, when he asks the question "What is truth?" the historical present marks his speech: "*legi autō ho Pilatos ti estin alētheia;*" (vv. 38). From this point, present tense verbs mark his subsequent speeches (19:4, 5, 6, 9, 10, 14, 15), while the outcries of the Jews against him are in aorist verbs (v.6, 7, 12).

In the trial scene, Pilate is the only person that the historical presents mark the speeches. John indicates other speeches, even those of Jesus, with aorist tense verbs, and clearly shows his intention that all eyes should be on what Pilate does and says. On the other hand, imperfect verbs introduce the background information in the trial scene: when they led Jesus to Praetorium, "it was (*ēn*) early" (18:28); the soldiers "were (*ērchonto*) coming up to him and were saying (*elegon*), Hail King of the Jews" (19:3); "it was (*ēn*) about the sixth hour" (19:14).

The heavy use of historical presents signifies that the described event is climatic in importance. In speaking of the chain of historical

---

131. Levinsohn said that in narrative, "the imperfect tends to correlate with background information and the aorist with foreground events, because of their inherent nature." Levinsohn, *Discourse Features*, 174.

132. Yamasaki, *Watching a Biblical Narrative*, 167–68.

presents in the unveiling of the identity of the betrayer (13:24–27), Mavis M. Leung noted that "This cluster of historical presents brings the entire event to the foreground so that the reader is alerted to what is most important in the storyline."[133]

Summary

This chapter demonstrated that readers can compare the Fourth Gospel with the Old Testament narratives with fruitful results. This comparison is possible because the Old Testament enlightens the New Testament not only in the contents, but also in terms of the form. Old Testament narratives are a rich depository of literary poetics and rhetoric, and the exploration in the point of view, character and characterization, plot, gaps and ambiguities, and narrative time amply demonstrated the point. apostle John, along with other New Testament writers, was a beneficiary of this great treasury. John intentionally crafted the narrative in the point of view of Jesus and endowed him with many names. The characters in John represent the grand story of God's love, human depravity, and saving faith in Jesus. John's three-and-four and six-and-seven patterns carry the plot in what appears to be a passionate plea for the truth of Christ, and many intentional gaps create bewildering ambiguities that unsettle readers but they are once again recognized as transformational agencies. Finally, John's skillful use of time draws the reader into the story at the critical points of Jesus' story. Now, the discussion will turn to the third type of literature of the Old Testament that is also characteristic of John, the prophets, for John is indeed a prophetic gospel in addition to being poetic and narrative gospel.

---

133. Leung, "Narrative Function and Verbal Aspect," 716.

5

The Gospel of John in Light of the Poetics of Old Testament Prophets

THE THIRD SET OF lens that brings the Gospel into its proper view is the poetics of Old Testament prophetic writings. Hanson's observation that John is a "prophetic Gospel" needs an exploration here.[1] The prophetic corpus comprises a major part of the Hebrew Scripture. The Jewish designation of Former Prophets (Joshua, Judges, Samuels, and Kings) and Latter Prophets (Isaiah, Jeremiah, Ezekiel, and the Twelve Minor Prophets) bears witness to the importance of prophets and their activities in the Old Testament time. Prophets and their writings exercised a profound impact upon the Fourth Gospel. Scholars have variously recognized the influences of Isaiah, Ezekiel, Jeremiah, and the Minor Prophets in the Gospel of John.[2] Moses is an important character in John,[3] and John presents Jesus as "the Prophet" in a stronger way than any of the other Gospels.[4]

---

1. Hanson, *Prophetic Gospel*, 342.

2. Cf. Griffiths, "Deutero-Isaiah and the Fourth Gospel," 355–60; Hamilton, "Influence of Isaiah on the Gospel of John," 139–62; Manning, *Echoes of a Prophet*, 100–197; McWhirter, *Bridegroom Messiah*, 46–78; Menken, "Allusions to the Minor Prophets in the Fourth Gospel," 67–84; Young, "Study of the Relation of Isaiah," 215–33.

3. Glasson, *Moses in the Fourth Gospel*; Harstine, *Moses as a Character*; Meeks, *Prophet-King*.

4. Aune, *Prophecy in Early Christianity*, 155.

Prophets played important roles in the New Testament also. Christian prophets had active presence in the life of the early churches. Agabus, by the Spirit of God, predicted that a famine was coming (Acts 11:28), and the disciples in Ephesus began to prophesy when Paul laid his hands on them (Acts 19:6). Through the Spirit, Agabus and unnamed believers warned Paul of what was awaiting him in Jerusalem (Acts 21:4, 10–11), and Philip's four daughters were prophetesses (Acts 21:9). Prophesying is a gift of the Holy Spirit (1 Cor 12:10), and Paul deals extensively with how Christians should use and think of prophesies within the church (1 Cor 14). "Prophet" is a church office, "God has appointed in the church, first apostles, second prophets, third teachers" (1 Cor 12:29; cf. Eph 2:20; 3:5), and Paul exhorts believers not to despise prophecies (1 Thess 5:19).[5]

Some scholars saw the influence of Christian prophets in the production of the Gospels. This view finds the support in the facts that prophets were active in the New Testament churches to bring "edification, exhortation, and consolation" (1 Cor 14:3), and that the Holy Spirit was a *paraklētos* who would guide believers into all truth (John 14:26; 15:26). In his *The Four Gospels*, therefore, B. H. Streeter said that John was like the Old Testament prophets: "The author of the Gospel claims that his interpretation of the Person and Work of Christ is a revelation of the Spirit. That claim must be set side by side with that of the Old Testament prophets that their message was in the same way derived direct from God."[6] Ernst Käsemann said that the Gospel's "actualization of the Christian proclamation" is the characteristic of Christian prophecy: "Just as this prophecy is determined by the particular situation as it teaches, admonishes, rebukes, comforts and interprets anew the tradition to its own time, so likewise John carried the Gospel with prophetic ruthlessness and one-sidedness into his present situation, using as much or as little of the tradition as suited his purpose."[7] According to these views, through the ministry of the Holy Spirit, John was able to take the traditions of Jesus and use them prophetically to shape his proclamation for the situation of his audience.

Deeply engrained in these positions, however, is the problematic notion that the discourses of Jesus merely contain the words of Jesus, and

---

5. Cf. Grudem, *Gift of Prophecy in 1 Corinthians*, 74–110.
6. Streeter, *Four Gospels*, 373.
7. Käsemann, *Testament of Jesus*, 38.

that they are only "organically" related to what Jesus said.[8] Bultmann in his seminal work, *The History of the Synoptic Tradition*, contended that Christian prophets were responsible for taking the sayings of Jesus and producing the Synoptic tradition. This was possible, he argued, because: "The Church drew no distinction between such utterances by Christian prophets and the sayings of Jesus in the tradition" because Jesus was "always a contemporary for the Church."[9] In this view, Christian prophets heavily redacted the "tradition" of Jesus to fit their contemporary situations. However, such stance does not harmonize with scriptural testimonies, because what set true prophets apart from false prophets was that they "did not speak his own words or 'words of his own heart,' but words which God had sent him to deliver."[10] M. Dibelius argued that Paul was careful to point out the difference between the Lord's words and his words (1 Cor 7:10, 12, 25),[11] and David Hill contended that the early church made a distinction between the words spoken through the Spirit and the words of the historical Jesus.[12] Aune agreed: "In spite of the theological attractiveness of the theory, however, the historical evidence in support of the theory lies largely in the creative imagination of scholars."[13]

In what sense, then, is John prophetic in character? It is possible to compare him with other New Testament prophets according to the way Hill defined New Testament prophets: "A Christian prophet is a Christian who functions within the church, occasionally or regularly, as a divinely called and divinely inspired speaker who receives intelligible and authoritative revelations or messages which he is impelled to deliver publicly, in oral or written form, to Christian individuals and/or the Christian community."[14]

---

8. Streeter, *Four Gospels*, 371. Scholars have argued for *ipsissima vox* (the very voice) of Jesus and not *ipsissima verba* (the exact word) of Jesus in the Gospels. See, Conzelmann, *Outline of the Theology*, 97–99; Jeremias, *New Testament Theology*, 1–3.

9. Bultmann, *History of the Synoptic Tradition*, 127–28. For a reiteration of this view, see von Wahlde, "Role of the Prophetic Spirit in John," 211–42.

10. Grudem, *Gift of Prophecy*, 15. See Deut 18:18–20; Jer 14:14; 23:16; 29:31–32; Ezek 13:1–3.

11. Dibelius, *Tradition to Gospel*, 241.

12. Hill, "Evidence for the Creative Role," 267; cf. Hill, "Prophecy and Prophets," 401–18.

13. Aune, *Prophecy in Early Christianity*, 245.

14. Hill, *New Testament Prophecy*, 8–9.

However, it is on a different ground that this chapter argues that John is prophetic in nature. The ability to associate apostle John with Old Testament prophets comes from the fact that they were authoritative spokesmen for God. Wayne A. Grudem made a keen observation that "in the NT the apostles are several times connected with the divinely authoritative OT prophets, but NT prophets, by contrast, are never connected with OT prophets in the same way."[15] In other words, the New Testament does not portray Christian prophets as authoritative in the same manner as the Old Testament prophets. Grudem pointed out again that the prophets in the Corinthian church were subject to Paul's apostolic authority (1 Cor 14:37), and that their words were subject to testing and censorship (1 Cor 14:29–32).[16]

In contrast to New Testament prophets, New Testament apostles were eyewitnesses of Christ's person and work, and they were his authoritative ambassadors like no other. Just as Moses was the minister of the old covenant, the apostle Paul was the minister of the new covenant (2 Cor 3:1–18). For this reason, Paul says, "For we are not like many, peddling the word of God, but as from sincerity, but as from God, we speak in Christ in the sight of God" (2 Cor 2:17). Peter equated the authority of the apostles' words with the words of Old Testament prophets and said, "You should remember the words spoken beforehand by the holy prophets and the commandment of the Lord and Savior *spoken* by your apostles" (2 Pet 3:2).[17] Regarding the apostle Paul, Christopher Rowland made the observation that "his sense of himself as an agent of God" and "to be a prophetic emissary is key to Paul's self-understanding."[18] As an apostle, John was an authoritative spokesman for Christ, and in this way, his Gospel is analogous to the writings of Old Testament prophets. There are certainly many areas of difference,[19] but the following discussions reveal that John and the Gospel he wrote are prophetic at heart.

15. Grudem, *Gift of Prophecy*, 45; cf. Myers and Freed, "Is Paul Also Among the Prophets?," 40–53; Best, "Prophets and Preachers," 129–50.

16. Grudem, *Gift of Prophecy*, 54–74.

17. Grudem, *Gift of Prophecy*, 45.

18. Rowland, "Prophecy and the New Testament," 420.

19. Old Testament prophets differed widely. Willen A. Vangemeren argued that prophetism was diverse in the history of Israel and said, "Oversimplification has often led to a disregard of the distinctive features of the prophet as a human being in a historical context and as God's messenger sent to meet the particular needs of God's people in that context. In reality, the prophetic phenomenon was diverse as to *place* (Israel or Judah), *time* (preexilic, exilic, postexilic), *message*, and *language*."

The Word of the LORD

One reason that this chapter argues that John's Gospel is a prophetic gospel is that it presents Jesus as the word (*logos*) of God and this echoes in many ways the prophetic proclamation of the word of God in the Old Testament. Prophets in the Old Testament were people who were "called out" by God to proclaim the word of the LORD, and this is what John set out to do in the beginning of his Gospel. Although the exact meaning of the Hebrew word *nabi'* is contestable, generally it means "called out one" in a passive sense.[20] The phrase *debar-yhwh* ("the word of the LORD") in the Old Testament almost synonymously denotes prophetic proclamation: out of its 241 occurrences, 221 of them are related to the prophetic word of God.[21] The most important trait of prophetic literature is that it is the *word* of the LORD. J. Lindblom noted, "The chief mission of the prophets was to carry Yahweh's words to their people. Yahweh had charged them with his words."[22]

The word of God has a special place in the prophets of the Old Testament. The first notable aspect of the word of God is that it *came* to the prophets. God's word is said to have come to various prophets. The word came to Moses (Exod 3:15; 4:22; 8:1; 20:22; Num 9:1), to Joshua (7:13), to unnamed prophets (Judg 6:8; 1 Sam 2:27; 1 Kgs 13:1–2), to Samuel (1 Sam 10:17–18), to Nathan (2 Sam 7:4), to Shemaiah the man of God (1 Kgs 12:22–24), and to Elijah (1 Kgs 18:1, 21:17, 28). The writing prophets regarded the coming of the word of the LORD with a great significance, because it was what inaugurated and substantiated their prophetic ministry.[23] At the beginning of prophetic books, the prophets indicate how the word of the LORD came (*hayah*) to them: it came to Jeremiah (1:2), Hosea (1:1), Joel (1:1), Amos (1:1), Jonah (1:1), Micah (1:1), Zephaniah (1:1), Haggai (1:1), Zechariah (1:1), and Malachi (1:1).[24] Instead of speaking of the coming of the word of the LORD, some prophets relate the visionary

---

Vangemeren, *Interpreting the Prophetic Word*, 42. Italics are original.

20. Peisker and Brown, "Prophet," 3:77.
21. Klappert, "Word," 3:1087.
22. Lindblom, *Prophecy in Ancient Israel*, 109.
23. von Rad, *Theology of Israel's Prophetic Traditions*, 80.
24. Amos says it is the "words of Amos" in the beginning, but later confirms that it is the word of the LORD (i.e., 1:3, 6, 9, 11, 13; 2:1). In Haggai's case, the wording is slightly different. The word of the LORD came "by the prophet" to Zerubbabel and to Joshua. In Malachi, it is the "oracle" of the word of the LORD that came to Israel through Malachi.

experiences which they saw. Isaiah relates the vision he saw (1:1), Ezekiel saw the visions of God (1:1), the message of Obadiah is a vision (1:1), Nahum is the book of vision (1:1), and Habakkuk is an oracle for what he saw (1:1). In these visionary experiences, what they saw was not visual image but a word from God, because God spoke in the visions.[25] Vision is "a word of revelation,"[26] or "a divine communication;"[27] so Lindblom remarked, "In the prophetic literature no definitive dividing-line is drawn between visions, auditions, and inspired ideas in general. Everything which came to a prophet in the inspired state may be called 'vision.'"[28] Whether the message came in an audible voice or in a visionary experience, writing prophets were careful to show in the beginning of their writings that the *word* came from the LORD. In this light, opening the Gospel with the statement of the *coming* of the Word of God (1:1–18) is the most appropriate way to establish the Gospel as a prophetic proclamation of the LORD.

The second notable aspect of the word of God in the Old Testament prophets is that they viewed the coming of the word of the LORD as a historical event. When the prophets receive the word of God, the phrase, "*wayehi dibar-yhwh ʾel*," "and the word of the LORD came to" (i.e. Jer 16:1) or "*debar-yhwh ʾasher hayah ʾel*," "the word of the LORD which came to" (i.e. Mic 1:1) repeatedly designates the occasion. The basic meaning of the verb *hyh* is "to be," "to occur," or "to become,"[29] and it carries the sense of coming into existence. When the word of God came to the prophets, it was as if the word became an existing reality, effectuating its potency in human history. Walther Zimmerli noted this special conception of the word of God in the Prophets:

> As regards the content of this formula we must see in it a derivation from a very well developed conception of the "word of Yahweh." We can, perhaps, speak of a prophetic "theology of word," which emerged in prophetic circles. Instead of a direct encounter by the personal address of God, the "word" is understood almost as an objective entity with its own power of *entry*.[30]

25. Jepsen, "חָזָה, *chāzāh*," 4:283–84.
26. Koehler et al., "חָזוֹן," 1:301–2.
27. Brown et al., "חָזוֹן," 302–3.
28. Lindblom, *Prophecy in Ancient Israel*, 108.
29. Koehler et al., "היה," 1:243–44.
30. Zimmerli, *Ezekiel 1*, 1:144. Italics are added for emphasis. Of course, this would not mean that the word had a separate power apart from the One who spoke it. It is

According to Thorlief Boman, this verb denotes active and dynamic existence which finds its ultimate reality in the *hyh* of God:

> To Jahveh is ascribed an unalterable (i.e. eternal) *hayah*, and this *hayah* is a dynamic, energetic, effective, personal being 'who carries out his will and achieves his purpose, and who thereby advances the good fortune and salvation of his people,' the obedience of the people being naturally presupposed. *The one who is*, i.e. the eternally effective Jahveh, *is the creator.*[31]

The coming of the word (or literally, "the word of the Lord was to") almost has an event-like character and the phrase may be translated as "the word of God became active reality with" or as "the word assumed effective shape in," and it stresses "the eminently historical character of the word of God in partaking of the nature of an event."[32] Horst Dietrich Preuss said that when "these prophets may have 'seen the words' of YHWH . . . this means that to them an event has become a word . . . The ancient Israelite, therefore, called both a 'word' and an 'event' a דבר (*dābār*)."[33] God is the One who *is* and effects the existence of beings.[34] The fact that the word of the LORD "came to be" to the prophets reveals the prophetic conception of the word of God. As the word befalls on the historical arena, it *becomes*—completely proceeding from and yet completely dependent in its effectiveness on the one who spoke it—and achieves the will of the LORD.[35] This is how John envisioned the coming of the Word of God. The Word *became* (*egeneto*) flesh and dwelt among "us" (John 1:14). The Word came into the world and it *became* a reality (of a man) to do the will

---

God who acts in the words which he speaks, and the words do not have independent power. In this way, God and the words he sends are intimately correlated.

31. Boman, *Hebrew Thought Compared with Greek*, 49. Cf. Boman, *Hebrew Thought*, 188–89. Italics are in the original. For a criticism of Boman's handling of the linguistics, see Barr, *Semantics of Biblical Language*, 58–72.

32. Klappert, "Word," 3:1090–91; cf. von Rad, *Old Testament Theology*, 87n15.

33. Preuss, *Old Testament Theology*, 2:74.

34. W. F. Albright argued, although not always accepted, that the tetragrammaton of the LORD's name should be taken in a causative sense. Albright, *Yahweh and the Gods of Canaan*, 168–72.

35. The concept of inherent power of the word of God is often compared to the belief in the magical power of words in the Ancient Near East. This view has been rightly challenged. Fretheim, "Word of God," 6:961–62. Frank Ritchel Ames said, "Hypostatization of the divine word is attested in ANE literature . . . but personification of Yahweh's word in [Psalms] 147:15 and elsewhere in the OT does not imply a belief in the presence of magical or dynamistic forces." Ames, "דָּבָר (dābar II)," 1:914.

of the one who sent him (i.e. 3:34; 4:34; 5:23, 24; 5:30, 36, 37, 38; 6:29). Jesus is the emissary of the Father to do his will, and John presents Jesus as the embodiment of the prophetic word of God.

The third notable aspect of the word of God in the prophets is that it possessed and effectuated the power of God that creates and destroys. Because of the omnipotence and the complete faithfulness of the one who stands behind his word, the word had great power. This fact is well attested in the Genesis's creation account (chs. 1–2) and in its recounts in Psalms (33:6, 9; 148:5). God spoke the word and all things came to be. The prophetic corpus displays the essential quality of the word of God as creative and sometimes as punitive. God infused his destructive and creative power into the words of Jeremiah and said, "Behold, I have put My words in your mouth. See, I have appointed you this day over the nations and over the kingdoms, to pluck up and to break down, to destroy and to overthrow, to build and to plant" (Jer 1:9–10). God made his word in Jeremiah's mouth a fire and the people wood (5:14), and he declared that his word is like a fire that consumes and a hammer that shatters (23:29). In the prophetic proclamations of the word of God, God decisively enacted his power. Hosea says that the LORD hews people by the word of the prophets (6:5), and when Ezekiel prophesied God's word to Pelatiah, he fell dead on the spot (11:13). The word of God was also full of creative power. At the delegated proclamation of his word, the dry bones became alive: "Again He said to me, 'Prophesy over these bones and say to them, "O dry bones, hear the word of the LORD." "Thus says the Lord GOD to these bones, 'Behold, I will cause breath to enter you that you may come to life'" (Ezek 37:4–5).[36]

Personified wisdom, Torah, and Targumic Memra form important background for the Johannine idea of *logos*, and Brown noted that the prophetic word of God is a proper context to understand the *logos* of John. Just as the word of God in the Old Testament had special roles, he said, "we see here many of the functions [of the word in the Old Testament] ascribed to the Word in the Prologue." The Word is the creator of all things (Ps 33:6; John 1:3), giver of life (Deut 32:46–47; John 1:4), light of men (Pss 119:105, 130; 19:8; John 1:4–5), and the healer (Ps 107:20; John 1:9–13).[37] The Word in the Fourth Gospel presents himself as the mighty power of God to give life (i.e. John 6:39, 40, 44, 54).

---

36. These examples are from Lindblom, *Prophecy in Ancient Israel*, 118–19. Cf. von Rad, *Old Testament Theology*, 80–87.

37. Brown, *John*, 1:521.

The fourth notable aspect of the word of God in the prophets is the notion that it comes from the LORD and effects change in the world. In Psalm 148:15–18, the psalmist speaks of the word coming from the LORD and making changes on the face of the earth: "He sends forth His command to the earth, His word runs very swiftly. He gives snow like wool, He scatters the frost like ashes. He casts forth His ice as fragments, who can stand before His cold? He sends forth His word and melts them, He causes His wind to blow and the waters to flow" (Ps 148:15–18). It is, however, in Isaiah where this idea receives its full articulation:

> For as the rain and the snow come down from heaven, and do not return there without watering the earth and making it bear and sprout, and furnishing seed to the sower and bread to the eater, so will My word be which goes forth from My mouth; it will not return to Me empty, without accomplishing what I desire, and without succeeding in the matter for which I sent it. (Isa 55:10–11)

In this passage, just as rain comes down from heaven ("*katabē . . . ek tou ouranou*," Septuagint) and brings forth fruit on the earth, the word of God "goes out" (*exelthē*) from the mouth of God and accomplishes (*suntelestē*) what he desires. The parallel construction of these two entities implies that the function of both the rain and the word of God is to give life to the world.[38] Having accomplished the purpose, then, the rain and the Word return to their place of origin.[39]

It is interesting that the ideas of coming down from heaven, finishing the work (of giving life to the world), and returning to the place of origin are central to Johannine concept of Jesus. Brown observed, "We have here the same cycle of coming down and returning that we encounter in the Prologue."[40] John V. Dahms observed that these ideas are prevalent in the rest of the Gospel, especially in John 13–17: "The influence of Is. 55:11 is to be seen particularly in the motif of coming from God and going to God, a motif which is only used concerning Christ, and which is

---

38. John Oswalt observed, "Each one achieves the purposes of blessing and the life-giving for which it was intended." Oswalt, *Book of Isaiah*, 2:446.

39. Oswalt said, "The grammar supports the idea of both the rain and the word returning to heaven after accomplishing their respective purposes." But he continued, "But the idea of return is not the important point. The point is the achieving of the purposes of God." Oswalt, *Isaiah*, 446.

40. Brown, *John*, 1:521.

especially characteristic of John 13–17."⁴¹ There are numerous references to Jesus as having come from God (*exerchomai*) and going away to the Father (13:1, 33, 36; 14:2–5, 12, 28; 16:5–10, 27–30; 17:8, 11, 13), and finishing the work (*teleioō*) that the Father has given to him (4:34; 5:36; 17:4; 19:28, 30).⁴² This was certainly an important concept of the word of God which the prophetic corpus foreshadowed and anticipated, and John is careful to show that Jesus fulfilled this purpose of the word of God. For this reason, John is truly a prophetic gospel proclaiming Jesus as the word of God in the spirit of the Prophets.

The fifth notable aspect of the word of God in the prophets is that the lives of the prophets often embodied the words they proclaimed. Ahijah's tearing of his cloak into twelve pieces symbolized tearing of the kingdom of Israel (1 Kgs 11:29–31), the false prophet Zedekiah made iron horns to speak the message of victory (1 Kgs 22:11), and Elisha used arrows to speak of Israel's military victory over Arameans (2 Kgs 13:14–19).⁴³

Such symbolic actions, however, find fuller significance in the writing prophets. The naming of Isaiah's sons as Shear-jashub, "a remnant shall return" (Isa 7:3), and Maher-shalal-has-baz, "swift is the booty, speedy is the prey" (8:3), was a way of embodying God's message for Israel. God commanded Ezekiel to proclaim his judgment over Israel through his symbolic actions (chaps 4–5; 12:3–7; 21:19–23). For the prophets, these symbolic acts were ways of visualizing the word of the LORD. Daniel I. Block observed, "Sign-acts are best interpreted as dramatic performances designed to visualize a message and in the process to enhance its persuasive force so that the observers' perceptions of a given situation might be changed and their beliefs and behavior modified."⁴⁴

By means of these symbolic actions, the prophets themselves came to be intimately involved with the actions they performed, so that the word of the LORD became identified not only with their words, but with themselves. Isaiah walked about naked for three years (Isa 20:2), Jeremiah was to remain celibate (Jer 16:2), and God commanded Ezekiel not to cry at the death of his wife (Ezek 24:15–24). It is, however, Hosea who demonstrates most clearly how the prophet's life personified the word of God. When the word of the LORD came to Hosea, the LORD commanded

---

41. Dahms, "Isaiah 55:11 and the Gospel of John," 78.
42. Dahms, "Isaiah 55:11 and the Gospel of John," 78–88.
43. Zimmerli, *Ezekiel*, 156.
44. Block, *Book of Ezekiel*, 1:166.

Hosea to marry a wife of harlotry and have children of harlotry, because "the land commits flagrant harlotry, forsaking LORD" (Hos 1:2). The prophet subsequently took Gomer as his wife and had children through her (Hos 1:3–11). Thus his whole life, his marital relationship with his wife, and the bearing of his children became the revelatory message for the people of Israel. In Hosea's case, the prophet himself was the symbolic proclamation of the word of God, so that, in a sense, the word of God became the life of the prophet and vice-versa.

In this way, the *logos* becoming flesh and dwelling among men is not surprising. The lives of the prophets embodying the word of God anticipated the incarnation of Christ as the Word of God. There was no better way of introducing Christ than as the Word of God who "became flesh" and "dwelt" among men (John 1:14). The writer of the Hebrews affirmed: "God, after He spoke long ago to the fathers in the prophets in many portions and in many ways, in these last days has spoken to us in His Son" (Heb 1:1). John shows that the word of God embodied in Jesus.

Prophetic Self-consciousness

The peculiar aspect of the self-designations of "we" and "I" (1:14; 21:24–25) in the Fourth Gospel (which has no parallel in the Synoptic Gospels) must be understood in light of the prophets' awareness of themselves in their writings. When the prophets of the Old Testament speak the word of God, the strong presence of prophetic "I" accompanies these proclamations, and this is most likely the background for the strong self-awareness of John in the Fourth Gospel.

The prophetic self-consciousness speaks of the prophet's awareness of himself, and this self-consciousness deals with the way he projects himself in his writing. The prophet's self-awareness had an important function in his role as the announcer of God's message. In many cases, the prophets speak of the way God commissioned them in order to authenticate their messages. Isaiah said that he saw the LORD sitting on his throne in heaven and heard him say, "Whom shall I send and who will go for us?" (Isa 6:8). Jeremiah heard from the LORD and he wrote what he said to him: "Before I formed you in the womb I knew you, and before you were born I consecrated you; I have appointed you a prophet to the nations" (Jer 1:4). In like manner, Ezekiel saw the vision of the throne room of God and reported his words: "Son of man, I am sending you to the sons of Israel, to a rebellious people who have rebelled against Me" (Ezek 2:3). Amos similarly testified, "The LORD took me from following the flock, and the LORD said to me, 'Go, prophesy to my people Israel'" (Amos 7:15).

False prophets, on the other hand, went on their own initiatives when the LORD did not send them. Regarding them, the LORD said, "I did not send these prophets, but they ran. I did not speak to them, but they prophesied" (Jer 23:21). N. Habel argued that the classical prophets Isaiah, Jeremiah, and Ezekiel appropriated a traditional calling formula such as of Moses and Gideon in their calling narratives, and thereby established their authority as servants of the LORD. He said, "The goal of the prophetic formulation of the call in this *Gattung* [traditional type] is to announce publicly that Yahweh commissioned the prophet in question as His representative."[45] Although it is questionable whether such call formula existed as an entity or the prophets appropriated it cognitively,[46] his observation that the calling account is for the credential of the prophet is certainly correct. Von Rad observed the importance of the reference to self in the calling accounts. He said:

> But the "I" the prophets speak of is expressly exclusive. The men who speak to us in these accounts were men who had been expressly called upon to abandon the fixed orders of religion which the majority of the people still considered valid—a tremendous step for a man of the ancient east to take—and because of it the prophets, in their new and completely unprecedented situation, were faced with the need to justify themselves both in their own and in other people's eyes . . . The call commissioned the prophet: the act of writing down an account of it was aimed at those sections of the public in whose eyes he had to justify himself.[47]

The prophets needed to establish their messages as having come from the LORD, and they accomplished this purpose through their calling accounts and the strong presence of prophetic "I."

The prophets, therefore, do not retract from speaking about themselves in their visionary encounters with God. Ezekiel said, "These are the living beings that I saw beneath the God of Israel by the river Chebar"

---

45. Habel, "Form and Significance of the Call Narratives," 323.

46. von Rad said, "The event which led to a man's call to be a *nabi'* is described in a considerable number of different ways, and it is also plain that there was no conventional fashion in which it came about." von Rad, *Old Testament Theology*, 56.

47. von Rad, *Old Testament Theology*, 54–55.

(Ezek 10:20; cf. 43:3); Amos said, "I saw the LORD standing beside the altar and He said to me" (Amos 9:1); and Zechariah said, "I saw at night, and behold, a man was riding on a red horse" (Zech 1:8). Because the prophets themselves had close ties to the message they received and proclaimed in their writings, they often speak in the most personal and sometimes autobiographical style. Jeremiah said, "Then *I* took Jaazaniah the son of Jeremiah, son of Habassiniah . . . *I* brought them into the house of the LORD . . . then *I* set before the men of the house of the Rechabites pitchers full of wine and cups, and *I* said to them, 'Drink wine!'" (Jer 35:3–5; cf. 36:5; 42:4).[48] Concerning this preference of first person references in the prophetic writings, Preuss said, "The vision and call reports are mostly stylized as first person accounts in order to emphasize that these are not reports by strangers about the prophets but rather are reports presented in the form of self-reflection in which the prophets set forth their experiences in ways that avoid ecstasy."[49] For this reason, the prophetic "I" in the prophetic literature had an important function of authenticating the messages by way of presenting self as a legitimate witness of the word of God.

In light of this discussion, the apostle's self-awareness in the Fourth Gospel is astonishing. As a sent-out one (*apostolos*) of Christ, it was important to John that the readers understand that he was bearing a truthful witness to what he had seen, as he recounts his personal *visionary* experience to the readers.[50] In John 1:14, he says: "And the Word became flesh, and dwelt among us, and *we saw* His glory, glory as of the only begotten from the Father, full of grace and truth."[51] In John 19:34–35, the apostle bears an eyewitness account: "But one of the soldiers pierced His side with a spear, and immediately blood and water came out. And he who has seen has testified, and his testimony is true; and he knows that he is telling the truth, so that you also may believe." In John 21:24, John testifies: "This is the disciple who is testifying to these things and wrote

48. Italics are added for emphasis.

49. Preuss, *Old Testament Theology*, 2:74.

50. Of course, the nature of John vision experience is different from those of Isaiah and Ezekiel. John's experience was through his physical eyes concerning the physical person Jesus while the OT prophets' vision was no doubt through the Spirit in spiritual realms. However, the object of that vision remains the same in both cases. All of them saw Christ (albeit in different realms) who is the outward manifestation of the glory of God (cf. John 12:39–41; Col. 1:15). John's language of "seeing" is thus strongly reminiscent of the prophetic voices.

51. Italics are added for emphasis.

these things, and *we* know that his testimony is true." When he compared the Fourth Gospel and Revelation, Rowland said, "Both in different senses involve claims to be linked with eyewitnesses, both, it is true, of a heavenly vision, one of that heavenly Word made flesh; the other of the awesome consequences of the heavenly vision of the enthroned divinity and the terrible lamb in the midst of the throne."[52] In the earthly life and ministry of the Lord Jesus, the disciples saw the glory of Jesus,[53] and John's autobiographical voice in the Gospel has the function of sealing credibility to his narrative as eyewitness accounts.[54] Craig S. Keener made note of the disciples' prophet-like perception of the glory of the Lord in the "we" account of John. He said:

> The most natural construal of the first person plural, if all source theories are held in suspension, is that John includes himself among the eyewitnesses. The eyewitnesses of the Word's glory do not evoke the initiates of Hellenistic Mysteries, but Moses, who beheld God's glory on Mount Sinai . . . In other words, Jesus' eyewitnesses, including John, are mediators of a revelation greater than that of Moses but in a manner analogous to Moses . . . Whereas many commentators . . . compare Jesus in the Fourth Gospel with Moses, it is actually particularly his disciples who represent Moses, while Jesus parallels the glory that Moses witnessed on the mountain.[55]

Apostle John testifies to the readers that he has seen the glory of the Lord with his strong narrative voice.

Probably the most unique (and controversial) self-conscious feature of the Fourth Gospel is the phrase, "the disciple whom Jesus loved" (13:23; 19:26; 20:2; 21:7, 20). In the Old Testament, when the writings project the prophetic self-consciousness, it was often presented in an affected and overwhelmed state by the message. The message overcame them. Prophets proclaimed the messages of God because they could not do otherwise. Amos 3:8 says: "The lion has roared; who will not fear? The

---

52. Rowland, "Prophecy and the New Testament," 425.

53. The word "glory" in John 1:14 may be comparable to what Isaiah and Ezekiel saw. The word signifies "a visible and powerful manifestation of God" and it refers to the "continuous glory in the earthly life of Jesus, notably in his miracles." Ridderbos, *Gospel according to John*, 52–53. John's experience of seeing the glory of Jesus was not lesser than that of Old Testament prophets.

54. Those who regard source theories for John think differently about this first person account of "we." Cf. Smith, "Johannine Christianity," 236.

55. Keener, *Gospel of John*, 1:412.

LORD God has spoken; who can but prophesy?" Jeremiah says in 20:8–9: "For each time I speak, I cry aloud; I proclaim violence and destruction, Because for me the word of the LORD has resulted In reproach and derision all day long. But if I say, 'I will not remember Him Or speak anymore in His name,' Then in my heart it becomes like a burning fire Shut up in my bones; And I am weary of holding *it* in, And I cannot endure *it*." These examples show that the word of the LORD powerfully swayed the prophet's consciousness. When Jeremiah *ate* the word of God, it became a joy and delight in his heart (Jer 15:16), and when Ezekiel *ate* the scroll, it was sweet as honey in his mouth (Ezek 3:3).

But sometimes, when the word of God came to the prophets, they experienced anguish and terror because of the nature of the message. Isaiah says, "For this reason my loins are full of anguish, Pains have seized me like the pains of a woman in labor. I am so bewildered I cannot hear, so terrified I cannot see. My mind reels, horror overwhelms me, The twilight I longed for has been turned for me into trembling" (Isa 21:3–4). Jeremiah cries out, "My soul, my soul! I am in anguish! Oh, my heart! My heart is pounding in me, I cannot be silent, Because you have heard, O my soul, The sound of the trumpet, The alarm of war" (Jer 4:19). Jeremiah became so terrorized by the words of the judgment of God that it was as if he was mortally wounded: "Why has my pain been perpetual and my wound incurable, refusing to be healed?" (15:18). When Habakkuk heard the sound of the coming judgment, he said, "I heard and my inward parts trembled, At the sound my lips quivered. Decay enters my bones, And in my place I tremble" (Hab 3:16). When the word of God came to the prophets, their consciousness was overwhelmed by the nature of the message, whether in joy or terror.

B. D. Napier called this phenomenon "the psychology of captivity," where the word of God exercised the "power of seizure" over the prophet.[56] He said that "the prophetic anguish is the product of the prophets' inevitable sense of participation in and consequently responsibility for the negative Word."[57] Abraham J. Heschel called this experience of the prophets as the participation in the divine *pathos*. He said:

> An analysis of prophetic utterances shows that the fundamental experience of the prophet is a fellowship with the feelings of God, a *sympathy with the divine pathos*, a communion with the

---

56. Napier, "Prophet, Prophetism," 3:896–919.
57. Napier, "Prophet, Prophetism," 3:896–919.

divine consciousness which comes about through the prophet's reflection of, or participation in, the divine pathos. The typical prophetic state of mind is one of being taken up into the heart of the divine pathos.[58]

As the heart of God against sinners so affected and overwhelmed them, "they speak and act as if the sky were about to collapse ... The prophet's words are outbursts of violent emotions. His rebuke is harsh and relentless."[59] The prophets were in fellowship with God's powerful pathos.

It is astounding that this "typical prophetic state of mind ... of being taken up into the heart of the divine pathos"[60] is what characterizes the Gospel of John. John speaks as one whose heart was in *captivity* with the message he was proclaiming—and the message was in essence the *love* of Jesus demonstrated at the cross. It is no wonder therefore that he frequently speaks of himself as "one whom Jesus loved" in the most significant places (13:23; 19:26; 20:2–8; 21:7, 20–23)—thus the designation as the 'beloved disciple.' This designation is not a cryptic strategy intended to hide his identity or even to misguide the reader, but instead, it is a mark of his overwhelmed prophetic self-consciousness according to the Old Testament precedents. John was simply weighed down and captivated by the divine *pathos* in the message he proclaimed. The theme of love is profound in the Gospel. When Jesus knew that he was going back to the Father, Jesus loved his disciples to the end (13:1).[61] Just as the Father loved him, Jesus loved them (15:9, 12). Because of his love, Jesus was laying down his life for them (15:13). John personally witnessed the love of Jesus. John was there when Jesus washed the disciples' feet as a servant (13:23), he was there at the foot of the cross beholding the one who died for him (19:26), he was there at the empty tomb witnessing Jesus' resurrection (20:2–8), and he was there by the Sea of Tiberias when the risen Lord came back to them (21:7). John identifies himself as one Jesus deeply loved in these significant events of Jesus. In proclaiming "God so loved the world" (3:16), John himself felt the depth of God's love in Jesus.

---

58. Heschel, *Prophets*, 26. Italics in original.

59. Heschel, *Prophets*, 4.

60. Heschel, *Prophets*, 20.

61. James H. Charlesworth noted that the introduction of the Beloved Disciple comes between "Jesus' absolute love for his disciples" (13:1–20) and "Jesus' new commandment to love as he loved them" (13:31–35). Charlesworth, *Beloved Disciple*, 51–52.

Although the author's anonymity has troubled many scholars, his self-designation as the "disciple whom Jesus loved" is a prophetic self-consciousness, and it reveals the state of his heart which the love of Jesus has overwhelmed. In comparison with the Synoptics, John shows a propensity for the idea of love in his Gospel. The noun *agapē* appears twice in the Synoptics, but seven times in John. The Synoptics use *phileō* eight times, and John uses it fifteen times. Concerning the verb *agapaō*, it occurs twenty-six times in the Synoptics in twelve morphological forms, but John uses it an overwhelming seventy-two times in twenty-three morphological forms. Jocelyn McWhirter observed that the Gospel resounds with echoes of marriage theme from Genesis 29:1–20, Jeremiah 33:10–11, and Song of Songs 1:12, 3:1–4.[62] The Gospel is elated with the fragrance of love.

Ann Roberts Winsor showed that the Gospel of John alludes to the Song of Songs in many places. In *A King is Bound in the Tresses: Allusions to the Song of Songs in the Fourth Gospel*, she said that John alludes to the Song of Songs in Jesus being at the table (John 12:1; Song 1:12), anointing with perfume (John 12:3; Song 1:3, 4, 12, 13), Mary wiping his feet with her hair (John 12:3; Song 5:3; 7:5), the tomb (John 20:1,11; the "chambers" in Song 1:4; 3:4; 8:2), the garden (John 19:41; Song 4:12, 16; 5:1; 8:13), Mary's search (John 20:1, 15; Song 3:1–4), and Jesus' voice to Mary (John 20:16; Song 5:2, 6).[63] For this reason, the aroma of love fills the pages of the Gospel of John. Johns Varghese also observed the prominence of the theme of love in the Fourth Gospel and pointed out that the topic of love relationship appears in the motifs of bridegroom and bride (2:1–11; 3:27–30; 4:1–26; 12:1–8; 20:1–2, 11–18), friendship (11:1–44; 12:1–8; 13:21–30; 19:25–27; 20:1–10; 21:1–14; 21:20–24; 15:13–15), and the covenant relationship (5:41–44; 8:41b–42; 13:34–35; 14:15–24; 15:9–17; 21:15–17).[64] John was an apostle who was profoundly transformed by the love of God in the death and resurrection of Jesus, and in this light, it is not strange that John should address himself as a disciple whom Jesus loved in his prophetic self-consciousness.

---

62. McWhirter, *Bridegroom Messiah*, passim.

63. Winsor, *King Is Bound*, passim.

64. Varghese, *Imagery of Love in the Gospel of John*, passim. Cf. Fensham, "Love in the Writings," 67–77; van Tilborg, *Imaginative Love in John*; Segovia, *Love Relationships in the Johannine Tradition*; Voorwinde, *Jesus' Emotions in the Fourth Gospel*, 150–61, 232–52.

Prophetic Persuasion

Prophets were the spokesmen of God who spoke on behalf of God to deliver the message of exhortation, repentance, judgment, and salvation. The heart of God for his people has always been that they would turn from their sinful ways and live: "'I know the plans that I have for you,' declares the LORD, 'plans for welfare and not for calamity to give you a future and a hope'" (Jer 29:11). For this reason, in all their proclamations, the prophets' task was *persuading* them to return to the LORD. Yehoshua Gitay recognized that prophets are persuasive in nature so that rhetorical criticism is helpful in analyzing prophetic literature. Concerning Isaiah, he said, "Since [Deutero-Isaiah's] prophecy is a public address, it should be studied as a communicative discourse designed to appeal to its audience."[65] Michael V. Fox stated that "for by any definition prophecy is rhetoric," and that the "prophets were intensely concerned with persuasion, and they are indeed persuasive."[66] Richard J. Clifford also observed that prophets are persuading and said: "His eloquent monotheism, his skill in consoling, the force of his ideas and images, long celebrated by commentators, are all subordinate to his task of persuading."[67]

Because of their persuasive role, prophets are the preachers of God's message. Peisker and Brown said that the Old Testament prophet "is a proclaimer of the word, called by God to warn, exhort, comfort, teach and counsel."[68] P. A. Verhoef noted that the "prophets were first and foremost preachers of God's word."[69] Charles S. Shaw observed that Demosthenes' description of Greek political orator is applicable to Hebrew prophets. Demosthenes said:

> Make as strict an inquiry as you will into everything for which an orator is responsible; I ask no indulgence. But for what is he responsible? For discerning the trend of events at the outset, for forecasting results, for warning others. That I have always done. Further, he ought to reduce to a minimum those delays and hesitations, those fits of ignorance and quarrelsomeness,

---

65. Gitay, *Prophecy and Persuasion*, 26–27.

66. Fox, "Rhetoric of Ezekiel's Vision," 179.

67. Clifford, *Fair Spoken and Persuading*, 4, 6. However, one should not see that the contents are subordinate to the task of persuasion. It is the importance and the urgency of the messages that occasion the persuasion of the prophets.

68. Peisker and Brown, "Prophet," 3:79.

69. Verhoef, "Prophecy," 4:1075.

which are the natural and inevitable failings of all free states, and on the other hand to promote unanimity and friendliness, and whatever impels a man to do his duty.[70]

Lindblom, furthermore, stated that the prophets' proclamations were often "caused by the apostasy and the sins of the people in general. Thus, the prophets appear as ordinary but inspired preachers of repentance and heralds of doom or bliss."[71]

This persuasive nature of the prophets and their writings probably in some measure has to do with the orality of their messages. When prophets delivered God's message, they often proclaimed it publicly.[72] Jeremiah 17:19–20 records: "Thus the LORD said to me, 'Go and stand in the public gate, through which the kings of Judah come in and go out, as well as in all the gates of Jerusalem and say to them.'" Jeremiah 26:2 states: "Stand in the court of the LORD's house, and speak to all the cities of Judah who have come to worship in the LORD's house all the words that I have commanded you to speak to them" (cf. Jer 22:1; 28:2–11; Ezek 14:1–11; 20:1–4). Many of the prophetic messages were, therefore, "delivered as public speeches or sermons."[73]

The prophetic persuasion was a matter of life and death for the listeners. If people heeded to the message, they lived; but if they refused, God brought judgment upon them. Prophets, therefore, often urged repentance from the people in the face of impending doom. Amos, Hosea, and Isaiah in some chapters (chaps 36–39) forged their messages at the wake of Neo-Assyrian invasion, and Habakkuk, Jeremiah, and Ezekiel at the menace of Chaldeans.[74] He said that the "prophets in Israel were associated with crucial moments in its existence," and that their activities during the time of stability "were far less prominent than they were during times of crisis."[75]

---

70. Demosthenes, "De Corona," 181; Shaw, *Speeches of Micah*, 21.
71. Lindblom, *Prophecy in Ancient Israel*, 153.
72. Boadt, "Poetry of Prophetic Persuasion," 6.
73. Lindblom, *Prophecy in Ancient Israel*, 153. Boadt, however, noted that "This does not rule out the possibility that some prophecy was written down before being delivered (suggested by Jeremiah 36), or that much of it was written down after it was delivered (see Isa 8:16; Hab 2:2). Whether oracles were written or not, however, they were normally proclaimed aloud." Boadt, "Poetry of Prophetic Persuasion," 6. See also, Ong, *Interfaces of the Word*, 114–16.
74. Petersen, "Prophet, Prophecy," 4:628–33.
75. Petersen, "Prophet, Prophecy," 633.

God always sent his prophets to the people to save them from coming destructions, although people often rejected them: "I have spread out My hands all day long to a rebellious people, Who walk in the way which is not good, following their own thoughts, A people who continually provoke Me to My face" (Isa 65:2–3); "Since the day that your fathers came out of the land of Egypt until this day, I have sent you all My servants the prophets, daily rising early and sending them, yet they did not listen to Me" (Jer 7:25). God's purpose was to turn them from their evil ways: "I have sent to you all My servants the prophets, sending them again and again, saying, 'Turn now every man from his evil way and amend your deeds, and do not go after other gods to worship them'" (35:15; cf. 25:4–5, 44:4).[76] Shalom M. Paul and S. David Sperling, therefore, observed that the essence of prophetic proclamations was persuading people to repent and have faith in the LORD:

> They demanded piety and faithfulness to the covenant between God and Israel, and threatened punishment and fulfillment of the covenant's curses for those who were disloyal to it. Yet all of their denunciations and frightful maledictions were not meant as ends in themselves. They were, rather, a vain attempt to arouse the people from their lethargic status quo; they were didactic means to achieve the desired end—repentance. The objective of the prophetic threat of dire punishment was that it should not take place. Paradoxically, the prophets wished to make their own calling self-defeating by persuading man to return to God. They censured, warned, and admonished their audiences to forsake their immoral ways in order to avoid imminent destruction.[77]

Prophets were men of God who carried God's history-altering messages to change the course of the people and deliver them from destruction and death. Their message was marked with severest threats and most urgent pleas. Prophets, for this reason, do not embed their intentions underneath narratives. Their presence and intentions come to the fore of their speeches aggressively and intrusively. So much hangs on the decisions of the people that they cannot leave anything to chance; they have urgency to persuade people with divine zeal to turn them to the LORD. At the impending destructions, prophets earnestly pleaded to win the

---

76. Jeremias, "נָבִיא," 2:709.
77. Paul and Sperling, "Prophets and Prophecy," 16:579.

audience. This is why prophetic discourses are different from narrative speeches. Gitay observed the difference:

> We can distinguish between two types of speeches: direct and oral, narrative and written. The narrative discourse is designed normally for a variety of audiences, and is composed, consequently, in a way which secures its meaning in some future time. By contrast, the direct discourse faces a specific audience in an actual situation, and includes, therefore, nonlinguistic clues to the speaker's intention; clues which may not be familiar any more to the later listener or reader.[78]

In contrast to narrative stories, prophetic discourses proclaim God's message directly to the audience.

As Heschel identified God's prophet as a "strange, one-sided," and "an unbearable extremist,"[79] John is so eager to move his audience. His stark contrasts of light and darkness, life and death, and truth and lie originate from his passionate desire to persuade in light of the eschatological consequences. In presenting the life and ministry of Jesus Christ, John pleads sincerely: "These have been written so that you may believe that Jesus is the Christ, the Son of God, and that by believing you may have life in His name" (John 20:30–31). John does not write a normal narrative; his style borders on the *direct* speech with his strong authorial voice protruding frequently in telling the story of Jesus. Concerning this unique persuasive voice of John, Teresa Okure made this observation:

> Though the Evangelist believes in the historicity of the events recorded ... he is clearly not writing history for its own sake, nor is he necessarily recording the selective events in the chronological order in which they occurred. Rather the presentation is governed ... according to the norms of rhetoric, by the need to persuade and convince the reader to take a faith stance towards Jesus.[80]

While John writes the historical events of Jesus, he is presenting them to persuade the readers to have faith in Jesus.

In the process of condemning sinful actions and persuading people to return to the LORD, prophets often employed legal accusations and

---

78. Gitay, "Reflections on the Study of Prophetic Discourse," 207.
79. Heschel, *Prophets*, 16.
80. Okure, *Johannine Approach to Mission*, 41.

lawsuit themes. Recognized as an important speech form of the prophets,[81] judicial motif dominates prophetic utterances: "The LORD arises to contend, And stands to judge the people. The LORD enters into judgment with the elders and princes of His people" (Isa 3:13); "Hear now what the LORD is saying, 'Arise, plead your case before the mountains, And let the hills hear your voice. Listen, you mountains, to the indictment of the LORD, And you enduring foundations of the earth, Because the LORD has a case against His people, Even with Israel He will dispute" (Mic 6:1); "Listen to the word of the LORD, O sons of Israel, For the LORD has a case against the inhabitants of the land" (Hos 4:1). Prominence of judicial themes in the Prophets is appropriate because the LORD is completely righteous in his judgments, and it becomes the ground from which the prophets exhort the people to repent before the LORD. Jeremiah 42:19 states: "The LORD has spoken to you, O remnant of Judah, 'Do not go into Egypt!' You should clearly understand that today I have testified against you" (cf. Amos. 3:13; Zeph 3:8; Mal 3:5).

The Gospel of John is strongly judicial in its nature. Andrew T. Lincoln pointed out that John uses the noun *marturia* fourteen times but Synoptic Gospels use it four times, and the verb *marturein* appears thirty-three times in John when other Gospels has it only twice.[82] Other legal terms in John are *krisis, krinein, krima, katēgoria, katēgorein, apokrinesthai, apokrisis, bēma, zētēsis, elegchein, homologein, arneisthai, aitia, heuriskein,* and *schism*.[83] Allison A. Trites said that the Fourth Gospel strongly resembles Isaiah 40–55 and pointed out that "the controversy between Yahweh and the false gods turns out to be a lawsuit between God and the world... Similarly, in the Fourth Gospel God incarnate has a lawsuit with the world."[84] She continued that "John, like his Old Testament counterpart, has a case to present, and for this reason he advances his arguments, challenges his opponents and presents his witnesses after the fashion of the Old Testament legal assembly."[85] John presents evidences and makes a case before the world that Jesus is the Son of God. In view of

---

81. Westermann, *Basic Forms of Prophetic Speech*.
82. Lincoln, *Truth on Trial*, 12.
83. Trites, *New Testament Concept of Witness*, 80–81.
84. Trites, *Witness*, 79.
85. Trites, *Witness*, 79–80.

The Gospel of John in Light of the Poetics of Old Testament Prophets

the testimonial and evidential character of the Gospel, the prominence of the term "belief" or "believing" is not surprising.[86]

Just as the prophets called the people to hear the LORD's case against them, John calls his audience to enter into the court room to evaluate the evidences he presents. As he presents the testimonies and affirms his truthfulness, he urges the audience in the spirit of the Old Testament prophets to believe in Jesus so that they would have life believing in his name. In this regard, John is truly *persuasive*, and it is a *prophetic* Gospel at heart.

Prophetic Mode of Speaking

The last aspect of the Gospel treated in this chapter is John's prophetic mode of speaking which was briefly noted earlier. Speaking of John 3:13–21, Morris voiced the ambiguity of John's style in this way:

> All are agreed that from time to time in this Gospel we have the meditations of the Evangelist, but it is difficult to know where they begin and end. In the first century there were no devices like quotation marks to show the precise limits of quoted speech. The result is that we are always left to the probabilities and we must work out for ourselves where a speech or quotation ends. In this passage Jesus begins to speak in verse 10, but John does not tell us where this speech ends . . . Most agree that somewhere we pass into the reflections of the Evangelist.[87]

In reading the Gospel, it is not clear whether John intended the readers to know the precise limits of the quoted speeches.

As noted above, the mark of true prophet is the faithful representation of the word of God. When the LORD appointed Aaron as the spokesman for Moses, their relationship clearly shows this function of the prophet: "You are to speak to him and put the words in his mouth; and I, even I, will be with your mouth and his mouth, and I will teach you what you are to do. Moreover, he shall speak for you to the people, and he will be as a mouth for you and you will be as God to him" (Exod 4:15–16). However, what happens often is that their speeches are presented in indistinguishable manners. It is the nature of the prophetic literature of the

---

86. Trites, *Witness*, 81.
87. Morris, *John*, 202.

Old Testament that the voices of the prophets and the LORD are often intertwined indiscriminately.

The fact that this manner of presenting speeches in the Prophets was troubling is attested through the Targumic paraphrase of the Old Testament. The exegetical tradition did not know how to handle this ambiguity, so that when there were uncertainties, it added, "the prophet said" (*'emar nebiya'*) in the text. Thus, Isaiah 9:6 has, "the prophet said, for a child will be born to us" and 28:23 has, "the prophet said, 'Give ear and hear my voice, listen and hear my words;'" 61:1 has, "The prophet said, 'The Spirit of the LORD God is upon me;'" and Jeremiah 8:22 has, "Jeremiah prophet said . . . Is there no balm in Gilead?"[88]

In his excellent study, Samuel A. Meier observed this phenomenon in the Prophets and showed that there are many places in the Prophets where the prophetic "I" and the "I" of the LORD exist side by side without distinction. A clear example of this is in Micah 1:1–8. After introducing the prophet in verse 1 (without showing who is speaking), verse 2 opens with this call, "Hear, O peoples, all of you; listen, O earth and all it contains" (v. 2a). From verses 2b–5, the prophet addresses God with his personal name LORD and with third person pronouns, so one can presume that it is the prophet who speaks in these verses: "behold, the LORD is coming forth from His place" (v. 3). Suddenly in verses 6–7, however, the speech changes to the voice of the LORD ("For I will make Samaria a heap of ruins in the open country . . . all her images I will make desolate"), and in verse 8, it changes to the prophet's voice again ("Because of this I must lament and wail, I must go barefoot and naked; I must make a lament like the jackals and mourning like the ostriches").[89] The writer does not indicate the change of speakers, and he lays the speeches side by side. Concerning this method, Meier said:

> What is crucial to observe is that there is little concern to distinguish the words of God from the words of the prophet. In these books it is frequently difficult to determine when God speaks and when the prophet speaks, for the voices blend and merge with a freedom that is disorienting for one who wishes greater precision in knowing the source of each articulation.[90]

---

88. Kaufman, *Targum Jonathan to the Prophets*. See also, Isa 24:16; 33:15; 35:3; Jer 4:19; 5:7; Ezek 19:14; 32:16; Hos 12:4,13. Samuel A. Meier observed this Targumic approach. Meier, *Speaking of Speaking*, 207.

89. For this example, see Meier, *Themes and Transformations*, 72–73.

90. Meier, *Prophecy*, 71.

The Gospel of John in Light of the Poetics of Old Testament Prophets 165

The situation perhaps is that the words of the LORD became the words of the prophets and so the distinction is sometimes impossible.

In Habakkuk 2, God's speech clearly begins in verse 2, but it is not certain when it ends in that chapter. The whole chapter seems to be God's speech, but its ending sounds like the voice of the prophet: "But the LORD is in His holy temple. Let all the earth be silent before Him" (v. 20). Marvin A. Sweeney said that verses 18–20 are the prophet's summary comments, but this demarcation is also arbitrary.[91]

In Joel 1, verses 1–3 show that the following verses are the LORD's speech: "The word of the LORD that came to Joel, the son of Pethuel: Hear this, O elders, And listen, all inhabitants of the land." The LORD continues his speech in verse 4 saying that the locusts have completely devastated the land; so that from verse 5, he commands his people to awake and weep: "Awake, drunkards, And weep; and wail, all you wine drinkers, On account of the sweet wine That is cut off from your mouth" (v. 5). These verbs and expressions continue to reverberate in the following verses (the reference of "the LORD" in v. 9 could be taken as God's self-reference, or as the prophet's voice), but in verse 13, it is the prophet who speaks suddenly: "Gird yourselves *with sackcloth* And lament, O priests; Wail, O ministers of the altar! Come, spend the night in the sackcloth O ministers of my God, For the grain offering and the drink offering Are withheld from the house of your God." There are thematic and linguistic connections of this verse to the previous verses ("wail" [v. 13 and vv. 5, 8, 11], "priests" [v. 13 and v. 9], "ministers" [v.13 and v. 9], "gird yourself" [v. 13 and v. 8]). In other words, the speeches of the LORD and of the prophet are tangled so closely together without clear signs of delineation, and the vocabulary of the prophet most likely owes itself to the words of the LORD.

In Hosea 9:8–17, the altering voices of the prophet and the LORD proceed against the people, and its effect is remarkable (Hosea [vv. 8–9], the LORD [vv. 10–13], Hosea [v. 14], the LORD [vv. 15–16], Hosea [v. 17]). The LORD and the prophet speak together to the people to accuse them and to woo them.[92] Francis I. Andersen and David N. Freedman

---

91. Sweeney, *Twelve Prophets*, 477.

92. Meier identified such mingling of voices in: Habakkuk (divine [1:5–11; 2:2ff], human [1:2–4, 12ff; 2:1; 3:2, 16–19]); Micah (divine [e.g., 1:6–7, 15; 2:12; 4:13; 7:15], human [e.g., 1:8; 4:12; 6:6; 7:1]); Obadiah [demarcations for divine's in vv.1, 8, 18]; Joel (divine [e.g. 1:6–7; 2:1a, 12, 25, 27; 3:1–3; 4:1–8, 12, 17, 21a], human [e.g., 1:13, 19; 4:11]); Hosea (divine [e.g., 6:4; 9:10, 15; 12:9], human [e.g., 6:1; 9:8–9, 14, 17; 12:2–6,

commented that "so intricately combined and blended are the two stories—of God and Israel, and Hosea and Gomer—that it is impossible to tell always where one stops and the other picks up."[93]

There are, however, opposite cases where the writer is careful to distinguish the word of the LORD from other words. In Haggai 1:1–8, phrases like "the Word of the LORD," and "says the LORD" occur so many times that the contrast with the former case is "stunning."[94] "In the second year of Darius . . . *the word of the LORD* came by the prophet Haggai to Zerubbabel . . . *saying, 'Thus says the LORD of hosts* . . . Then *the word of the LORD* came by Haggai the prophet, *saying* . . . Now therefore, *thus says the LORD of hosts*, 'Consider your ways!' . . . *Thus says the LORD of hosts . . . says the LORD.*"[95] There is no doubt who is speaking, and the specification is remarkably superfluous. The post-exilic condition of Judah may have demanded this seeming over-specification of "the word of the LORD" through the prophets.[96] In the case of Haggai, people's preoccupation with their own houses, at the expense of restoring God's house resulted in the failures in life, and it must have been necessary that the people know clearly that the LORD has done this and *he* is speaking to them through the prophet.

There are cases that such delineation is uneven within the book itself. In Amos, Jeremiah, Ezekiel, and Isaiah, specifications of divine speeches from other voices are sometimes present and sometimes not.[97] Meier attributed the presence and non-presence of delineation markers to the characteristic of pre-exilic, exilic, and post-exilic periods, or to the poetic vs. prose style of different periods, but one should not strictly apply the classification.[98] Whatever the case may be, it is important to note that God entrenched the prophets with his words and with his heart that when God spoke, they spoke, and when they spoke, God spoke. In many

---

13–14; 14:9]); Nahum (it uncertain who is speaking in 2:4–13; 3:1–4, 8–19); Zephaniah (divine [e.g., 1:2–4, 8b–12, 17a; 2:5b, 9, 12; 3:6–12a, 18–20], human [e.g., 1:7, 18; 2:1–3, 5a, 10–11, 13–14; 3:5, 15, 17]). Meier, *Speaking of Speaking*, 209–22.

93. Andersen and Freedman, *Hosea*, 46–47. See also Fretheim, *Suffering of God*, 155–56.

94. Fretheim, *Suffering of God*, 222.

95. See Meier, *Themes and Transformations*, 73–74. Italics are added for emphasis.

96. Meier pointed out that Haggai, Zechariah 1–8, and Malachi are careful to mark the direct discourse of the LORD.

97. See Meier, *Speaking of Speaking*, 226–29, 230–72.

98. See Meier, *Themes and Transformations*, 70–77.

cases, prophets did not specify the voices because they knew that it was God who was speaking through them. This consciousness is, however, different from prophets taking liberty to speak from their own hearts. The heart of a true prophet was a captivated heart; when it was most free, it was most captured and confined (Amos 3:8; Jer 20:8–9; cf. 2 Cor 5:14).

In the Gospel of John, there are places where the identity of the voice is hard to discern especially in John 3:13–21 and 3:31–36. There are different views on this phenomenon,[99] but in light of the foregoing discussions, this is John's prophetic manner of speaking according to the Old Testament precedents. John speaks freely from his captivated heart, so that his voice and Jesus' voice mingle together to become God's voice ultimately.[100]

Summary

This last chapter showed that the prophets of the Old Testament had profound influence on the poetics of the Fourth Gospel. Although the discussion investigated the prophetic nature of the Gospel on limited scope, comparing the Gospel with the Old Testament prophetic writings has been fruitful. The mentioning of the *logos* in the opening section was comparable to the openings of the prophetic writings,[101] and Gospel's presentation of the Word finds its root in the concept of word of God in the Old Testament. This chapter identified that John's self-awareness, persuasive zeal, and his way of presenting his own reflections are Old Testament prophets' methods of communicating God's message. John is therefore a truly *prophetic* Gospel.

---

99. Cf. Barrett, *John*, 178; Beasley-Murray, *John*, 46; Haenchen, *John 1*, 204; Morris, *John*, 202, 215; Michaels, *John*, 200, 221–22; Bernard, *John*, 1:xxiii; Bultmann, *John*, 160; Schnackenburg, *John*, 1:380–92; and Ridderbos, *John*, 149.

100. This mode of speaking is also prominent in Pss 50:4–15; 81:2–17; 82:1–8; 91:11–16; and 95:7–11. Meier, *Speaking on Speaking*, 222. Sigmund Mowinckel called such psalms as *prophetic* psalms. Mowinckel, *Psalms in Israel's Worship*, 2:70.

101. It should not trouble the readers that the word *logos* does not appear again in the rest of the Gospel. *Logos* functions to set the rest of the Gospel as the Word of God revealed and incarnate.

Bibliography

Abbott, Edwin A. *Johannine Grammar.* London: Adam and Charles Black, 1906.

———. *Johannine Vocabulary: A Comparison of the Words of the Fourth Gospel with Those of the Three.* London: Adam and Charles Black, 1905.

Abbot, Ezra, et al. *The Fourth Gospel: Evidences External and Internal of Its Johannine Authorship; Essays by Ezra Abbot, Andrew P. Peabody and Bishop Lightfoot.* New York: C. Scribner's Sons, 1891.

Abrams, Meyer H. *A Glossary of Literary Terms.* 6th ed. Fort Worth, TX: Harcourt Brace Jovanovich College Publishers, 1993.

———. *The Mirror and the Lamp: Romantic Theory and the Critical Tradition.* New York: Oxford University Press, 1953.

Adams, Hazard. *Critical Theory Since Plato.* 2nd ed. New York: Harcourt Brace Jovanovich, 1971.

Adams, Hazard, and Leroy Searle. *Critical Theory Since Plato.* 3rd ed. Boston: Thomson Wadsworth, 2005.

Aichele, George, and Bible and Culture Collective. *The Postmodern Bible.* New Haven: Yale University Press, 1995.

Albright, W. F. *Yahweh and the Gods of Canaan.* Garden City, NY: Doubleday, 1968.

Alexander, Philip S. "Rabbinic Judaism and the New Testament." *ZNW* 74 (1983) 237–46.

Alter, Robert. *The Art of Biblical Narrative.* 2nd ed. New York: Basic, 2011.

———. *The Art of Biblical Poetry.* 2nd ed. New York: Basic, 2011.

———. *The World of Biblical Literature.* New York: Basic, 1992.

Alter, Robert, and Frank Kermode. *The Literary Guide to the Bible.* Cambridge, MA: Belknap, 1987.

Amit, Yairah. *Reading Biblical Narratives: Literary Criticism and the Hebrew Bible.* Minneapolis: Fortress, 2001.

Andersen, Francis I., and A. D. Forbes. "'Prose Particle' Counts of the Hebrew Bible." In *The Word of the Lord Shall Go Forth: Essays in Honor of David Noel Freedman in Celebration of His Sixtieth Birthday*, edited by C. L. Meyers and M. O'Connor, 165–83. Winona Lake, IN: Eisenbrauns, 1983.

Andersen, Francis I., and David Noel Freedman. *Hosea*. AB 24. Garden City, NY: Doubleday, 1980.

The Ante-Nicene Fathers. Edited by Alexander Roberts and James Donaldson. 10 vols. Peabody, MA: Hendrickson, 1994.

Arnold, Bill T., and H. G. M. Williamson, eds. *Dictionary of the Old Testament: Historical Books*. Downers Grove, IL: InterVarsity, 2005.

Arp, Thomas R. *Perrin's Story and Structure*. 9th ed. Fort Worth, TX: Harcourt Brace College, 1998.

Ashton, John. "The Transformation of Wisdom: A Study of the Prologue of John's Gospel." *NTS* 32 (1986) 161–86.

———. *Understanding the Fourth Gospel*. Oxford: Clarendon, 1991.

Attridge, Harold W. "Ambiguous Signs, an Anonymous Character, Unanswerable Epistemology." *NTS* 65.3 (July 2019) 267–88.

———. "Genre Bending in the Fourth Gospel." *JBL* 121.1 (2002) 3–21.

Auerbach, Erich. *Mimesis: The Representation of Reality in Western Literature*. Translated by Willard Trask. Garden City, NY: Doubleday, 1957.

Aune, David E. *The New Testament in Its Literary Environment*. Library of Early Christianity Series. Philadelphia: Westminster, 1987.

———. *Prophecy in Early Christianity and the Ancient Mediterranean World*. Grand Rapids: Eerdmans, 1983.

———. *The Westminster Dictionary of New Testament and Early Christian Literature and Rhetoric*. Louisville: Westminster John Knox, 2003.

Baker, David W., and T. Desmond Alexander, eds. *Dictionary of the Old Testament: Pentateuch*. Downers Grove, IL: InterVarsity, 2003.

Ball, C. J. "Had the Fourth Gospel an Aramaic Archetype?" *ExpTim* 21 (1909) 91–93.

Bar-Efrat, Shimon. *Narrative Art in the Bible*. Sheffield: Almond, 1989.

Barr, James. *The Semantics of Biblical Language*. Oxford: Oxford University Press, 1961.

Barrett, C. K. *The Gospel according to St. John: An Introduction with Commentary and Notes on the Greek Text*. 2nd ed. Philadelphia: Westminster, 1978.

Bauckham, Richard. "Historiographical Chracteristics of the Gospel of John." *NTS* 53 (2007) 17–36.

———. *The Testimony of the Beloved Disciple: Narrative, History, and Theology in the Gospel of John*. Grand Rapids: Baker Academic, 2007.

Beasley-Murray, George R. *John*. WBC 36. Waco, TX: Word, 1987.

Beattie, James. *Essays on Poetry and Music as They Affect the Mind*. 3rd ed. London: E. & C. Dilly, 1779.

Beirne, Margaret M. *Women and Men in the Fourth Gospel: A Discipleship of Equals*. London: Sheffield Academic, 2003.

Belle, Gilbert van. "Repetition, Variation and Amplification: Thomas Popp's Recent Contribution on Johannine Style." *ETL* 79.1 (2003) 166–78.

———. "Repetitions and Variations in Johannine Research: A General Historical Survey." In *Repetitions and Variations in the Fourth Gospel: Style, Text, Interpretation*, edited by G. van Belle et al., 33–85. BETL 223. Walpole, MA: Peeters, 2009.

Belle, Gilbert van, et al., eds. *Repetitions and Variations in the Fourth Gospel: Style, Text, Interpretation*. Walpole, MA: Peeters, 2009.

Bennema, Cornelis. "A Comprehensive Approach to Understanding Character in the Gospel of John." In *Characters and Characterization in the Gospel of John*, edited by Christopher W. Skinner, 36–58. LNTS 461. London: Bloomsbury, 2013.

———. *Encountering Jesus: Character Studies in the Gospel of John*. Minneapolis: Fortress, 2014.

Benson, Thomas W., and Michael H. Prosser, eds. *Readings in Classical Rhetoric*. Bloomington: Indiana University Press, 1972.
Bergen, Robert D. *1, 2 Samuel*. NAC 7. Nashville: Broadman and Holman, 2001.
———, ed. *Biblical Hebrew and Discourse Linguistics*. Dallas, TX: Summer Institute of Linguistics, 1994.
Berlin, Adele. *Biblical Poetry through Medieval Jewish Eyes*. Bloomington: Indiana University Press, 1991.
———. *The Dynamics of Biblical Parallelism*. Rev. ed. Grand Rapids: Eerdman, 2008.
———. "Introduction to Hebrew Poetry." In *1 and 2 Maccabees, Introduction to Hebrew Poetry, Job, Psalms*, 301–15. NIB 4. Nashville: Abingdon, 1996.
———. *Poetics and Interpretation of Biblical Narrative*. BLS. Sheffield: Almond, 1983.
———. "Reading Biblical Poetry." In *The Jewish Study Bible: Jewish Publication Society Tanakh Translation*. Edited by Adele Berlin, Marc Zvi Brettler, and Michael A. Fishbane. Oxford: Oxford University Press, 2004.
Bernard, J. H. *A Critical and Exegetical Commentary on the Gospel according to St. John, Volumes 1 and 2*. ICC. Edinburgh: T&T Clark, 1928.
Best, Ernest. "Prophets and Preachers." *SJT* 12.2 (1959) 129–50.
Black, C. Clifton. "Keeping up with Recent Studies, Pt 16: Rhetorical Criticism and Biblical Interpretation." *ExpTim* 100.7 (1989) 252–58.
———. *The Rhetoric of the Gospel: Theological Artistry in the Gospels and Acts*, 2nd ed. Louisville, KY: Westminster John Knox, 2013.
Black, C. Clifton, and Duane F. Watson, eds. *Words Well Spoken: George Kennedy's Rhetoric of the New Testament*. Waco, TX: Baylor University Press, 2008.
Black, David Alan. "On the Style and Significance of John 17." *CTR* 3.1 (1988) 141–59.
Black, Matthew. *An Aramaic Approach to the Gospels and Acts*. Oxford: Clarendon, 1954.
Black, Max. "Metaphor." *PAS* 55 (1954) 273–94.
———. "More about Metaphor." In *Metaphor and Thought*, edited by Andrew Ortony, 19–43. New York: Cambridge University Press, 1979.
Bloch, Renée. "Midrash." In *Approaches to Ancient Judaism: Theory and Practice*, edited by William Scott Green, 29–50. Brown Judaic Studies 1. Missoula: Scholars, 1978.
Block, Daniel I. *The Book of Ezekiel*. 2 vols. NICOT. Grand Rapids: Eerdmans, 1997.
———. *Judges, Ruth*. NAC 6. Nashville: Broadman and Holman, 2001.
Boadt, Lawrence. "The Poetry of Prophetic Persuasion: Preserving the Prophet's Persona." *CBQ* 59.1 (1997) 1–21.
Boman, Thorlief. *Hebrew Thought Compared with Greek*. Philadelphia: Westminster, 1960.
Boodberg, Peter A. "On Crypto-Parallelism in Chinese Poetry." In *Cedules from a Berkeley Workshop in Asiatic Philology*, nos. 001–540701. Berkeley, CA: N.P., 1954–55.
———. "Syntactical Metaplasia in Stereoscopic Parallelism." In *Cedules from a Berkeley Workshop in Asiatic Philology*, nos. 017–541210. Berkeley, CA: N.P., 1954–55.
Boos, David. "The Historical Present in John's Gospel." *Selected Technical Articles Related to Translation* 11 (1989) 17–24.
Booth, Steve. *Selected Peak Marking Features in the Gospel of John*. AUS 178. New York: Peter Lang, 1996.
Booth, Wayne C. *The Rhetoric of Fiction*. 2nd ed. Chicago: The University of Chicago Press, 1983
Borchert, Gerald L. *John 1–11*. NAC 25A. Nashville: Broadman and Holman, 1996.
———. *John 12–21*. NAC 25B. Nashville: Broadman and Holman, 2002.

Borgen, Peder. *Bread from Heaven: An Exegetical Study of the Concept of Manna in the Gospel of John and the Writings of Philo.* Leiden: Brill, 1965.

———. "Observation on the Midrashic Character of John 6." *ZNW* 54 (1963) 232–40.

Boring, M. Eugene. "The Influence of Christian Prophecy on the Johannine Portrayal of the Paraclete and Jesus." *NTS* 25 (1978–79) 113–23.

Born, J. B. "Literary Features in the Gospel of John [3:1–21]." *Direction* 17 (1988) 3–17.

Botterweck, G. Johannes, and Helmer Ringgren, eds. *Theological Dictionary of the Old Testament.* Translated by David E. Green. Grand Rapids: Eerdmans, 1980.

Bradley, Mark Alan. *The Functions of Questions in the Fourth Gospel: A Narrative-Critical Inquiry.* PhD diss., Golden Gate Baptist Theological Seminary, 1994.

Braine, David D. C. "The Inner Jewishness of St. John's Gospel as the Clue to the Inner Jewishness of Jesus." *SNTSU* 13 (1988) 101–55.

Brant, Jo-Ann A. *Dialogue and Drama: Elements of Greek Tragedy in the Fourth Gospel.* Peabody: Hendrickson, 2004.

———. "Divine Birth and Apparent Parents: The Plot of the Fourth Gospel." In *Ancient Fiction and Early Christian Narrative*, edited by Ronald F. Hock et al., 199–211. SBLSymS 6. Atlanta: Scholars, 1998.

Brichto, Herbert. *Toward a Grammar of Biblical Poetics: Tales of the Prophets.* New York: Oxford University Press, 1992.

Briggs, Charles A. *General Introduction to the Study of Holy Scripture.* New York: Scribner's, 1899.

Brodie, Thomas L. *The Gospel according to John: A Literary and Theological Commentary.* New York: Oxford University Press, 1993.

———. *The Quest for the Origin of John's Gospel: A Source-Oriented Approach.* New York: Oxford University Press, 1993.

Brown, Colin, ed. *The New International Dictionary of New Testament Theology.* 3 vols. Grand Rapids: Zondervan, 1978.

Brown, Francis, et al. "חָזוֹן." In *BDB* 302–3.

Brown, Raymond E. *The Community of the Beloved Disciple.* New York: Paulist, 1979.

———. *The Gospel according to John (I–XII) Introduction, Translation, and Notes.* AB 29. Garden City, NY: Doubleday, 1966–70.

———. *The Gospel according to John (XIII–XXI) Introduction, Translation, and Notes.* AB 29A. New Haven: Yale University Press, 2008.

———. *An Introduction to the Gospel of John.* Edited by Francis J. Moloney. ABRL. Garden City, NY: Doubleday, 2003.

Brown, Schuyler. "From Burney to Black: The Fourth Gospel and the Aramaic Question." *CBQ* 26 (1964) 323–39.

Bruce, F. F. *Biblical Exegesis in the Qumran Texts.* Grand Rapids: Eerdmans, 1959.

———. *The Gospel of John: Introduction, Exposition, and Notes.* Grand Rapids: Eerdmans, 1983.

Bultmann, Rudolf. *The Gospel of John: A Commentary.* Translated by G. R. Beasley-Murray et al. Philadelphia: Westminster, 1971.

———. *The History of the Synoptic Tradition.* Translated by John Marsh. New York: Harper and Row, 1963.

———. *Primitive Christianity in Its Contemporary Setting.* Translated by R. H. Fuller. New York: Meridian, 1956.

Burnett, Fred W. "Characterization and Reader Construction of Characters in the Gospels." *Semeia* 63 (1993) 3–78.

Burney, C. F. *The Aramaic Origin of the Fourth Gospel.* Oxford: Clarendon, 1922.

———. *The Poetry of Our Lord: An Examination of the Formal Elements of Hebrew Poetry in the Discourses of Jesus Christ.* Oxford: Clarendon, 1925.

Burridge, Richard A. *What Are the Gospels? A Comparison with Graeco-Roman Biography.* SNTSMS 70. Cambridge: Cambridge University Press, 1992.

Buth, Randy. "Mark's Use of the Historical Present." *Notes* 65 (1977) 7–13.

Buttrick, George A., ed. *The Interpreter's Dictionary of the Bible.* 4 vols. Nashville: Abingdon, 1962.

Caird, George B. *The Language and Imagery of the Bible.* Philadelphia: Westminster, 1980.

Campbell, Constantine R. *Advances in the Study of Greek: New Insights for Reading the New Testament.* Grand Rapids: Zondervan, 2015.

———. *Basics of Verbal Aspect in Biblical Greek.* Grand Rapids: Zondervan, 2008.

———. *Verbal Aspect, the Indicative Mood, and Narrative.* New York: Peter Lang, 2007.

Carson, D. A. *The Gospel according to John.* PNTC. Grand Rapids: Eerdmans, 1991.

———. "Understanding Misunderstandings in the Fourth Gospel." *TynBul* 33 (1982) 59–91.

Carson, D. A., and Douglas J. Moo. *An Introduction to the New Testament.* 2nd ed. Grand Rapids: Zondervan, 2005.

Carter, Warren. "Ideological Readings of the Fourth Gospel." In *The Oxford Handbook of Johannine Studies*, edited by Judith M. Lieu and Martinus C. de Boer, 203–19. Oxford: Oxford University Press, 2018.

Casanowicz, Immanuel M. *Paronomasia in the Old Testament.* Baltimore: Johns Hopkins University Press, 1892.

Cassiodorus. *Explanation of the Psalms.* Translated by P. G. Walsh. New York: Paulist, 1990.

———. *Institutions of Divine and Secular Learning and On the Soul.* Translated by James W. Halporn. Liverpool: Liverpool University Press, 2004.

Ceresko, Anthony R. "Janus Parallelism in Amos's 'Oracles Against the Nations' (Amos 1:3—2:16)." *JBL* 113.3 (1994) 485–90.

Chang, Peter S. C. *Repetitions and Variations in the Gospel of John.* PhD diss., Universite des Sciences Humaines de Strasbourg, 1975.

Charlesworth, James H. *The Beloved Disciple: Whose Witness Validates the Gospel of John?* Vallex Forge, PA: Trinity, 1995.

———. *Literary Setting, Textual Studies, Gnosticism, the Dead Sea Scrolls and the Gospel of John.* Vol. 1 in *Critical Reflections on the Odes of Solomon.* JSPSup 22. Sheffield: Sheffield Academic, 1998.

———. "Reinterpreting John: How the Dead Sea Scrolls Have Revolutionized Our Understanding of the Gospel of John." *BRev* 9.1 (1993) 18–25, 54.

Chatman, Seymour Benjamin. *Story and Discourse: Narrative Structure in Fiction and Film.* Ithaca, NY: Cornell University Press, 1980.

Chilton, Bruce. *Targumic Approaches to the Gospels: Essays in the Mutual Definition of Judaism and Christianity.* SJ. New York: University Press of America, 1986.

Chisholm, Robert B. "A Rhetorical Use of Point of View in Old Testament Narrative." *BSac* 159.636 (2002) 404–14.

———. "Wordplay in the Eighth-century Prophets." *BSac* 144.573 (1987) 44–52.

Clifford, Richard J. *Fair Spoken and Persuading: An Interpretation of Second Isaiah.* New York: Paulist, 1984.

Coggins, Richard J. "Keeping up with Recent Studies, 10: The Literary Approach to the Bible." *ExpTim* 96.1 (October 1984) 9–14.

Collins, Raymond F. "Representative Figures." In *These Things Have Been Written: Studies in the Fourth Gospel*, 1–45. Grand Rapids: Eerdmans, 1990.

———. "The Representative Figures of the Fourth Gospel, Part I." *DRev* 94 (1976) 26–46.

———. "The Representative Figures of the Fourth Gospel, Part II." *DRev* 94 (1976) 118–32.

Coloe, Mary L. *God Dwells with Us: Temple Symbolism in the Fourth Gospel*. Collegeville, MN: Liturgical, 2001.

———. "The Structure of the Johannine Prologue and Genesis 1." *ABR* 45 (1997) 40–55.

Cohen, Shaye J. D. *From the Maccabees to the Mishnah*. Louisville: Westminster John Knox, 1987.

Cole, Thomas. *The Origins of Rhetoric in Ancient Greece*. Baltimore: Johns Hopkins University Press, 1991.

Collins, C. John. *Reading Genesis Well: Navigating History, Poetry, Science, and Truth in Genesis 1–11*. Grand Rapids: Zondervan, 2018.

Colwell, Ernest Cadman. *The Greek of the Fourth Gospel: A Study of Its Aramaisms in the Light of Hellenistic Greek*. Chicago: Chicago University Press, 1931.

Conroy, Charles. *Absalom Absalom! Narrative and Language in 2 Sam 13–20*. Rome: Biblical Institute, 1978.

Conway, Colleen M. *Men and Women in the Fourth Gospel*. Atlanta: Society of Biblical Literature, 1999.

———. "Speaking through Ambiguity: Minor Characters in the Fourth Gospel." *BibInt* 10.3 (2002) 324–41.

Conzelmann, Hans. *An Outline of the Theology of the New Testament*. Translated by John Bowden. New York: Harper and Row, 1969.

Cross, Frank M. *The Ancient Library of Qumran and Modern Biblical Studies*. Garden City, NY: Doubleday, 1958.

Cross, Frank M., and D. N. Freedman. *Studies in Ancient Yahwistic Poetry*. 2nd ed. Grand Rapids: Eerdmans, 1997.

Crossan, John D. "It is Written: A Structuralist Analysis of John 6." *Semeia* 26 (1983) 3–21.

———. "'Ruth amid the Alien Corn': Perspectives and Methods in Contemporary Biblical Criticism." In *Biblical Mosaic: Changing Perspectives*, edited by Robert Polzin and Eugene Rothman, 199–210. Philadelphia: Fortress, 1982.

Culler, Jonathan. *On Deconstruction: Theory and Criticism After Structuralism*. Ithaca, NY: Cornell University Press, 1982.

———. *Structuralist Poetics: Structuralism, Linguistics and the Study of Literature*. 2nd ed. New York: Routledge, 2002.

Culpepper, R. Alan. *Anatomy of the Fourth Gospel: A Study in Literary Design*. Philadelphia: Fortress, 1983.

———. *The Gospel and Letters of John*. Nashville: Abingdon, 1998.

———. *John: The Son of Zebedee, the Life of a Legend*. Columbia, SC: University of South Carolina Press, 1994.

———. "The Pivot of John's Prologue." *NTS* 27 (1980–81) 1–31.

Culpepper, R. Alan, and C. C. Black, eds. *Exploring the Fourth Gospel: In Honor of D. Moody Smith*. Louisville: Westminster John Knox, 1996.

Culpepper, R. Alan, and Fernando F. Segovia, eds. *The Fourth Gospel from a Literary Perspective*. Semeia 53. Atlanta: Society of Biblical Literature, 1991.

Dahms, John V. "Isaiah 55:11 and the Gospel of John." *EvQ* 53.2 (1981) 78–88.
Danker, Frederick W., et al. *Greek-English Lexicon of the New Testament and Other Early Christian Literature*. 3rd ed. Chicago: University of Chicago Press, 2000.
Davies, Margaret. *Rhetoric and Reference in the Fourth Gospel*. JSNTSup 69. Sheffield: Sheffield Academic, 1992.
Day, John, *Prophecy and Prophets in Ancient Israel: Proceedings of the Oxford Old Testament Seminar*. New York: T&T Clark, 2010.
Déaut, Roger Le. "Apropos a Definition of Midrash." *Int* 25.3 (1971) 259–82.
Deeks, D. "The Structure of the Fourth Gospel." In *The Gospel of John as Literature: An Anthology of Twentieth-Century Perspectives*, edited by Mark W. G. Stibbe, 107–29. New York: Brill, 1993.
Deissmann, Adolf. *Light from the Ancient East: The New Testament Illustrated by Recently Discovered Texts of the Graeco-Roman World*. Translated by Lionel R. M. Strachan. Rev. ed. New York: George H. Doran, 1927.
Demosthenes, "De Corona." In *De Corona, De Falsa Legatione (18, 19)*, vol. 2, trans. C. A. Vince and J. H. Vince, 3–231. Cambridge, MA: Harvard University Press, 1971.
Derrida, Jacques. *Of Grammatology*. Translated by Gayatri Chakravorty Spivak. Baltimore: Johns Hopkins University Press, 1976.
———. *Writing and Difference*. Translated by Alan Bass. Chicago: University of Chicago Press, 1978.
Dibelius, M. *From Tradition to Gospel*. Greenwood, SC: Attic, 1971.
Dillenberger, John, ed. *Martin Luther: Selections from His Writings*. Garden City, NY: Anchor, 1962.
Dodd, C. H. *Historical Tradition in the Fourth Gospel*. Cambridge: Cambridge University Press, 1965.
———. *The Interpretation of the Fourth Gospel*. Cambridge: Cambridge University Press, 1953.
Duke, Paul. *Irony in the Fourth Gospel*. Atlanta: John Knox, 1985.
Eitan, Israel. "La Repetition de la Racine en Hebreu." *JPOS* (1921) 171–86.
Eliot, T. S. *Selected Essays*. New York: Harcourt, Brace and World, 1964.
Ellenburg, B. Dale. "A Review of Selected Narrative-Critical Conventions in Mark's Use of Miracle Material." *JETS* 38.2 (1995) 171–80.
Ellis, Peter. "Understanding the Concentric Structure of the Fourth Gospel." *SVTQ* 47.1 (2003) 131–54.
Elowsky, Joel C., ed. *John 1–10*. ACCS 4a. Downers Grove, IL: InterVarsity, 2006.
———. *John 11–21*. ACCS 4b. Downers Grove, IL: InterVarsity, 2007.
Emerton, John A. "Relations between Poetry and Prose in the Book of Jeremiah with Special Reference to Jeremiah iii 6–11 and xii 14–17." In *Congress Volume, Vienna, 1980*. Leiden: Brill, 1981.
Empson, William. *Seven Types of Ambiguity: A Study of Effects in English Verse*. 3rd ed. New York: Meridian, 1955.
Ensor, Peter W. "The Johannine Sayings of Jesus and the Question of Authenticity." In *Challenging Perspectives on the Gospel of John*, edited by John Lierman, 14–33. WUNT 2. Reihe 219. Tübingen: Mohr Siebeck, 2006.
Enz, Jacob J. "The Book of Exodus as a Literary Type for the Gospel of John." *JBL* 76 (1957) 208–15.
Estes, Daniel J. "The Hermeneutics of Biblical Lyric Poetry." *BSac* 152.608 (1995) 428.

Estes, Douglas. *The Temporal Mechanics of the Fourth Gospel: A Theory of Hermeneutical Relativity in the Gospel of John*. Boston: Brill, 2008.
Eusebius. *Preparation for the Gospel*. Translated by Edwin H. Gifford. Oxford: Clarendon, 1903.
Evans, Craig A., and Stanley E. Porter, eds. *Dictionary of New Testament Background*. Downers Grove, IL: InterVarsity, 2000.
Fanning, Buist M. *Verbal Aspect in New Testament Greek*. OTM. Oxford: Clarendon, 1990.
Farelly, Nicolas. *The Disciples in the Fourth Gospel: A Narrative Analysis of Their Faith and Understanding*. WUNT 2. Reihe 290. Tübingen: Mohr Siebeck, 2010.
Feldman, Louis H. *Judaism and Hellenism Reconsidered*. Supplements to the Journal for the Study of Judaism 107. Leiden: Brill, 2006.
Fenton, J. C. *The Gospel according to John*. Oxford: Clarendon, 1970.
Firth, D. G. "Ambiguity." In *DOTWPW* 11–13.
Fisch, Harold. *Poetry with a Purpose*. Bloomington: Indiana University Press, 1988.
Fish, Stanley. *Is There a Text in This Class? The Authority of Interpretive Communities*. Cambridge, MA: Harvard University Press, 1980.
Fishbane, Michael. *Biblical Interpretation in Ancient Israel*. Oxford: Clarendon, 1985.
———. "Recent Work on Biblical Narrative." *Prooftexts* 1 (1980) 99–104.
Floyd, Michael H. *Minor Prophets, Part 2*. FOTL 22. Grand Rapids: Eerdmans, 2000.
Fohrer, Georg. "Twofold Aspects of Hebrew Words." In *Words and Meanings: Essays Presented to David Winton Thomas*, edited by Peter R. Ackroyd, 95–103. Cambridge: Cambridge University Press, 1968.
Fokkelman, J. P. *Narrative Art and Poetry in the Books of Samuel*. 4 vols. Assen: Van Gorcum, 1981–93.
———. *Narrative Art in Genesis: Specimens of Stylistic and Structural Analysis*. Assen: Van Gorcum, 1975.
———. *Reading Biblical Narrative: An Introductory Guide*. Translated by Ineke Smit. Louisville, KY: Westminster John Knox, 1999.
———. *Reading Biblical Poetry: An Introductory Guide*. Translated by Ineke Smit. Louisville, KY: Westminster John Knox, 2001.
Forster, E. M. *Aspects of the Novel*. New York: Harcourt, Brace and Company, 1927.
Fortna, Robert. *The Gospel of Signs: A Reconstruction of the Narrative Source Underlying the Fourth Gospel*. London: Cambridge University Press, 1970.
Fowler, Robert. *Let the Reader Understand: Reader-Response Criticism and the Gospel of Mark*. Minneapolis: Fortress, 1991.
France, R. T. "Jewish Historiography, Midrash, and the Gospels." In *Gospel Perspectives: Studies in Midrash and Historiography*, edited by R. T. France and David Wenham, 3:99–127. Sheffield: JSOT Press, 1983.
Freed, Edwin D. "Another Look at Biblical Hebrew Poetry." In *Directions in Biblical Hebrew Poetry*, edited by Elaine R. Follis, 11–28. JSOTSup 40. Sheffield: JSOT Press, 1987.
———. *Old Testament Quotations in the Gospel of John*. NovTSup 11. Leiden: Brill, 1965.
———. "Pottery, Poetry, and Prophecy: An Essay on Biblical Poetry." *JBL* 96.1 (1977) 5–26.
Frei, Hans. *The Eclipse of Biblical Narrative: A Study in Eighteenth and Nineteenth Century Hermeneutics*. New Haven: Yale University Press, 1974.

Fretheim, Terence E. *The Suffering of God: An Old Testament Perspective*. Philadelphia: Fortress, 1984.
Friedman, Norman. "Imagery." In *NPEPP* 559–66.
Frye, Northrop. *Anatomy of Criticism: Four Essays*. 3rd ed. Princeton: Princeton University Press, 1957.
———. *The Great Code: The Bible and Literature*. New York: Harvest, 1982.
Funk, Robert W. *The Poetics of Biblical Narrative*. Sonoma, CA: Polebridge, 1988.
Geller, Stephen A. *Parallelism in Early Biblical Poetry*. HSM 20. Missoula, MT: Scholars, 1979.
Genette, Gérard. *Narrative Discourse: An Essay in Method*. Translated by Jane E. Lewin. Ithaca, NY: Cornell University Press, 1980.
Gevirtz, Stanley. "Of Patriarchs and Puns: Joseph at the Fountain Jacob at the Ford." *HUCA* 46 (1975) 33–54.
Gibbs, J. W. M., ed. *Early Essays by John Stuart Mill*. London: George Bell & Sons, 1897.
Gilfillan, George. *The Bards of the Bible*. New York: Harper, 1874.
Gillingham, Susan E. *The Image, the Depths, and the Surface: Multivalent Approaches to Biblical Study*. New York: Sheffield Academic, 2002.
———. *The Poems and Psalms of the Hebrew Bible*. Oxford Bible Series. Oxford: Oxford University Press, 1994.
Gitay, Yehoshua. *Prophecy and Persuasion: A Study of Isaiah 40–48*. Bonn: Lingustica Biblica, 1981.
———. "Reflections on the Study of Prophetic Discourse: The Question of Isaiah 1:2–20." *VT* 33.2 (1983) 207–21.
Glasson, T. F. *Moses in the Fourth Gospel*. Naperville, IL: A. R. Allenson, 1963.
Golding, Thomas A. "The Imagery of Shepherding in the Bible, Part I." *BSac* 163.649 (2006) 18–28.
Goldingay, John. "Repetition and Variation in the Psalms." *JQR* 68.3 (1977–78) 146–51.
Gordon, Cyrus H. "New Directions." *BASP* 15 (1978) 59–66.
Gordon, Robert P. *"The Place Is Too Small for Us": The Israelite Prophets in Recent Scholarship*. Winona Lake, IN: Eisenbrauns, 1995.
Gray, George B. *The Forms of Hebrew Poetry: Considered with Special Reference to the Criticism and Interpretation of the Old Testament*. New York: Hodder and Stoughton, 1915.
Green, Joel B. *Hearing the New Testament: Strategies for Interpretation*. Grand Rapids: Eerdmans, 1995.
Green, Joel B., et al., eds. *Dictionary of Jesus and the Gospels*. Downers Grove, IL: InterVarsity, 1992.
Greenslade, S. L. *The West from the Reformation to the Present Day*. Vol. 3 of *The Cambridge History of the Bible*. Cambridge: Cambridge University Press, 1975.
Greenstein, E. L. "How Does Parallelism Mean?" In *A Sense of Text: The Art of Language in the Study of Biblical Literature; Papers from a Symposium*, edited by E. L. Greenstein, 41–70. Winona Lake, IN: Eisenbrauns, 1983.
———. "Wordplay, Hebrew." In *ABD* 6:968–71.
Greenwood, David. *Structuralism and the Biblical Text*. New York: Mouton, 1985.
Gregory, John Milton. *The Seven Laws of Teaching*. Rev. ed. Grand Rapids: Baker, 1954.
Griffiths, D. R. "Deutero-Isaiah and the Fourth Gospel: Some Points of Comparison." *ExpTim* 65 (1954) 355–60.
Groden, Michael, and Martin Kreiswirth, eds. *The Johns Hopkins Guide to Literary Theory & Criticism*. Baltimore: Johns Hopkins University Press, 1994.

Grossberg, Daniel. "Multiple Meaning: Part of a Compound Literary Device in the Hebrew Bible." *EAJT* 4.1 (1986) 77–86.

Grudem, Wayne A. *The Gift of Prophecy in 1 Corinthians.* Washington, DC: University Press of America, 1982.

Guillaume, A. "Paronomasia in the Old Testament." *JSS* 9 (1964) 282–90.

Habel, N. "The Form and Significance of the Call Narratives." *ZAW* 77.3 (1965) 297–323.

Haenchen, Ernst. *John 1: A Commentary on the Gospel of John, Chapters 1–6.* Hermeneia. Translated by Robert W. Funk. Philadelphia: Fortress, 1984.

Hallevi, Judah. *Kitab al Khazari.* Translated by Hartwig Hirschfeld. London: George Routledge & Sons, 1905.

Hamid-Khani, Saeed. "Johannine Expressions of Double Meaning: A Literary-Exegetical Analysis." ThM thesis, Dallas Theological Seminary, 1992.

———. *Revelation and Concealment of Christ: A Theological Inquiry into the Elusive Language of the Fourth Gospel.* WUNT 2. Reihe 120. Tübingen: Mohr Siebeck, 2000.

Hamilton, James M. "The Influence of Isaiah on the Gospel of John." *Perichoresis* 5.2 (2007) 139–62.

Hammermeister, Kai. *The German Aesthetic Tradition.* Cambridge: Cambridge University Press, 2002.

Han, Chul-Hee. *The Use of Misunderstanding in the Fourth Gospel.* ThM Thesis, Dallas Theological Seminary, 2009.

Hanson, Anthony T. *The Prophetic Gospel: A Study of John and the Old Testament.* Edinburgh: T&T Clark, 1991.

Harstine, Stanley Dwight. *The Functions of Moses as a Character in the Fourth Gospel and Responses of Three Ancient Mediterranean Audiences.* PhD diss., Baylor University, 1999.

———. *Moses as a Character in the Fourth Gospel: A Study of Ancient Reading Techniques.* New York: Sheffield Academic, 2002.

Harvey, W. J. *Character and the Novel.* Ithaca, NY: Cornell University Press, 1965.

Hawkins, John C. *Horae Synopticae.* 2nd ed. Grand Rapids: Baker, 1968.

Hays, Richard B. *Echoes of Scripture in the Letters of Paul.* New Haven: Yale University Press, 1989.

Hendriksen, William. *Exposition of the Gospel according to John: Two Volumes Complete in One.* NTC. Grand Rapids: Baker, 1979.

Hengel, Martin. *The Johannine Question.* Philadelphia: Trinity Press International, 1989.

———. *Judaism and Hellenism: Studies in Their Encounter in Palestine during the Early Hellenistic Period.* 2 vols. Philadelphia: Fortress, 1974.

———. "The Old Testament in the Fourth Gospel." *HBT* 12 (1990) 19–41.

Heschel, Abraham J. *The Prophets.* New York: Harper and Row, 1962.

Hill, David. *New Testament Prophecy.* Atlanta: John Knox, 1979.

———. "On the Evidence for the Creative Role of Christian Prophets." *NTS* 20.3 (1974) 262–74.

———. "Prophecy and Prophets in the Revelation of St John." *NTS* 18.4 (July 1972) 401–18.

Hirsch, E. D. *Aims of Interpretation.* Chicago: University of Chicago Press, 1976.

———. *Validity in Interpretation.* New Haven: Yale University Press, 1967.

Hoare, Frederick R. *The Original Order and Chapters of St. John's Gospel.* London: Burns, Oates & Washbourne, 1944.
Holladay, William L. "Prototype and Copies: A New Approach to the Poetry-Prose Problem in the Book of Jeremiah." *JBL* 79.4 (1960) 351–67.
Horace. *Art of Poetry.* Translated by Daniel Bagot. London: William Blackwood and Sons, 1863.
Hoskyns, Edwyn C. *The Fourth Gospel.* London: Faber & Faber, 1947.
House, Paul R., ed. *Beyond Form Criticism: Essays in Old Testament Literary Criticism.* Winona Lake, IN: Eisenbrauns, 1992.
Hrushovski, Benjamin. "Note on the Systems of Hebrew Versification." In *Penguin Book of Hebrew Verse,* edited by T. Carmi, 57–72. New York: Penguin, 1981.
Hunt, Steven A., D. Francois Tolmie, and Ruben Zimmermann, eds. *Character Studies in the Fourth Gospel: Narrative Approaches to Seventy Figures in John.* Grand Rapids: Eerdmans, 2016.
Hunter, Archibald M. *The Gospel according to John.* CBC. Cambridge: Cambridge University Press, 1965.
Hurd, Richard. *A Dissertation on the Idea of Universal Poetry.* London: A. Millar, 1766.
Iser, Wolfgang. *The Act of Reading: A Theory of Aesthetic Response.* Baltimore: Johns Hopkins University Press, 1978.
Jackson, H. J., and J. R. de J. Jackson, eds. *Shorter Works and Fragments.* 2 vols. *The Collected Works of Samuel Taylor Coleridge, Volume 11.* Princeton: Princeton University Press, 1995.
Jakobson, Roman. "Concluding Statement: Linguistics and Poetics." In *Style in Language,* edited by Thomas A. Sebeok, 350–77. Cambridge, MA: MIT Press, 1960.
———. "Grammatical Parallelism and Its Russian Facet." *Language* 42.2 (1966) 399–429.
———. "The Structuralists and the Bible." *Int* 28.2 (1974) 146–64.
———. *Word and Language. Selected Writings, Volume 2.* Gravenhage: Mouton, 1971.
James, J. Courtenay. *The Language of Palestine and Adjacent Regions.* Edinburgh: T&T Clark, 1920.
Jepsen, A. "חָזָה, *chāzāh.*" In *TDOT* 4:280–90.
Jeremias, Joachim. *New Testament Theology.* New York: Scribner's, 1971.
———. "נָבִיא." In *TLOT* 2:697–710.
Jones, L. P. *The Symbol of Water in the Gospel of John.* Journal for the Study of the New Testament Supplement Series 145. Sheffield: Sheffield, 1997.
Josephus. *Jewish Antiquities, Books 1–4.* Vol. 4 of *Joseph.* LCL. Translated by H. St. J. Thackerary. Cambridge, MA: Harvard University Press, 1961.
———. *Jewish Antiquities, Books 5–8.* Vol. 5 of *Joseph.* LCL. Translated by H. St. J. Thackerary. Cambridge, MA: Harvard University Press, 1958.
———. *The Life, Against Apion.* Vol. 1 of *Joseph.* LCL. Translated by H. St. J. Thackerary. Cambridge, MA: Harvard University Press, 1961.
———. *The Works of Josephus: Complete and Unabridged.* Edited by William Whiston. Peabody: Hendrickson, 1987.
Kalimi, Isaac. *The Reshaping of Ancient Israelite History in Chronicles.* Winona Lake: Eisenbrauns, 2005.
Kant, Immanuel. *Critique of Judgment.* Translated by J. H. Bernard. 2nd ed. London: Macmillan and Co., 1914.

Kaplan, Grant. *René Girard, Unlikely Apologist: Mimetic Theory and Fundamental Theology*. Notre Dame: University of Notre Dame Press, 2016.

Kaufman, Stephen A., ed. *Targum Jonathan to the Prophets*. Comprehensive Aramaic Lexicon. Cincinnati: Hebrew Union College, 2005.

Käsemann, Ernst. *The Testament of Jesus: A Study of the Gospel of John in the Light of Chapter 17*. Translated by Gerhard Krodel. Philadelphia: Fortress, 1968.

Kealy, Seán P. *John's Gospel and the History of Biblical Interpretation*. 2 vols. Lewiston, NY: Edwin Melen, 2002.

Keegan, Terence. *Interpreting the Bible: A Popular Introduction to Biblical Hermeneutics*. New York: Paulist, 1985.

Keener, Craig S. *The Gospel of John: A Commentary*. 2 vols. Peabody, MA: Hendrickson, 2003.

Kennedy, George A. "An Introduction to the Rhetoric of the Gospels." *Rhetorica* 1.2 (1983) 17–31.

———. *The Art of Persuasion in Greece*. Princeton: Princeton University Press, 1963.

———. *Comparative Rhetoric: An Historical and Cross-Cultural Introduction*. New York: Oxford University Press, 1997.

———. *New Testament Interpretation through Rhetorical Criticism*. Chapel Hill, NC: University of North Carolina Press, 1984.

Kermode, F. "St. John as Poet." *JSNT* 28 (1986) 3–16.

Kerr, Alan R. *The Temple of Jesus' Body: The Temple Theme in the Gospel of John*. Journal for the Study of the New Testament Supplement Series 220. New York: Sheffield Academic, 2002.

Kikawada, Isaac. *Before Abraham Was: The Unity of Genesis 1–11*. Nashville: Abingdon, 1985.

Kingsbury, Jack. *Matthew as Story*. Philadelphia: Fortress, 1986.

Klappert, K. "Word." *NIDNTT* 3:1081–146.

Knight, Douglas A., and Gene M. Tucker, eds. *The Hebrew Bible and Its Modern Interpreters*. Philadelphia: Fortress, 1985.

Koehler, Ludwig et al. "חָזוֹן." In *HALOT* 1:301–2.

———. "היה." In *HALOT* 1:243–44.

Koester, Craig. *Symbolism in the Fourth Gospel: Meaning, Mystery, Community*. Minneapolis: Fortress, 1995.

Köstenberger, Andreas J. *John*. BECNT. Grand Rapids: Baker Academics, 2004.

Krieger, Murray. *A Window to Criticism: Shakespeare's Sonnets and Modern Poetics*. Princeton: Princeton University Press, 1964.

Kselman, John S. "Janus Parallelism in Psalm 75:2." *JBL* 121.3 (2002) 531–32.

Kugel, James L. *The Idea of Biblical Poetry: Parallelism and Its History*. New Haven: Yale University Press, 1981.

Kümmel, Werner Georg. *Introduction to the New Testament*. Translated by Howard Clark Kee. Nashville: Abingdon, 1975.

———. *The New Testament: The History of the Investigation of its Problems*. Nashville: Abingdon, 1972.

Kwon, Jongseon. *A Rhetorical Analysis of the Johannine Farewell Discourse*. PhD diss., Southern Baptist Theological Seminary, 1993.

Kysar, Robert. "Coming Hermeneutical Earthquake in Johannine Interpretation." In *"What Is John?" Readers and Readings of the Fourth Gospel*, edited by Fernando F. Segovia, 1:185–98. SBLSymS 3. Atlanta: Scholars, 1996.

———. *The Fourth Evangelist and His Gospel: An Examination of Contemporary Scholarship*. Minneapolis: Augsburg, 1975.

Lampe, G. W. H. *The West from the Fathers to the Reformation*. Vol. 2 of *The Cambridge History of the Bible*. Cambridge: Cambridge University Press, 1975.

Lanser, Susan Sniader. *The Narrative Act: Point of View in Prose Fiction*. Princeton: Princeton University Press, 1981.

Larsen, Kasper Bro. "Introduction: The Gospel of John as Genre Mosaic." In *The Gospel of John as Genre Mosaic*, edited by Kasper Bro Larsen, 13–24. Bristol, CT: Vandenhoeck & Ruprecht, 2015.

Lea, Thomas D. "The Reliability of History in John's Gospel." *JETS* 38.3 (1995) 387–402.

Lee, Dorothy A. *Flesh and Glory: Symbol, Gender, and Theology in the Gospel of John*. New York: Crossroad, 2002.

———. *The Symbolic Narratives of the Fourth Gospel: The Interplay of Form and Meaning*. JSNTSup 95. Sheffield: Sheffield Academic, 1994.

Leon, Judah Messer. *The Book of the Honeycomb's Flow*. Edited by Isaac Rabinowitz. Ithaca, NY: Cornell University Press, 1983.

Lehtipuu, Outi. "Characterization and Persuasion: The Rich Man and the Poor Man in Luke 16:19–31." In *Characterization in the Gospels: Reconceiving Narrative Criticism*, edited by David Rhoads and Kari Syreeni, 73–105. JSNTSup 184. Sheffield: Sheffield Academic, 1999.

Leung, Mavis M. "The Narrative Function and Verbal Aspect of the Historical Present in the Fourth Gospel." *JETS* 51.4 (2008) 703–20.

Lévi-Strauss, Claude. *Structural Anthropology*. New York: Basic, 1963.

Levinsohn, Stephen H. *Discourse Features of New Testament Greek: A Coursebook on the Information Structure of New Testament Greek*. 2nd ed. Dallas: SIL International, 2000.

Lightfoot, Joseph B. *Biblical Essays*. London: Macmillan, 1904.

Lightfoot, R. H. *St. John's Gospel: A Commentary*. Oxford: Clarendon, 1956.

Lincoln, Andrew T. *The Gospel according to Saint John*. BNTC. London: Continuum, 2005.

———. *Truth on Trial: The Lawsuit Motif in the Fourth Gospel*. Peabody, MA: Hendrickson, 2000.

Lindars, Barnabas. *The Gospel of John*. NCB. Grand Rapids: Eerdmans, 1972.

———. *New Testament Apologetic*. London: SCM, 1961.

———. "Traditions Behind the Fourth Gospel." In *L'Evangile de Jean: Sources, rédaction, théologie*, edited by Marinus de Jonge, 107–24. BETL 44. Leuven: Leuven University Press, 1977.

Lindblom, J. *Prophecy in Ancient Israel*. Philadelphia: Fortress, 1962.

Lipson, Carol S., and Roberta A. Binkley, eds. *Rhetoric Before and Beyond the Greeks*. Albany: State University of New York Press, 2004.

Longenecker, Bruce W. *Rhetoric at the Boundaries: The Art and Theology of the New Testament Chain-Link Transitions*. Waco, TX: Baylor University Press, 2005.

Longenecker, Richard N. *The Christology of Early Jewish Christianity*. 1970. Reprint, Grand Rapids: Baker, 1981.

Longinus. "On the Sublime." In *Aristotle, the Poetics; "Longinus" on the Sublime; Demetrius on Style*, translated by W. Hamilton Fyfe, 143–308. LCL. Cambridge, MA: Harvard University Press, 1982.

Longman, Tremper, III. *How to Read Daniel*. Downers Grove, IL: IVP Academic, 2020.

———. *How to Read Exodus*. Downers Grove, IL: IVP Academic, 2009.

———. *How to Read Genesis*. Downers Grove, IL: IVP Academic, 2005.

———. *How to Read Proverbs* (Downers Grove, IL: IVP Academic, 2002

———. "The Literary Approach to the Study of the Old Testament: Promise and Pitfalls." *JETS* 28.4 (1985) 385–98.

———. "Terseness." *DOTWPW* 791–94.

Longman, Tremper, III, and Peter Enns, eds. *Dictionary of the Old Testament: Wisdom, Poetry and Writings*. Downers Grove, IL: InterVarsity, 2008.

Louis, Kenneth R. R. Gros. *Literary Interpretations of Biblical Narratives*. 2 vols. Nashville: Abingdon, 1982.

Louw, Johannes P. "On Johannine Style." *Neot* 20 (1986) 5–12.

Louw, Johannes P., and Eugene A. Nida. *Greek-English Lexicon of the New Testament Based on Semantic Domains*. 2nd ed. New York: United Bible Society, 1989.

Lowth, Robert. *Isaiah: A New Translation with a Preliminary Dissertation and Notes*. Glasgow: Glasgow University Press, 1822.

———. *Lectures on the Sacred Poetry of the Hebrews*. 2 vols. Translated by G. Gregory. Boston: Joseph T. Buckingham, 1815.

Lucas, E. C. "Poetics, Terminology." In *DOTWPW* 520–25.

Lund, N. W. *Chiasmus in the New Testament*. Chapel Hill: University of North Carolina Press, 1942.

———. "The Influence of Chiasmus upon the Structure of the Gospels." *AThR* 13 (1931) 27–48, 405–33.

Lundbom, Jack R. *Jeremiah: A Study in Ancient Hebrew Rhetoric*. Winona Lake, IN: Eisenbrauns, 1997.

MacGregor, G. H. C., and A. Q. Morton. *The Structure of the Fourth Gospel*. Edinburgh: Oliver & Boyd, 1961.

Malbon, Elizabeth Struthers. "Structuralism, Hermeneutics, and Contextual Meaning." *JAAR* 51.2 (1983) 207–30.

Malherbe, Abraham J., et al., eds. *The Early Church in Its Context: Essays in Honor of Everett Ferguson*. Boston: Brill, 1998.

Manning, Gary T. *Echoes of a Prophet: The Use of Ezekiel in the Gospel of John and in Literature of the Second Temple Period*. New York: T&T Clark, 2004.

Martin, W. J. "'Dischronologized' Narrative in the Old Testament." *Congress Volume Rome*. VTSup 17. Leiden: Brill, 1969.

Martin, Wallace. "Metaphor." *NPEPP* 760–66.

Maynard, Arthur H. *The Function of Apparent Synonyms and Ambiguous Words in the Fourth Gospel*. PhD diss., University of Southern California, 1950.

Menken, Maarten J. J. *Old Testament Quotations in the Fourth Gospel*. Kampen: Pharos, 1996.

McFague, Sallie. *Metaphorical Theology: Models of God in Religious Language*. Philadelphia: Fortress, 1982.

McKnight, Edgar V. *The Bible and the Reader: An Introduction to Literary Criticism*. Philadelphia: Fortress, 1985.

———. *Meaning in Texts: The Historical Shaping of a Narrative Hermeneutics*. Philadelphia: Fortress, 1978.

———. *Post-Modern Use of the Bible: The Emergence of Reader-Oriented Criticism*. Nashville: Abingdon, 1990.

———. "Structure and Meaning in Biblical Narrative." *PRSt* 3.1 (March 1976) 4–20.

McKnight, Edgar V., and Elizabeth Struthers Malbon, eds. *The New Literary Criticism and the New Testament*. Valley Forge, PA: Trinity Press Internaitonal, 1994.

McKnight, Scot, and Grant R. Osborne, eds. *The Face of New Testament Studies: A Survey of Recent Research*. Grand Rapids: Baker Academic, 2004.

Manning, Gary T. *Echoes of a Prophet: The Use of Ezekiel in the Gospel of John and in Literature of the Second Temple Period*. JSNTSup 270. London: T&T Clark, 2004.

McWhirter, Jocelyn. *The Bridegroom Messiah and the People of God: Marriage in the Fourth Gospel*. SNTSMS 138. New York: Cambridge University Press, 2006.

Meeks, Wayne A. *The Prophet-King: Moses Traditions and the Johannine Christology*. Leiden: Brill, 1967.

Meier, Samuel A. *Speaking of Speaking: Marking Direct Discourse in the Hebrew Bible*. VTSup. New York: Brill, 1992.

———. *Themes and Transformations in Old Testament Prophecy*. Downers Grove, IL: IVP Academic, 2009.

Melberg, Arne. "Plato's 'Mimesis.'" In *Theories of Mimesis*, 10–50. Cambridge: Cambridge University Press, 1995.

Menken, Maarten J. J. "Allusions to the Minor Prophets in the Fourth Gospel." *Neot* 44.1 (2010) 67–84.

Merenlahti, Petri. *Poetics for the Gospels? Rethinking Narrative Criticism*. New York: T. & T. Clark, 2002.

Michaels, J. Ramsey. *The Gospel of John*. NICNT. Grand Rapids: Eerdmans, 2010.

Miller, C. L. "Ellipsis." In *DOTWPW* 156–60.

Mitchell, W. J. T. "Image." In *NPEPP* 556–59.

Mlakuzhyil, George. *The Christocentric Literary Structure of the Fourth Gospel*. Analecta Biblica 117. Rome: Pontifical Biblical Institute, 1987.

Moloney, Francis J. *Belief in the Word: Reading the Fourth Gospel, John 1–4*. Minneapolis: Fortress, 1993.

———. *Glory Not Dishonor: Reading John 13–21*. Minneapolis: Fortress, 1998.

———. *The Gospel of John*. SP 4. Collegeville, MN: Liturgical, 1998.

———. *Signs and Shadows: Reading John 5–12*. Minneapolis: Fortress, 1996.

Möller, Karl. *Prophet in Debate: The Rhetoric of Persuasion in the Book of Amos*. Sheffield: Sheffield, 2009.

Moore, Stephen D. "Are There Impurities in the Living Water that the Johannine Jesus Dispenses? Deconstruction, Feminism, and the Samaritan Woman." *BibInt* 1.2 (July 1993) 207–27.

———. "Illuminating the Gospels Without the Benefit of Color: A Plea for Concrete Criticism." *JAAR* 60.2 (1992) 257–79.

———. *Literary Criticism and the Gospels: The Theoretical Challenge*. New Haven: Yale University Press, 1989.

Morgan, Richard. "Fulfillment in the Fourth Gospel." *Int* 11 (1957) 155–65.

Morris, Leon. *The Gospel according to John*. NICNT. Rev. ed. Grand Rapids: Eerdmans, 1995.

———. *Studies in the Fourth Gospel*. Grand Rapids: Eerdmans, 1969.

Moulton, J. H., and W. F. Howard. *A Grammar of New Testament Greek*. 4 vols. Edinburgh: T&T Clark, 1919–76.

Mowinckel, Sigmund. *The Psalms in Israel's Worship*. 2 vols. Nashville: Abingdon, 1962.

Muilenburg, James. "Form Criticism and Beyond." *JBL* 88.1 (1969) 1–18.

———. "A Study in Hebrew Rhetoric: Repetition and Style." In *Congress Volume: Copenhagen, 1953*, edited by G Anderson, 97–111. Leiden: Brill, 1953.

Myers, Alicia D. *Characterizing Jesus: A Rhetorical Analysis on the Fourth Gospel's Use of Scripture in Its Presentation of Jesus*. London: T&T Clark, 2012.

Napier, B. D. "Prophet, Prophetism." In *IDB* 3:896–919.

Neusner, Jacob, ed. *Tractate Shabbat*. Vol. 2 in *The Babylonian Talmud*. Peabody, MA: Hendrickson, 2005.

New International Dictionary of Old Testament Theology and Exegesis. Edited by William A. VanGemeren. 5 vols. Grand Rapids, MI: Zondervan, 2012.

New Oxford American Dictionary. 3rd ed. Edited by Angus Stevenson and Christine A. Lindberg. New York: Oxford University Press, 2010.

Ng, W.-Y. *Water Symbolism in John: An Eschatological Interpretation*. New York: P. Lang, 2001.

Niccacci, Alviero. *The Syntax of the Verb in Classical Hebrew Prose*. JSOTSup 86. Translated by Wilfred G. E. Watson. Sheffield: Sheffield Academic, 1990.

The Nicene and Post-Nicene Fathers, Series 1. Edited by Philip Schaff. 1886–1889. 14 vols. Reprint. Peabody, MA: Hendrickson, 1994.

The Nicene and Post-Nicene Fathers, Series 2. Edited by Philip Schaff. 1886–1890. 14 vols. Reprint. Peabody, MA: Hendrickson, 1994.

Nicol, Willem. *The Sēmeia of the Fourth Gospel: Tradition and Redaction*. Leiden: Brill, 1972.

———, ed. *Essays on the Jewish Background of the Fourth Gospel*. Pretoria: University of South Africa, 1972.

Nietzsche, Friedrich. *The Will to Power*. Translated by Walter Kaufmann. New York: Vintage, 1967.

Noegel, Scott B. "Janus Parallelism in Job and Its Literary Significance." *JBL* 115.2 (June 1996) 313–20.

———. *Janus Parallelism in the Book of Job*. JSOTSup 223. Sheffield: Sheffield Academic, 1996.

Noonan, Benjamin J. *Advances in the Study of Biblical Hebrew and Aramaic: New Insights for Reading the Old Testament*. Grand Rapids: Zondervan Academic, 2020.

O'Conner, M. *Hebrew Verse Structure*. Winona Lake, IN: Eisenbrauns, 1997.

O'Day, Gail R. "The Gospel of John." *NIB* 9. Nashville: Abingdon, 1995.

———. *Revelation in the Fourth Gospel*. Philadelphia: Fortress, 1986.

O'Rourke, John J. "Asides in the Gospel of John." *NovT* 21 (1979) 210–19.

———. "The Historic Present in the Gospel of John." *JBL* 93 (1974) 585–90.

Okure, Teresa. *The Johannine Approach to Mission: A Contextual Study of John 4:1–42*. WUNT 2. Reihe 31. Tübingen: J. C. B. Mohr, 1988.

Oliver, M. *A Poetry Handbook*. San Diego: Harcourt Brace, 1994.

Olson, Robert C. *The Contribution of John 12:38 to the Structure and Theology of the Fourth Gospel*. ThM diss., Trinity Evangelical Divinity School, 1999.

Olsson, Birger. *Structure and Meaning in the Fourth Gospel: A Text-Linguistic Analysis of John 2:1–11 and 4:1–42*. ConBNT 6. Translated by Jean Gray. Lund: CWK Gleerup, 1974.

Ong, Walter J. *Interfaces of the Word: Studies in the Evolution of Consciousness and Culture*. Ithaca, NY: Cornell University Press, 1977.

Osborne, Grant R. *The Hermeneutical Spiral: A Comprehensive Introduction to Biblical Interpretation*. Rev. ed. Downers Grove, IL: InterVarsity, 2006.

Oswalt, John N. *The Book of Isaiah*. 2 vols. Grand Rapids: Eerdmans, 1998.

Østenstad, Gunnar H. *Patterns of Redemption in the Fourth Gospel: An Experiment in Structural Analysis*. Lewiston, NY: E. Mellen, 1998.

———. "The Structure of the Fourth Gospel: Can It Be Defined Objectively?" *ST* 45 (1991) 33–55.
Painter, John. *John: Witness and Theologian*. London: SPCK, 1975.
Pardee, D. *Ugaritic and Hebrew Poetic Parallelism: A Trial Cut ('nt I and Proverbs 2)*. Leiden: Brill, 1988.
Parsenios, George L. *Departure and Consolation: The Johannine Farewell Discourses in Light of Greco-Roman Literature*. NovTSup 117. Leiden: Brill, 2005.
———. *Rhetoric and Drama in the Johannine Lawsuit Motif*. WUNT 258. Tübingen: Mohr Siebeck, 2010.
Parsons, Mikeal C., et al., eds. *Anatomies of the Gospels and Beyond: Essays in Honor of R. Alan Culpepper*. Leiden: Brill, 2018.
Pater, Walter H. *Studies in the History of the Renaissance*. London: Macmillan, 1873.
Patte, Daniel. *Structural Exegesis for New Testament Critics*. Minneapolis: Fortress, 1990.
———. *What Is Structural Exegesis?* Philadelphia: Fortress, 1976.
Patton, Matthew H., and Frederic Clarke Putnam. *Basics of Hebrew Discourse: A Guide to Working with Hebrew Prose and Poetry*. Edited by Miles V. Van Pelt. Grand Rapids: Zondervan Academics, 2019.
Paul, Shalom M., and S. David Sperling. "Prophets and Prophecy." *EncJud* 16:566–86.
Pedersen, Johannes. *Israel: Its Life and Culture*. Vol. 1. London: Oxford University Press, 1926.
Peisker, C. H., and Colin Brown. "Prophet." In *NIDNTT* 3:74–92.
Perrine, Laurence. *Sound and Sense: An Introduction to Poetry*. 7th ed. San Diego: Harcourt Brace Jovanovich, 1987.
Petersen, David L., and Kent Harold Richards. *Interpreting Hebrew Poetry*. Minneapolis: Fortress, 1992.
Petersen, David L. "Prophet, Prophecy." In *NIDB* 4:622–48.
Petersen, Norman R. *Literary Criticism for New Testament Critics*. Philadelphia: Fortress, 1978.
Phillips, Peter M. *The Prologue of the Fourth Gospel: A Sequential Reading*. New York: T&T Clark, 2006.
Philo. *The Works of Philo: Complete and Unabridged*. Translated by Charles Duke Yonge. Peabody, MA: Hendrickson, 1995.
Plato. *The Dialogues of Plato*. Vol. 1. Translated by B. Jowett. New York: Random House, 1920.
Plummer, Alfred. *The Gospel according to S. John*. CGTSC. Cambridge: Cambridge University Press, 1896.
Polzin, Robert. *Biblical Structuralism: Method and Subjectivity in the Study of Ancient Texts*. Philadelphia: Fortress, 1977.
Porter, Stanley E. "Discourse Analysis and New Testament Studies: An Introductory Survey." In *Discourse Analysis and Other Topics in Biblical Greek*, edited by Stanley E. Porter and D. A. Carson, 14–35. Sheffield: Sheffield Academic, 1995.
———, ed. *Handbook of Classical Rhetoric in the Hellenistic Period 330 B.C.–A.D. 400*. New York: Brill, 1997.
———, ed. *Hearing the Old Testament in the New Testament*. Grand Rapids: Eerdmans, 2006.
———. *Idioms of Greek New Testament*. Sheffield: JSOT Press, 1992.
———. "Prominence: An Overview." In *The Linguist as Pedagogue: Trends in the Teaching and Linguisitic Analysis of the Greek New Testament*, edited by Stanley E. Porter and Matthew Brook O'Donnell, 45–74. Sheffield: Sheffield Phoenix, 2009.

———. *Verbal Aspect in the Greek of the New Testament: With Reference to Tense and Mood.* SBG 1. New York: Peter Lang, 1989.

Porter, Stanley E., and Thomas H. Olbricht. *Rhetoric and the New Testament: Essays from the 1992 Heidelberg Conference.* Sheffield: JSOT Press, 1993.

Powell, Mark. *The Bible and Modern Literary Criticism: A Critical Assessment and Annotated Bibliography.* New York: Greenwood, 1992.

———. *What Is Narrative Criticism?* Minneapolis: Fortress, 1991.

Poythress, Vern S. "Structuralism and Biblical Studies." *JETS* 21 (1978) 221–37.

Preuss, Horst Dietrich. *Old Testament Theology.* 2 vols. Louisville: Westminster John Knox, 1992.

Propp, Vladimir. *Morphology of the Folktale.* 2nd ed. Austin: University of Texas Press, 1968.

Regt, L. J. de, et al., eds. *Literary Structure and Rhetorical Strategies in the Hebrew Bible.* Assen, the Netherlands: Van Gorcum, 1996.

Reim, Günter. *Studien zum alttestamentlichen hintergrund des Johannesevangeliums.* Cambridge: Cambridge University Press, 1974.

Reinhartz, A. "Jesus as Prophet: Predictive Prolepses in the Fourth Gospel." *JSNT* 36 (1989) 3–16.

Renan, Ernest. *Life of Jesus.* Boston: Little, Brown, & Co., 1915.

Rendsburg, Gary A. "Janus parallelism in Gen 49:26." *JBL* 99.2 (1980) 291–93.

Resseguie, James L. "A Narrative-Critical Approach to the Fourth Gospel." In *Characters and Characterization in the Gospel of John*, edited by Christopher W. Skinner, 3–17. LNTS 461. London: Bloomsbury, 2013.

———. *Narrative Criticism of the New Testament: An Introduction.* Grand Rapids: Baker Academic, 2005.

———. *The Strange Gospel: Narrative Design and Point of View in John.* Boston: Brill, 2001.

Rhoads, David M. *Israel in Revolution: 6–74 C.E.* Philadelphia: Fortress, 1976.

———. "Jesus and the Syrophoenician Woman in Mark: A Narrative-Critical Study." *JAAR* 62.2 (1994) 343–76.

———. "Narrative Criticism and the Gospel of Mark." *JAAR* 50.3 (1982) 411–34.

Rhoads, David M., and Donald Michie. *Mark as Story: An Introduction to the Narrative of a Gospel.* Philadelphia: Fortress, 1982.

Richard, E. "Expressions of Double Meaning and Their Function in the Gospel of John." *NTS* 31 (1985) 96–112.

Richards, I. A. *The Philosophy of Rhetoric.* New York: Oxford University Press, 1950.

———. *Principles of Literary Criticism.* London: Kegan Paul, Trench, Trubner & Co., 1930.

Ricoeur, Paul. *Time and Narrative.* Vol. 1. Chicago: University of Chicago Press, 1984.

Ridderbos, Herman, *The Gospel according to John: A Theological Commentary.* Translated by John Vriend. Grand Rapids: Eerdmans, 1997.

Rimmon-Kenan, S. *Narrative Fiction: Contemporary Poetics.* London: Methuen, 1983.

Robinson, John A. T. *Can We Trust the New Testament?* Grand Rapids: Eerdmans, 1977.

———. *The Priority of John.* Edited by J. F. Coakley. Oak Park, IL: Meyer-Stone Books, 1987.

———. "The Relation of the Prologue to the Gospel of St. John." *NTS* 9 (1962–63) 120–29.

Rossi, Azariah ben Moses dei. *The Light of the Eyes.* Yale Judaica Series 31. Translated by Joanna Weinberg. New Haven: Yale University Press, 2001.

Roth, Cecil, ed. *Encyclopaedia Judaica*. Jerusalem: Keter, 1972.
Ruckstuhl, E. *Die literarische Einheit des Johannesevangeliums*. Göttingen: Vandenhoeck und Ruprecht, 1987.
Runge, Steven E. *Discourse Grammar of the Greek New Testament: A Practical Introduction for Teaching and Exegesis*. Bellingham: Lexham, 2010.
———. "Pragmatic Effects of Semantically Redundant Anchoring Expressions in Biblical Hebrew Narrative." *JNSL* 32.2 (2006) 85–102.
Ryken, Leland. "The Bible as Literature. Pt 1, 'Words of Delight': The Bible as Literature." *BSac* 147.585 (1990) 3–15.
———. "The Bible as Literature. Pt 2, 'And It Came to Pass': The Bible as God's Storybook." *BSac* 147.586 (1990) 131–42.
———. "The Bible as Literature. Pt 3, 'I Have Used Similitudes': The Poetry of the Bible." *BSac* 147.587 (1990) 259–69.
———. "The Bible as Literature. Pt 4, 'With Many Parables': The Imagination as Means of Grace." *BSac* 147.588 (1990) 387–98.
———. *How Bible Stories Work: A Guided Study of Biblical Narrative*. Bellingham, WA: Lexham, 2015.
———. *How to Read the Bible as Literature*. Grand Rapids: Zondervan, 1984.
———. *Jesus the Hero: A Guided Literary Study of the Gospels*. Bellingham, WA: Lexham, 2016.
———. *Letters of Grace & Beauty: A Guided Literary Study of New Testament Epistles*. Bellingham, WA: Lexham, 2016.
———. "Metaphor in the Psalms." *Christianity and Literature* 31.3 (1982) 9–29.
———. *Short Sentences Long Remembered: A Guided Study of Proverbs and Other Wisdom Literature*. Bellingham, WA: Lexham, 2016.
———. *Sweeter than Honey, Richer than Gold: A Guided Study of Biblical Poetry*. Bellingham, WA: Lexham, 2015.
———. *Symbols and Reality: A Guided Study of Prophecy, Apocalypse, and Visionary Literature*. Bellingham, WA: Lexham, 2016.
———. *Words of Delight: A Literary Introduction to the Bible*. Grand Rapids: Baker, 1987.
———. *Words of Life: A Literary Introduction to the New Testament*. Grand Rapids: Baker, 1987.
Ryken, Leland, et al., eds. "Introduction." *DBIm* xiii–xxi.
Sabou, Marius. "A Critical Analysis of Rhetorical Method in the Fourth Gospel with Particular Reference to the Contribution of John 7:1–52." PhD diss., Queen's University Belfast, 2012.
Sacks, Sheldon. *On Metaphor*. Chicago: Chicago University Press, 1979.
Sakenfeld, Katharine Doob, ed. Vol. 4 in *The New Interpreter's Dictionary of the Bible*. Nashville: Abingdon, 2006.
Saussure, Ferdinand de. *Course in General Linguistics*. New York: McGraw-Hill, 1966.
Schlatter, A. *Die Sprache und Heimat des vierten Evangelisten*. Gütersloh: Bertelsmann, 1902.
Schmiedel, Paul W. *The Johannine Writings*. Translated by Maurice A. Canney. London: Adam and Charles Black, 1908.
Schnackenburg, Rudolf. *The Gospel according to St. John*. 3 vols. Translated by Kevin Smyth. New York: Herder & Herder, 1968–82.
Schneider, K. F. *Die Aechtheit des Johanneischen Evangeliums*. Berlin: Wiegandt und Grieben, 1854.

Schneiders, S. M. "History and Symbolism in the Fourth Gospel." In *L'Evangile de Jean: Sources, rédaction, théologie*, edited by Marinus de Jonge, 371–76. BETL 44. Leuven: Leuven University Press, 1977.

Schökel, Luis Alonso. *A Manual of Hebrew Poetics*. Rome: Editrice Pontificio Istituto Biblico, 1988.

Scholes, Robert, and Robert Kellogg. *The Nature of Narrative*. New York: Oxford University Press, 1966.

Scholes, Robert, et al. *The Nature of Narrative*. Rev. ed. New York: Oxford University Press, 2006.

Schubert, Kurt. *The Dead Sea Community: Its Origin and Teachings*. London: Adam & Charles Black, 1959.

Schuchard, B. G. *Scripture within Scripture: The Interrelationship of Form and Function in the Explicit Old Testament Citations in the Gospel of John*. SBLDS 133. Atlanta: Scholars, 1992.

Schweizer, E. *Ego Eimi: Die religionsgeschichtliche Herkunft und theologische Bedeutung der johanneischen Bildreden, Zugleich ein Beitrag zur Quellenfrage des vierten Evangeliums*. Göttingen: Vandenhoeck und Ruprecht, 1939.

Segovia, Fernando F. *Love Relationships in the Johannine Tradition*. Chico, CA: Scholars, 1982.

———. *"What Is John?" Volume I: Readers and Reading of the Fourth Gospel*. SBLSymS 3. Atlanta: Scholars, 1996.

———. *"What Is John?" Volume II: Literary and Social Readings of the Fourth Gospel*. SBLSymS 7. Atlanta: Scholars, 1998.

Shaw, Charles S. *The Speeches of Micah: A Rhetorical-Historical Analysis*. JSOTSup 145. Sheffield: Sheffield Academic, 1993.

Shedd, Russell. "Multiple Meanings in the Gospel of John." In *Current Issues in Biblical and Patristic Interpretation: Studies in Honor of Merill C. Tenney Presented by His Former Students*, edited by Gerald F. Hawthorne, 247–58. Grand Rapids: Eerdmans, 1975.

Sidney, Philip, et al. *The Defence of Poesie, A Letter to Q. Elizabeth, A Defence of Leicester*. THL. Edited by G. E. Woodberry. Boston: Merrymount, 1908.

Silva, Moisés, ed. *Foundations of Contemporary Interpretation*. Grand Rapids: Zondervan, 1996.

Sinclair, Scott Gambrill. *The Road and the Truth: The Editing of John's Gospel*. Vallejo, CA: Bibal, 1994.

Ska, Jean Louis. *"Our Fathers Have Told Us": Introduction to the Analysis of Hebrew Narratives*. Rome: Editrice Pontificio Instituto Biblico, 1990.

Skinner, Christopher W., ed. *Characters and Characterization in the Gospel of John*. LNTS 461. London: Bloomsbury, 2013.

———. "Introduction: Characters and Characterization in the Gospel of John: Reflections on the Status Quaestionis." In *Characters and Characterization in the Gospel of John*, edited by Christopher W. Skinner, xvii–xxxii. LNTS 461. London: Bloomsbury, 2013.

———. "Misunderstanding, Christology, and Johannine Characterization: Reading John's Characters through the Lens of the Prologue." In *Characters and Characterization in the Gospel of John*, edited by Christopher W. Skinner, 111–28. London: Bloomsbury, 2013.

Sloane, Thomas O. *Encyclopedia of Rhetoric*. New York: Oxford University Press, 2001.

Smalley, Stephen S. *John: Evangelist & Interpreter*. 2nd ed. Downers Grove, IL: InterVarsity, 1998.

———. "Keeping up with Recent Studies, Pt 12: St John's Gospel." *ExpTim* 97.4 (1986) 102–8.

Smith, Ben C. "The Latin Prologues: The Anti-Marcionite and Monarchian Prologues to the Canonical Gospels." http://www.textexcavation.com/latinprologues.html.

Smith, D. Moody. *The Composition and Order of the Fourth Gospel: Bultmann's Literary Theory*. New Haven: Yale University Press, 1965.

———. "Johannine Christianity: Some Reflections on Its Character and Delineation." *NTS* 21.2 (1975) 222–48.

———. *John*. ANTC. Nashville: Abingdon, 1999.

Sonek, Krzysztof. *Truth, Beauty, and Goodness in Biblical Narratives: A Hermeneutical Study of Genesis 21:1–21*. New York: Walter de Gruyter, 2009.

Soskice, Janet M. *Metaphor and Religious Language*. Oxford: Clarendon, 1985.

Spivey, Robert A. "Structuralism and Biblical Studies: The Uninvited Guest." *Int* 28.2 (April 1974) 133–45.

Stafford, John K. "The Call of Nathanael, John 1:49: A Rhetorical-Theological Study." *Perichoresis* 11.2 (2013) 50–61.

Staley, Jeffrey Lloyd. *The Print's First Kiss: A Rhetorical Investigation of the Implied Reader in the Fourth Gospel*. SBLDS 82. Atlanta: Scholars, 1988.

———. "The Structure of John's Prologue." *CBQ* 48 (1986) 241–64.

———. "Stumbling in the Dark, Reaching for the Light: Reading Character in John 5 and 9." Edited by R. Alan Culpepper and Fernando F. Segovia. *Semeia* 53 (1991) 55–80.

Stancil, Wilburn T. "Structuralism and New Testament Studies." *SwJT* 22.2 (March 1980) 41–59.

Stanzel, F. K. *A Theory of Narrative*. Translated by Charlotte Goedsche. Cambridge: Cambridge University Press, 1984.

Sternberg, Meir. "The Bible's Art of Persuasion: Ideology, Rhetoric, and Poetics in Saul's Fall." *HUCA* 54 (1983) 45–82.

———. *The Poetics of Biblical Narrative: Ideological Literature and the Drama of Reading*. Bloomington, IN: Indiana University Press, 1987.

Stibbe, Mark W. G. *The Artistry of John: The Fourth Gospel as Narrative Christology*. PhD diss., University of Nottingham, United Kingdom, 1989.

———, ed. *The Gospel of John as Literature: An Anthology of Twentieth-Century Perspectives*. New York: Brill, 1993.

———. *John: A Readings Commentary*. RNBC. Sheffield: Sheffield Academic, 1993.

———. *John as Storyteller: Narrative Criticism and the Fourth Gospel*. SNTSMS 73. Cambridge: Cambridge University Press, 1992.

———. *John's Gospel*. New York: Routledge, 1994.

———. "'Return to Sender': A Structuralist Approach to John's Gospel." *BibInt* 1.2 (July 1993) 189–206.

Strawn, B. A. "Imagery." *DOTWPW* 306–14.

———. "Keep/Observe/Do—Carefully—Today! The Rhetoric of Repetition in Deuteronomy." In *A God So Near: Essays on Old Testament Theology in Honor of Patrick D. Miller*, edited by B. A. Strawn and N. R. Bowen, 215–40. Winona Lake, IN: Eisenbrauns, 2003.

Streeter, B. H. *The Four Gospels: A Study of Origins*. London: Macmillan, 1956.

Stube, John C. *A Graeco-Roman Rhetorical Reading of the Farewell Discourse*, LNTS 309. New York: T&.T Clark, 2006.
Swartley, Willard M., ed. *Violence Renounced: René Girard, Biblical Studies, and Peacemaking*. Telford, PA: Pandora, 2000.
Sweeney, Marvin A. *Forms of Old Testament Literature: Isaiah 1–39 with an Introduction to Prophetic Literature*. Grand Rapids: Eerdmans, 1996.
———. *The Twelve Prophets*. BOSHNP. Collegeville, MN: Liturgical, 2000.
Swete, Henry B. *The Apocalypse of St. John*. CCGNT. 2nd ed. New York: Macmillan, 1906.
Talbert, Charles H. *Reading John: A Literary and Theological Commentary on the Fourth Gospel and the Johannine Epistles*. New York: Crossroad, 1992.
Tannehill, Robert. *The Narrative Unity of Luke-Acts: A Literary Interpretation*. 2 vols. Philadelphia: Fortress, 1986–90.
Tanner, J. Paul. "The Gideon Narrative as the Focal Point of Judges." *BSac* 149.594 (1992) 146–61.
Teeple, Howard M. *The Literary Origin of the Gospel of John*. Evanston: Religion and Ethics Institute, 1974.
Temple, William. *Readings in St. John's Gospel: First and Second Series*. London: Macmillan, 1945.
Tenney, Merrill C. "The Footnotes of John's Gospel." *BSac* 117.468 (1960) 350–64.
———. "The Imagery of John." *BSac* 121.481 (1964) 13–21.
———. *John: The Gospel of Belief; An Analytic Study of the Text*. Grand Rapids: Eerdmans, 1976.
———. "Literary Keys to the Fourth Gospel: Part I, The Symphonic Structure of John." *BSac* 120.478 (1963) 117–25.
———. "Literary Keys to the Fourth Gospel: Part III, The Old Testament and the Fourth Gospel." *BSac* 120.480 (1963) 300–308.
Thatcher, Tom. "Anatomies of the Fourth Gospel: Past, Present, and Future Probes." In *Anatomies of Narrative Criticism: The Past, Present, and Futures of the Fourth Gospel as Literature*, edited by Tom Thatcher and Stephen D. Moore, 1–38. Atlanta: Society of Biblical Literature, 2008.
———. "The Beloved Disciple, the Fourth Evangelist, and the Authorship of the Fourth Gospel." In *The Oxford Handbook of Johannine Studies*, edited by Judith M. Lieu and Martinus C. de Boer, 83–100. Oxford: Oxford University Press, 2018.
———. *Jesus the Riddler: The Power of Ambiguity in the Gospels*. Louisville, KY: Westminster John Knox, 2006.
———. "John's Memory Theater: The Fourth Gospel and Ancient Mnemo-rhetoric." *CBQ* 69.3 (2007) 487–505.
———. "A New Look at Asides in the Fourth Gospel." *BSac* 151.604 (1994) 428–39.
———, ed. *What We Have Heard from the Beginning: The Past, Present, and Future of Johannine Studies*. Waco, TX: Baylor University Press, 2007.
Theron, S. W. "A Multi-Faceted Approach to an Important Thrust in the Prayer of Jesus in John 17." *Neot* 21.1 (1987) 77–94.
Thiselton, Anthony C. "Keeping up with Recent Studies, 2: Structuralism and Biblical Studies: Method or Ideology?" *ExpTim* 89.11 (1978) 329–35.
———. *Thiselton on Hermeneutics: Collected Works with New Essays*. Grand Rapids: Eerdmans, 2006.
———. *The Two Horizons: New Testament Hermeneutics and Philosophical Description with Special Reference to Heidegger, Bultmann, Gadamer, and Wittgenstein*. 1980. Reprint, Grand Rapids: Eerdmans, 1993.

Thiselton, Anthony C., and Clarence Walhout. *The Responsibility of Hermeneutics*. Grand Rapids: Eerdmans, 1985.
Tilborg, Sjef van. *Imaginative Love in John*. New York: Brill, 1993.
Tobin, T. H. "The Prologue of John and Hellenistic Jewish Speculation." *CBQ* 52 (1990) 252–69.
Todorov, Tzvetan. *Introduction to Poetics*. Minneapolis: University of Minnesota Press, 1981.
———. *The Poetics of Prose*. Ithaca, NY: Cornell University Press, 1977.
Tompkins, Jane P. *Reader-Response Criticism from Formalism to Post-structuralism*. Baltimore: Johns Hopkins University Press, 1980.
Tovey, Derek. *Narrative Art and Act in the Fourth Gospel*. JSNTSup 151. Sheffield: Sheffield, 1997.
Trible, Phyllis. *Rhetorical Criticism*. Philadelphia: Fortress, 1994.
Trites, Allison A. *The New Testament Concept of Witness*. New York: Cambridge University Press, 1977.
Tsumura, David Toshio. "Janus Parallelism in Hab. iii 4." *VT* 54.1 (2004) 124–28.
———. "Janus Parallelism in Nah 1:8." *JBL* 102.1 (1983) 109–11.
Tucker, Gene. *Form Criticism of the Old Testament*. Philadelphia: Fortress, 1971.
Turner, Nigel. "The Language of the New Testament." In *Peake's Commentary on the Bible*, edited by Matthew Black, 659–62. New York: Thomas Nelson, 1962.
Ullmann, Stephen. *The Principles of Semantics*. Oxford: Basil Blackwell, 1963.
Uspensky, Boris. *A Poetics of Composition the Structure of the Artistic Text and Typology of a Compositional Form*. Berkeley: University of California Press, 1973.
Van der Watt, Jan G. "Double Entendre in the Gospel according to John." In *Theology and Christology in the Fourth Gospel: Essays by the Members of the SNTS Johannine Writings Seminar*, edited by G. Van Belle, J.G. van der Watt, and P. Maritz, 463–81. Leuven: Leuven University Press, 2005.
———. *Family of the King: Dynamics of Metaphor in the Gospel according to John*. BibInt 47. Boston: Brill, 2000.
———. "Johannine Style: Some Initial Remarks on the Functional Use of Repetition in the Gospel according to John." *IDS* 42.1 (April 2008) 75–99.
Vangemeren, Willem A. *Interpreting the Prophetic Word*. Grand Rapids: Zondervan, 1990.
———. *New International Dictionary of Old Testament Theology & Exegesis*. 5 vols. Grand Rapids: Zondervan, 1997.
Vanhoozer, Kevin J. "A Lamp in the Labyrinth: The Hermeneutics of 'Aesthetic' Theology." *TJ* 8.1 (1987) 25–56.
———. *Is There a Meaning in This Text? The Bible, the Reader, and the Morality of Literary Knowledge*. Grand Rapids: Zondervan, 1998.
Verheyden, Joseph, et al., eds. *Prophets and Prophecy in Jewish and Early Christian Literature*. WUNT 2. Reihe 286. Tübingen: Mohr Siebeck, 2010.
Verhoef, P. A. "Prophecy." In *NIDOTTE* 4:1067–78.
Via, Dan O. *Kerygma and Comedy in the New Testament: A Structuralist Approach to Hermeneutic*. Philadelphia: Fortress, 1975.
von Herder, Johann Gottfried. *The Spirit of Hebrew Poetry*. Translated by James Marsh. Burlington: Edward Smith, 1833.
Von Rad, Gerhard. *The Theology of Israel's Prophetic Traditions*. Vol. 2 in *Old Testament Theology*. Translated by D. M. G. Stalker. New York: Harper & Row, 1965.
von Wahlde, U. "Literary Structure and Theological Argument in Three Discourses with the Jews in the Fourth Gospel." *JBL* 103 (1984) 575–84.

Voorwinde, Stephen. *Jesus' Emotions in the Fourth Gospel: Human or Divine?* LNTS 284. New York: T&T Clark, 2005.
Walsh, Jerome T. *Old Testament Narrative: A Guide to Interpretation.* Louisville, KY: Westminster John Knox, 2010.
———. *Style & Structure in Biblical Hebrew Narrative.* Collegeville, MN: Liturgical, 2001.
Waltke, Bruce K., and M. O'Connor. *An Introduction to Biblical Hebrew Syntax.* Winona Lake, IN: Eisenbrauns, 1990.
Walton, John H., and Tremper Longman III, *How to Read Job.* Downers Grove, IL: IVP Academic, 2015.
Warner, Martin. *The Bible as Rhetoric: Studies in Biblical Persuasion and Credibility.* New York: Routledge, 1990.
Watson, Duane F. "The New Testament and Greco-Roman Rhetoric: A Bibliographical Update." *JETS* 33.4 (1990) 513–24.
———. "The New Testament and Greco-Roman Rhetoric: A Bibliography." *JETS* 31.4 (1988) 465–72.
———. ed. *Persuasive Artistry: Studies in New Testament Rhetoric in Honor of George A. Kennedy.* JSNTSup 50. Sheffield: JSOT Press, 1991.
———. *The Rhetoric of the New Testament: A Bibliographic Survey.* Leiderdorp: Deo, 2006.
Watson, Wilfred G. E. *Classical Hebrew Poetry: A Guide to Its Techniques.* JSOTSup 26. Sheffield: JSOT Press, 1984.
———. "Hebrew Poetry." In *Text in Context: Essays by Members of the Society for Old Testament Study*, edited by A. D. H. Mayes, 253–85. Oxford: Oxford University Press, 2000.
———. "The Study of Hebrew Poetry: Past-Present-Future." In *Sacred Conjectures: The Context and Legacy of Robert Lowth and Jean Astruc*, edited by John Jarick, 124–54. London: T&T Clark, 2007.
———. *Traditional Techniques in Classical Hebrew Verse.* JSOTSup 170. Sheffield: Sheffield Academic, 1994.
Watts, James W. "Rhetorical Strategy in the Composition of the Pentateuch." *JSOT* 68 (1995) 3–22.
Wead, David W. *The Literary Devices in John's Gospel.* Basel: Reinhardt, 1970.
———. *The Literary Devices in John's Gospel: Revised and Expanded Edition.* Edited by Paul N. Anderson and R. Alan Culpepper. Eugene, OR: Wipf and Stock, 2018.
Weima, Jeffrey A. D. "Literary Criticism." In *Interpreting the New Testament: Essays on Methods and Issues*, edited by David Alan Black and David S. Dockery, 150–66. Nashville: Broadman and Holman, 2001.
Weiss, Meir. *Bible from Within: The Method of Total Interpretation.* Jerusalem: Magnes, 1984.
Wellek, René, and Austin Warren. *Theory of Literature.* 3rd ed. San Diego: Harcourt Brace Jovanovich, 1977.
Wellhausen, J. *Das Evangelium Johannis.* Berlin: Georg Reimer, 1908.
Westcott, B. F. *The Gospel according to St. John.* London: John Murray, 1890.
Westermann, Claus. *Basic Forms of Prophetic Speech.* Translated by Hugh Clayton White. London: Lutterworth, 1967.
Wills, Lawrence M. *Quest of the Historical Gospel: Mark, John and the Origins of the Gospel Genre.* London: Routledge, 1997.

Wilson, Gerald H. *Psalms*. Vol. 1. Grand Rapids: Zondervan, 2002.
Witherington, Ben, III. *John's Wisdom: A Commentary on the Fourth Gospel*. Louisville: Westminster John Knox, 1995.
———. *New Testament Rhetoric: An Introductory Guide to the Art of Persuasion in and of the New Testament*. Eugene, OR: Cascade, 2009.
Whitenton, Michael R. "The Dissembler of John 3: A Cognitive and Rhetorical Approach to the Characterization of Nicodemus." *JBL* 135.1 (2016) 141–58.
Wimsatt, William K., and Monroe C. Beardsley. "The Affective Fallacy." *The Sewanee Review* 57.1 (1949) 31–55.
———. "The Intentional Fallacy." *The Sewanee Review* 54.3 (1946) 468–88.
Wolfers, D. "The Speech-Cycles in the Book of Job." *VT* 43 (1993) 385–402.
Wordsworth, William, and Samuel Taylor Coleridge. *Lyrical Ballads with Pastoral and Other Poems*. Vol. 1. London: Longman, Hurst, Rees, and Orme, 1805.
Wright, C. J. *Jesus the Revelation of God: His Mission and Message according to St. John*. London: Hodder & Stoughton, 1950.
Wright, William M. *Rhetoric and Theology: Figural Reading of John 9*. Berlin: Walter de Gruyter, 2009.
Wyller, Egil A. "In Solomon's Porch: A Henological Analysis of the Architectonic of the Fourth Gospel." *ST* 42 (1988) 151–67.
Votaw, Clyde Weber. *The Gospels and Contemporary Biographies in the Greco-Roman World*. Philadelphia: Fortress, 1970.
Yamasaki, Gary. *Watching a Biblical Narrative: Point of View in Biblical Exegesis*. New York: T. & T. Clark, 2007.
Young, F. W. "A Study of the Relation of Isaiah to the Fourth Gospel." *ZNW* 46 (1955) 215–33.
Zakovitch, Yair. *The Pattern of the Numerical Sequence Three-Four in the Bible*. PhD diss., Hebrew University of Jerusalem, 1977.
Zimmerli, Walther. *Ezekiel 1: A Commentary on the Book of the Prophet Ezekiel Chapters 1–24*. Herm. Translated by Ronald E. Clements. Philadelphia: Fortress, 1979.
Zimmermann, Ruben. "Imagery in John." In *Imagery in the Gospel of John: Terms, Forms, Themes, and Theology of Johannine Figurative Language*, edited by Jörg Frey, Jan G. Van der Watt, and Ruben Zimmermann, 1–43. WUNT 200. Tübingen: Mohr Siebeck, 2006.

Subject Index

Abbott, E. A., 84, 88–89
Abraham, 105–6
Abrams, Meyer H., 4, 12–23, 21n45, 43, 103, 118
Absalom, 134–35
Adams, Hazard, 19
Ad Herennium, 29
aesthetics, 17–18, 39
Against Apion (Josephus), 61
Albright, W. F., 147n34
Alexander, Philip S., 58
allegory, 96
Alter, Robert, 74, 111
ambiguities, 91, 95, 95n118, 129, 131
Ambrose, 63n82
American New Criticism, 22, 31
Ames, Frank Ritchel, 147n35
Amit, Yairah, 118–20, 130
Anatomy of the Fourth Gospel (Culpeper), 3, 32–33
Andersen, Francis I., 86, 165–66
Annual Meeting of the Society of Biblical Literature, 6–7, 39
anonymity, 51, 118, 157
anthropology, 36
antithetic parallelisms, 72, 75
aorist tenses, 138–39
An Apology for Poetry (Sidney), 16–17
apostles, 48, 144, 153

apostolic authorship of the Gospel of John, 45–50, 50n23
The Aramaic Origin of the Fourth Gospel (Burney), 53
Aramaism in the Gospel of John, 53–54
Aristobulus, 62, 63n79
Aristotelian rhetoric, 30, 67
Aristotle, 14, 16, 21n45, 26–28, 61, 97, 118
aspect, 109
asyndeton, 88–89
Attridge, Harold W., 6–7, 30n85
audience, 20
Auerbach, Erich, 14–16, 111
Augustine, 1, 63–64, 63n82
Aune, David E., 143
authorial intent, 22–23
authority, 38–39, 51, 144
authorship, 33–34, 45–51, 50n23

Ball, C. J., 53
Bar-Efrat, Shimon, 133
Barrett, C. K., 2, 89n90
Beardsley, Monroe C., 22–23
Beattie, James, 17
beauty, 17–18, 21–22
Belle, G. van, 82–83, 83n55
beloved disciple, 49–50, 156–57, 156n61
Bennema, Cornelis, 116

Berlin, Adele, 8, 60, 72n2, 74, 78–79, 83n55, 85–86, 104, 112n40, 114
Beutler, Johannes, 56
Bible. *See* Scripture
biblical characterizations, 110–18
biblical exegesis, 23
biblical literature, 4–9, 25–26
biblical parallelisms, 71–72
biblical poetry, 71–101
Biblical Poetry through Medieval Jewish Eyes (Berlin), 60
biblical scholarship, 23–24
biblical studies, 14–15, 102–3
Binkley, Roberta A., 30
Black, C. Clifton, 29–30
Black, David Alan, 90
Black, Matthew, 53, 57
Black, Max, 97–98
blanks, 127–28
Bloch, Renée, 57
Block, Daniel I., 150
Boadt, Lawrence, 159n73
Boismard, M. É, 83
Boman, Thorlief, 147
Boodberg, Peter A., 74
Book of Ruth, 113
Book of the Honeycomb's Flow (Leon), 66–68
Booth, Steve, 118n64
Booth, Wayne, 34
Borchert, Gerald L., 82
Braun, F. M., 83
Brodie, Thomas L., 6
Brown, Colin, 158
Brown, Raymond E., 47, 49, 82, 148–49
Bruce, F. F., 47
Bultmann, Rudolf, 48, 52, 75, 143
Burney, C. F., 53, 75, 89, 89n91

Caird, George B., 96
calling narratives, 152
Campbell, Constantine R., 109
Casanowicz, Immanuel M., 91–92
Cassiodorus, 64–65
Celsus, 62
Chang, Peter S. C., 84–85
change, 119
character and characterization, 34, 110–18, 112n40, 131–32

Charlesworth, James H., 156n61
Chatman, Seymour, 32
Chilton, Bruce, 57
Christianity, 52, 63
Christian prophets, 142–44
Christology, 59
Chrysostom, John, 1–2
Cicero, 29
classic rhetoric, 30
Clement of Alexandria, 1, 63, 63n79
Clifford, Richard J., 158
Cohen, Shaye J., 59
Coleridge, Samuel Taylor, 21–22
Collins, C. John, 8, 8n36
Colwell, Ernest, 53
coming of the word, 145–51
communication, 20–21, 23, 27–30, 31, 41, 43, 66, 129
complete parallelisms, 73
composition theories, 24
conjunctions, 86
Conroy, Charles, 135n118
context, defined, 12
contextual ellipsis, 89
convictions, 37
couplets followed by explanatory and prose-style comments, 75
Course in General Linguistics (de Saussure), 35
Critique of Judgment (Kant), 17
Cross, Frank M., 52
Crossan, John D., 37
Crossman, John D., 24
Culpepper, R. Alan, 3–5, 32–34, 33n98, 49, 95n118, 111, 115
cultural sensitivity, 100

Dahms, John V., 149–50
David, 61, 63
dead metaphor, 100
Dead Sea Scrolls, 5, 52
Déaut, Roger Le, 57
debar-yhwh ("the word of the LORD"), 145
deconstructionism, 38, 41–43
deconstructionist criticism, 41–43
De doctrina christiana, (On Christian Doctrine) (Augustine), 64
Deissmann, Adolf, 53

deliberative rhetoric, 28
Demosthenes, 158–59
Derrida, Jacques, 38, 41–42
desire, 14n9, 42–43
Dibelius, M., 143
Dinah, 105
discourse analysis, 109–10, 109n27, 110n28, 132n111
divine pathos, 155–56
divine speeches, 166–67
Dodd, C. H., 46–47, 52, 99
double meanings, 71, 90–95, 95n118
Duke, Paul, 95n117

The Eclipse of Biblical Narrative (Frei), 34–35
economy of words, 93
Egyptian Hermetic texts, 52
Ehud's story, 130
elder John, 46–47
Eliot, T. S., 22
ellipsis, 87–88, 89–90
Empson, William, 91
Ensor, Peter W., 88n88
enteuthen, 108–9n22
Enz, Jacob J., 55
epideictic rhetoric, 28
Epilogue of the Gospel of John, 48
epithetic descriptions, 116–17
Estes, Daniel J., 92
Estes, Douglas, 136
Eusebius of Caesarea, 46, 62–63
excellence of Old Testament poetics, 60–69
Exodus generation, 114
Exodus narrative, 55
Explanation of the Psalms (Cassiodorus), 64–65
expression in Scripture, 64
expressive theory, 13, 19–21
external evidences for apostolic authorship, 45–47
eyewitnesses, 34, 48–49, 153–54, 153n50

false prophets, 152
Fanning, Buist M., 109, 109n23
Feldman, Louis H., 62
feminist readings, 40
fiction, 33–34

fiction and Scripture, 15
figurative interpretation of history, 15
figurative language, 95–101
first person references in the prophetic writings, 152–53
Firth, D. G., 91
Fish, Stanley, 38–39
Fishbane, Michael, 6
flashbacks, 134
flat characters, 110
focalization, 103–4
Fohrer, Georg, 93
Forbes, A. Dean, 86
form criticism, 6, 23, 26–27
"Form Criticism and Beyond" (Muilenburg), 26–27
Former Prophets, 141
Forster, E. M., 110
four categories according to Abram, 12–23
The Four Gospels (Streeter), 142–43
Fourth Gospel (John). *See* Gospel of John
The Fourth Gospel (Hoskyns), 2
Fowlers, Robert, 131n109
Fox, Michael V., 158
Freedman, David N., 72, 86, 165–66
Frei, Han W., 34–35
Frye, Northrop, 26

gaps, 127–32, 128n97, 131n109
Genette, Gérard, 103–4
genre, 8, 8n36
genre bending, 7
"Genre Bending in the Fourth Gospel" (Attridge), 7
Gentile Christians, 59–60
Girard, René, 14n9
Gitay, Yehoshua, 158, 161
giving life to the world, 149
glory, 154n53
God
    Christian prophets, 142–44
    Old Testament characters, 114–15
    prophetic mode of speaking, 163–67
    prophetic persuasion, 158–63
    prophetic self-consciousness, 151–57
    word of, 51, 65, 145–51, 147n35, 155, 163–67

Golding, Thomas A., 96
Goldingay, John, 79
Gordis, Robert, 98
Gordon, C. H., 92–93
Gospel of John
   apostolic authorship, 45–50, 50n23
   Aramaic origin of, 53–54
   authoritative voice, 4
   autobiographical voice, 154
   characters and characterization, 111, 116–18, 131–32
   Christology, 59
   deconstructionist criticism, 42–43
   descriptions of, 1–2
   divine pathos, 156
   double meanings, 90–95
   economy of words, 93
   emotional response to, 40
   expressive theory, 20–21
   eyewitnesses, 34, 48–49, 153–54, 153n50
   generic conventions in, 7–8
   genre, 7–8, 7n30
   Greek language, 53–55
   Hebrew Scripture, 55–56
   hermeneutics, 57–59
   historical presents, 136–40
   history of the text, 2–3
   imagery in, 98–101
   importance of authorship, 50–51, 50n23
   Jewish character of, 5
   Jewishness of, 52–60
   as judicial, 162
   literary nature of, 2–9
   literary tradition of the Old Testament, 5–6
   Midrashic character of, 57–58
   modern literary theories, 23–43
   narrative criticism, 32–35, 32n96, 102–3
   narrative structure, 5–6
   narrative time, 136–40
   nature of, 7
   parallelisms, 72–78
   perspectives in, 103–10, 106n17
   plot, 123–27
   poetic approach to, 51
   as poetic narrative, 71–101
   poetics of Old Testament prophetic writings, 141–67
   point of view, 106–9
   postmodern understanding of, 4
   as prophetic, 55–56
   prophetic mode of speaking, 163–67
   prophetic persuasion, 161–63
   prophetic self-consciousness, 151–57
   prophetic word of God, 145–51
   Qumran, 58
   reader-response criticism, 39–41
   repetition and variation, 80–85
   rhetorical criticism, 29
   Semitisms of, 53–55
   source theories, 47–48
   structuralist criticism, 36–37
   structure, 5–6, 32, 74–78, 78n24, 80, 83, 118–27, 126n92, 127n93
   style of, 8, 20–21, 29–30, 45, 48–49, 74–75, 102, 161
   terseness, 85–90
   truth claim of, 2–3, 20–21, 34
   use of Scripture, 56
Gospels, 112
Gospels and narrative, 30–31
Gospels and rhetorical criticism, 29–30
Gray, George B., 73
Greco-Roman rhetoric, 5, 27, 29, 53
Greek and Hebraic characters, 110–11
Greek language, 53–55
Greek psaltery, 63
Greek rhetoric, 28–30
Greeks, 62–64, 69
Greek tenses, 138
Grudem, Wayne A., 144

Habel, N., 152
Hallevi, Judah, 65–66, 68
Hamid-Khani, Saeed, 94
Hanson, Anthony T., 56, 141
Hays, Richard B., 57–58
Hebrew Bible, 6
Hebrew language, 66, 81, 93, 110
Hebrew narratives, 123
Hebrew parallelisms, 72–78
Hebrew poetry, 72–101
   double meaning, 90–95
   imagery, 95–101
   meter in, 66

parallelism, 72–78
poetics of the Old Testament, 68–69
repetition and variation, 78–85
terseness, 85–90, 87n78
Hebrew rhetoric, 68
Hebrews, 62, 65–66, 80–81
Hebrew Scripture, 55–56, 62–63, 67–68, 141
Hellenism, 52
hendiadys, 76n23
Hengel, Martin, 46
Herder, Johann G. von, 73
hermeneutics, 57–59
Heschel, Abraham J., 155–56, 161
Hill, David, 143
Hirsch, E. D., 51
historical criticism(s), 23–25, 27, 33n98
historical presents, 136–40, 136n125
The History of the Synoptic Tradition (Bultmann), 143
Holland, Norman, 38
Horace, 16
Hosea, 150–51
Hoskyns, Edwyn, 2
Howard, W. F., 53
Hurd, Richard, 17
hymns of the Old Testament, 61

"I am" statements, 99–100
The Idea of Biblical Poetry (Kugel), 60, 73–74
ideological criticism, 41
idiomatic ellipsis, 89
imagery, 87–88, 95–101
imitation, Aristotle on, 16
imitation in literature. *See* mimetic theory
imperfective aspect, 109
imperfect tenses, 138–39
implied author, 31–34, 40
implied reader, 31, 40
inclusio structures, 82–83
incomplete parallelisms, 73
indicative verbs, 109
individuality of the poet, 19, 22
informational blanks, 127–28
informational gaps, 127–32
informational omission in a story, 127–32

Institutions of Divine and Secular Learning and On the Soul (Cassiodorus), 64
"The Intentional Fallacy" (Wimsatt and Beardsley), 22–23
intermediate kingdom, 72
internal evidences for apostolic authorship, 47–50
interpretation of Christ, 58–59
interpretive community, 38–39, 38n129
Ion (Plato), 13
Irenaeus, 45
Iser, Wolfgang, 39, 129
Ishmael, 106
Israelites, 93

Jakobson, Roman, 12n2, 35–36, 43
James, J. Courtenay, 53–54
Janus parallelisms, 92–93
Jerome, 68
Jerusalem, 49
Jesus
    characters and characterization, 117–18
    Hebrew Scriptures, 55–56
    historical presents, 139
    "I am" statements, 99–100
    importance of authorship, 51
    interpretation of, 58–59
    living water discourse, 42
    Old Testament prophetic writings, 141–43
    parallelisms, 75–77
    point of view, 106–9
    prophetic self-consciousness, 156–57
    responses to, 115–16
    as the word of God, 145–51
Jewish hermeneutics, 57–59
Jewishness of the Gospel of John, 5, 47–48, 52–60
Jews and Samaritans, 117, 117n61
Job, 121–22
Johannine community, 47
Johannine study, 2–5
Johannine study/scholarship, 52
John. *See* Gospel of John
John, son of Zebedee, 45, 46, 49–50
John the Baptist, 75, 77, 82, 88, 116–17n57, 125, 131

John the Elder, 46–47
Joseph's dream, 104
Josephus, 61, 68
Jotham, 120
Judaea, 49
Judaism, 52
judicial rhetoric, 28
judicial themes in the Prophets, 162
Jung, Carl Gustav, 40

kai, 89
Kalimi, Isaac, 122
Kant, Immanuel, 17, 21–22
Käsemann, Ernst, 142
Keener, Craig S., 5, 59, 154
Kellogg, Robert L., 4, 110–11
Kennedy, George, 27–30
A King is Bound in the Tresse (Winsor), 157
Kitab al Khazari (Hallevi), 65–66
Kitzberger, Ingrid Rosa, 40
Kneale, J. Douglas, 42, 42n147
Koester, Craig R., 40, 99
Krieger, Murray, 33
Kugel, James L., 60–61, 63–64, 71–72, 73–74, 85, 87
Kysar, Robert, 4, 40

Lampe, G. W. H., 58–59
language, 35–36, 42, 53–54, 65
Latter Prophets, 141
Lea, Thomas D., 3–4
Lectures on the Sacred Poetry of the Hebrews (Loweth), 72–73
Lehtipuu, Outi, 112
Leon, Judah Messer, 66–68
Leung, Mavis M., 140
Levinsohn, Stephen H., 137
Lévi-Strauss, Claude, 36
lexical double meanings, 94–95
Lightfoot, Joseph B., 54
Light of the Eyes (Rossi), 68–69
Lincoln, Andrew T., 83, 162
Lindars, Barnabas, 57
Lindblom, J., 145–46, 159
linear time in biblical narratives, 135–36
linguistics, 109
Lipson, Carol S., 30

literary art of the Gospel of John, 2–9, 12–43
literary strategies, 71–72
literary study of Scripture, 14–15, 25–26
literary theories, 102–40
literature
 biblical, 4–9, 25–26
 character and characterization, 110–18
 deconstructionist criticism, 41–43
 expressive theory, 19–21
 gaps and ambiguities, 127–32
 mimetic theory, 13–16
 narrative criticism, 3, 30–35
 narrative time, 132–40
 objective theory, 21–23
 plot, 118–27
 point of view, 103–10
 pragmatic theory, 16–18
 prophetic, 145–46, 153, 158, 163–64
 reader-response criticism, 37–41
 rhetorical criticism, 26–30
 structuralist criticism, 35–37
living water discourse, 42
logocentrism, 41
logos, 148–51, 167n101
Loisy, A., 56
Longenecker, Bruce W., 29
Longinus, 16, 19, 68
Longman, Tremper, 43, 85, 87, 95
Louw, Johannes P., 108n22
love, 156–57
Lowth, Robert, 72–75, 78
Lucian, 29
Luther, Martin, 2
Lyrical Ballads (Wordsworth), 19

"The Making of Metaphor" (Kysar), 40
Mandaean Gnostic dualism, 52
marriage, 157
Maynard, H., 84
McWhirter, Jocelyn, 157
medieval period, 64–66
Meier, Samuel A., 164, 165n92, 166
Merenlahti, Petri, 34
metaphor, 96–101, 97n133
meter, 66
metonymy, 96
Michaels, J. Ramsey, 50n23

Subject Index

Mill, John Stuart, 20
Miller, Carolyn, 8n36
Miller, C. L., 87
Mimesis (Auerbach), 14–15
mimetic theory, 13–16, 14n9, 19–20
Minor Prophets, 141
Mlakuzhyil, George, 78n24, 127n93
mnemotechnique, 29
modern literary theories, 23–43
Moloney, Francis J., 116
Moore, Stephen D., 42–43
Morphology of the Folktale (Propp), 36
Morris, Leon, 50n23, 84, 163
Moses, 60–61, 141
Moulton, J. H., 53
Mowinckel, Sigmund, 167n100
Muilenburg, James, 26, 78, 80–81
multiple meanings, 90–95
multiple readings of the text, 4
multivalent conjunction, 87n78
myths, 36

Naccacci, Alviero, 136n124
namelessness, 114, 118n62
naming, 113–14
Napier, B. D., 155
narrative criticism, 3, 30–35, 32n96, 102–3
narrative situation, 104n4
narrative speeches, 126n92, 161
narrative speed, 136
narrative structure, 5–6, 78n24, 118–27, 126n92, 127n93
narrative techniques, 103–10
narrative time, 132–40
narrative voice, 107–9, 120, 138, 154
narrator. *See* point of view
New Criticism, 33, 37
Newheart, Michael W., 40
New Testament, 27–29, 30, 50, 52, 53, 58, 114–15, 142–44
New Testament Interpretation through Rhetorical Criticism (Kennedy), 27
Nicodemus, 117, 131–32
Nicol, Willem, 82
Nida, Eugene A., 108n22
Nietzsche, Friedrich, 42
Noegel, Scott B., 93

novel, 3–4
Numenius of Apamea, 62, 63n79

objective theory, 13, 21–23, 50–51
objectivity and subjectivity, 38–39
O'Day, Gail, 6
offenbarungsreden ("Revelation-speech" source material), 75
Okure, Teresa, 161
Old Testament poetics, 6–9
 centrality of Hebrew Scripture, 55–56
 character and characterization, 110–18
 double meaning, 90–95
 excellence of, 60–69
 gaps and ambiguities, 127–32
 narrative time, 132–40
 plot, 118–27, 132n111
 point of view, 103–10
 prophetic mode of speaking, 163–67
 prophetic persuasion, 158–63
 prophetic self-consciousness, 151–57
 prophetic writings, 141–67, 144n19
 prophets, 58–59
 repetition and variation, 78–85
 terseness, 86
 wisdom literature, 98–99
 word of God, 145–51
Olsson, Birger, 32n96, 57
omissions, 127–28
orality of prophets' messages, 159
order of events, 134–36
Origen, 62
Østenstad, Gunnar, 124
Oswalt, John, 149nn38–39
overspecification, 117
Oxyrhynchus papyrus, 62

Painter, John, 100–101
Palestinian Jew as author of the Gospel of John, 47–48
Palestinian Targum of the Pentateuch, 53
Papias, 46
parallelisms, 71–78, 78n24, 87–88, 92–93, 123
Parallelismus Membrorum, 72
paratactic constructions, 87–89, 131
parataxis, 89nn91–92
paronomasia, 91–92

Pater, Walter, 17–18, 39
patristic period, 62–64
Patte, Daniel, 37
Paul, 60
Paul, Shalom M., 160
Pedersen, Johannes, 81
Peisker, C. H., 158
Pentateuch, 55
perfective aspect, 109
Perrin, Laurence, 90–91
personification, 96, 148
perspectives in the Gospel of John, 103–10, 106n17
persuasion, 125–27, 158n67
persuasive or confrontational structure, 120–23
Pesharism of the Qumran Community, 58
Peter, 49–50, 89, 144
Peterson, Norman R., 24
Phelan, James, 4
Philo of Alexandria, 60–61
Plato, 13–14, 16, 62, 63n79, 63n82
plot, 112–13, 118–27, 132n111
Plummer, Alfred, 88
poetic devices, 85–90
poetics. *See* Old Testament poetics
Poetics (Aristotle), 14
poetry, 9n39, 13–14, 16–17, 19–20, 63, 71–72, 72n2. *See also* Old Testament poetics
point of view, 31–32, 103–10
Polycrates, 45–46
polysemous parallelisms, 92–93
Porter, Stanley E., 109n23, 137
power, 148
pragmatic theory, 13, 16–18, 19–20, 26
present tenses, 138–39
Preuss, Horst Dietrich, 147, 153
The Print's First Kiss (Staley), 40
Prologue of the Gospel, 75–76, 83, 116, 124, 131–32
prophets/prophetism
  Gospel of John as prophetic, 55–56
  interpretation of Scripture, 58–59
  poetics of Old Testament prophetic writings, 141–44, 144n19
  prophetic discourses, 161
  prophetic "I," 152–53, 164
  prophetic mode of speaking, 163–67
  prophetic persuasion, 158–63, 158n67
  prophetic proclamations, 159–60
  prophetic self-consciousness, 151–57
  prophetic word of God, 145–51
  prophetic writings, 141–67, 144n19
  word of God, 145–51
  writing prophets, 145–46, 150
Propp, Vladimir, 36
prose and poetry, 9n39, 71–72
prose particles, 86, 88
Psalms, 55, 61, 64–65, 68
Psalms of David, 63
Pythagoras, 62

Quintilian, 29, 96
Qumran, 52, 58

rabbinic Midrash, 57–58
Rabinowitz, Isaac, 66–67
rationalism, 23
reader-response criticism, 37–41
readers, 17–18, 37–41
"Reading Myself, Reading the Text" (Staley), 40
reading strategies, 4, 25
real author, 31–32
reality of Scripture, 14–16
real readers, 31–32, 51
redaction criticism, 23
reference to self, 152–53
referential function of the Scripture, 32–33, 51
renaissance period, 66–69
repetition and variation, 78–85, 83n55
repetitions, 123–24
Repetitions and Variations in the Gospel of John (Chang), 84
Resseguie, James L., 106n17, 116
Revelation, 1
Revelation and John, 154
"Revelation-speech" source material (*offenbarungsreden*), 75
rhetorical conventions, 8–9
rhetorical criticism, 26–30, 66–68, 158
Rhoads, David, 31
Richard, E., 94, 95n118

Subject Index

Richards, I. A., 18, 25, 97
Rossi, Azariah de', 68–69
round characters, 110
Rowland, Christopher, 144, 154
Ruckstuhl, E., 48–49, 83
Runge, Steven E., 117
Russian Formalism, 22, 30–31
Ryken, Leland, 95, 97–98, 100

Samaritans, 117, 117n61
Samaritan Woman, 125–26
Saussure, Ferdinand de, 35–36, 41
scenic structure, 119–20, 124
Schlatter, A., 53
Schnackenburg, Rudolf, 5, 46
Schökel, Luis Anonso, 79–80, 95
Scholes, Robert, 4, 110–11
Schubert, Kurt, 52
Schweizer, E., 48–49, 83
scriptural mimesis, 13–16
scriptural reality, 14–16
Scripture
    authorship, 50–51
    blanks, 128
    characters and characterization, 111–12
    as communication, 23
    deconstructionist criticism, 43
    figurative language in, 96–97
    language of the New Testament, 54
    literary study of, 14–15, 25–26
    literary theories, 102–40
    mimetic theory, 14–16
    modern literary theories on, 25
    narrative criticism, 30–35
    overspecification, 117
    poetics, 65
    pragmatic theory, 16–18
    prose and poetry, 71–72
    reality of, 14–15
    referential function of, 32–33, 51
    songs in, 68–69
    sublimity, 63–64, 68
Second Temple period, 57, 60–61
secular learning, 63, 65
Segovia, Fernano F., 39–40
selected testimonies on Old Testament poetics, 60–69
self-consciousness in Gospel of John, 151–57
semitization of the Greek language, 53–54
Septuagint, 62, 98
Shaw, Charles S., 158–59
Sidney, Philip, 16–17
simile, 96–97
singular perspective, 105
six-and-seven structure, 122–23, 125–26, 126n92
Ska, Jean Louise, 104n8
Society of Biblical Literature, 26–27, 39
Sonek, Krzysztof, 129
Song of Moses, 61
Song of Songs, 157
Soskice, Janet M., 97n133
source criticism, 23
source materials, 75
source theories, 48–49
space, use of, 108–9
"The Spectrum of Johannine Readers" (Koester), 40
Sperling, S. David, 160
spiritual Gospel, 1
staircase parallelisms, 75–76
Staley, Jeffrey L., 31n94, 40, 111n35
Stanzel, F. K., 104n4, 106n17
step-parallelisms, 75
Sternberg, Meir, 6, 24–25, 105, 105n8, 112–13, 127–29
Stibbe, Mark W. G., 5, 34
Story and Discourse (Chatman), 32
storytelling, 123, 133
Streeter, B. H., 142–43
Stromateis (or *Miscellanies*) (Clement of Alexandria), 63
Structural Exegesis for New Testament Critics (Patte), 36–37
structuralist criticism, 35–37
structure(s), 5–6, 32, 41, 68–69, 74–78, 78n24, 80, 83, 118–27, 126n92, 127n93
Studies in the History of the Renaissance (Pater), 17–18
"The Style of John" (Turner), 54–55
stylistic studies, 27
subjectivism, 38–39
sublimity, 16, 19, 63–64, 68, 86, 89, 90

summaries, 133
Sweeney, Marvin A., 165
symbolism, 99
symmetry, 123–24
symphonic structure, 80
synchronic reading, 24
synecdoche, 96
synonymous parallelisms, 72, 75, 78–80
synonyms, 84
Synoptic Gospels, 85, 89, 107, 143, 157, 162
synthetic parallelisms, 73, 75

Talbert, Charles H., 116–17n57
Targum, 57
Targumic Memra, 148
Teeple, H. M., 83
temporal aspects of the Gospel of John, 136–40
Tenney, Merrill C., 55, 80, 107–8
terseness, 85–90, 87n78
text-oriented approach. *See* narrative criticism
Thatcher, Tom, 29, 32, 50n22
theological purpose in characterization, 114
Thielman, Frank, 29
Thiselton, Anthony, 33
thought patterns of the Hebrew people, 80–81
three-and-four structure, 121–23, 125–26, 126n92
time in biblical narratives, 132–40
Torah, 148
totality, 81, 83, 85
Tovey, Derek, 106n17
"Toward a Psycho-Literary Reading of the Fourth Gospel" (Newheart), 40
transcendental signified, 41–43
Trible, Phyllis, 27
Trites, Allison A., 162–63
truth claim of the Gospel of John, 2–3, 20–21, 34
Turner, Nigel, 54

Uspensky, Boris, 103

value, 18
Van der Watt, Jan G., 100
Vangemeren, Willen A., 144n19
Vanhoozer, Kevin J., 33, 42n145
Varghese, Johns, 157
verbal aspects, 109–10, 109n23
verbal tenses, 136n124, 137–40
Verhoef, P. A., 158
victimization, 40, 40n139
visions, 145–46
Von Rad, Gerhard, 152, 152n46

Walhout, Clarence, 15
Walsh, Jerome T., 123, 123n83, 128–30
Warren, Austin, 22
Watson, Wilfred G. E., 79
Wellek, René, 22
Westcott, B. F., 47–48, 52, 75
Western philosophy, 41
"What is John?" (Segovia), 39–40
Wilhoit, James C., 95–96
Wilson, G. H., 74
Wimsatt, William K., 22–23
Winsor, Ann Roberts, 157
wisdom literature, 98–99
Witherington, Ben III, 28
word of God, 51, 65, 145–51, 147n35, 155, 163–67
word of the LORD, 145–51, 165–66
"the word of the LORD" *(debar-yhwh)*, 145
wordplay, 90–95
Wordsworth, William, 19–20
writing prophets, 145–46, 150
Wyller, Egil A., 123–24

Yamasaki, 138–39

Zakovitch, Yair, 122
Zimmerli, Walther, 146
Zimmermann, Ruben, 98–99

Scripture Index

OLD TESTAMENT

Genesis

1	131–32
1–2	148
3	133
3:1	112
6:9	112
11:1–9	119
11:4	119
11:6	119
11:7–8	119
11:9	119
20:8	134
21:9	106
21:11	106
22	105
22:1–2	128
25:25	112
25:27	106
27:1	112
28:12	55–56
29:1–20	157
29:32	133
34	105
34:1	105
34:5	105
34:7	105, 106
34:13	105
34:25	105
34:27	105
35:20	105
37	104
37:3	104
37:4	104
37:8–11	104
37:18–31	104
37:32–35	104
38	104n8, 115
42–45	105
49:10	59, 96
49:26	92n108

Exodus

2:11	55
3:1–6	55
3:12—13:16	104n8
3:15	55
4:4	145
4:15–16	55
4:22	163
4:29	145
4:30	55
8:1	55
12	144
	59

Exodus (*cont.*)

12:40	133
14:8	55
15	43, 61
16–40	55
16:15	56
20:22	145
32–33	55
40:33	55

Leviticus

1–5	59

Numbers

9:1	145
21:5–9	56

Deuteronomy

18:18–20	143n10
32	61
32:46–47	148

Joshua

2:2–14	115
6:15–25	115
7:13	145
7:26	120
8:28	105

Judges

3:7–11	120
3:12–30	130
3:15–17	113
4:19	86
5:25	86
6:8	145
9:7–15	120
9:56–57	106
16:1–3	120
16:4–21	120
18:12	105
19:22	106

1 Samuel

2:27	145
9:1—10:16	133
9:2	106
10:17–18	145
16:7	112
16:18	112
17:12–14	122
17:38	44
25:3	113
28:14	111

2 Samuel

2:18	113
7:4	145
12:1–7	96
12:1–9	128
14:4–20	133
14:25–26	134
15–19	114
15:33	114
15:37	114
16:2	114
16:6	114
16:11	114
16:13	114
16:23	106
17:14	106, 134
17:24–28	134–35
18:18	105
18:24–32	104n8
19:17	114
19:18	114
19:19	114

1 Kings

1:5–7	135–36
1:13	130
2:13–18	130
2:27	106
9:21	105
10:1–10	130
10:1–13	130
10:11–12	130
10:13	130
11:6	106
11:29–31	150

12:22–24	145	35:3	164n88
13	113	40–55	162
13:1–2	145	40:1	79
13:33	106	40:13–14	79
15:11	106	40:30–31	79
18:1	145	51:6	79
21:2–3	119–20	52:1	79
21:4–10	120	54:7–8	79
21:11–14	120	55:11	149
21:15–16	120	61:1	164
21:17	145	65:2–3	160
21:17–27	120		
21:28	145		
22:11	150		

2 Kings

5:1	113		
13:14–19	150		
14:12	96		
23:3	51		
23:25	106		

Isaiah

	166
1:1	146
1:2	79
2:3	87
3:13	162
5:7	79
5:20	79
6:8	151
7:3	150
8:3	150
8:16	159n73
9:6	164
9:11	92
20:2	150
21:3–4	155
22:22	79, 96
23:7	96
24:16	164n88
28:10	79
28:23	164
29:4	92
30:1	92
33:15	164n88
33:22	79

Jeremiah

	166
1:2	145
1:4	151
1:9–10	148
4:12	92
4:19	155, 164n88
5:7	164n88
5:14	148
7:25	160
8:22	164
14:14	143n10
15:16	155
15:18	155
16:1	146
16:2	150
17:19–20	159
20:8–9	155, 167
22:1	159
23:16	143n10
23:21	152
23:29	148
25:4–5	160
26:2	159
28:2–11	159
29:11	158
29:31–32	143n10
33:10–11	157
35:3–5	153
35:15	160
36	159n73
36:5	153
42:4	153
42:19	162
44:4	160
49:1	79

Ezekiel

	166
1:1	146
2:3	152
3:3	155
4–5	150
10:20	153
11:13	148
12:3–7	150
13:1–3	143n10
14:1–11	159
19:14	164n88
20:1–4	159
21:19–23	150
24:15–24	150
32:16	164n88
37:4–5	148
43:3	153
47	59

Hosea

1:1	145
1:2	151
1:3–11	151
4:1	162
6:1	165n92
6:4	165n92
6:5	148
9:8–9	165, 165n92
9:8–17	165
9:10	165n92
9:10–13	165
9:14	165n92
9:15	165n92
9:17	165n92
11:4	92
12:2–6	165n92
12:4	164n88
12:9	165n92
12:13	164n88
12:13–14	166n92
13:14	96
14	165
14:9	166n92
15–16	165
17	165

Joel

1:1	145
1:1–3	165
1:5	165
1:6–7	165n92
1:8	165
1:9	165
1:11	165
1:13	165, 165n92
1:19	165n92
2:1a	165n92
2:12	165n92
2:25	165n92
2:27	165n92
3:1–3	165n92
4:1–8	165n92
4:11	165n92
4:12	165n92
4:17	165n92
4:21a	165n92

Amos

	166
1–2	79
1:1	145
1:3	145n24
1:6	145n24
1:9	145n24
1:11	145n24
1:13	145n24
2:1	145n24
3:8	154–55, 167
3:13	162
4:6–11	79
7:15	152
9:1	153

Obadiah

1:1	146, 165n92
1:8	165n92
1:18	165n92

Jonah

1:1	145

Micah

1:1	145, 146, 164
1:1–8	164
1:2	164
1:2a	164
1:3	164
1:6–7	165n92
1:8	164, 165n92
1:15	165n92
2b–5	164
2:12	165n92
4:12	165n92
4:13	165n92
6–7	164
6:1	162
6:6	165n92
7:1	165n92
7:15	165n92

Nahum

1:1	146
2:4–13	166n92
3:1–4	166n92
3:8–19	166n92

Habakkuk

1:1	146
1:2–4	165n92
1:5–11	165n92
1:12	165n92
2	165
2:1	165n92
2:2	159n73, 165, 165n92
2:18–20	165
2:20	165
3:2	165n92
3:16	155
3:16–19	165n92

Zephaniah

1:1	145
1:2–4	166n92
1:7	166n92
1:8b–12	166n92
1:17a	166n92
1:18	166n92
2:1–3	166n92
2:5a	166n92
2:5b	166n92
2:9	166n92
2:10–11	166n92
2:12	166n92
2:13–14	166n92
3:5	166n92
3:6–12a	166n92
3:8	162
3:15	166n92
3:17	166n92
3:18–20	166n92

Haggai

	145n24
1:1	145
1:1–8	166

Zechariah

1–8	166n96
1:1	145
1:8	153
12:10	59
13:7	59
14:8	59

Malachi

	145n24, 166n96
1:1	145
3:5	162

Psalms

5:10	92
8	79
8:2	79
8:10	79
13:2–3	79
15:3	92
18:10	92
19:7	51
19:7–11	70
19:8	148
23:1	86, 96

Psalms (cont.)

24	79
25:10	51
29	79
33:6	148
42–43	79
46	79
49	79
50:4–15	167n100
56	79
57	79
59	79
62	79
78:56	51
78:61	96
80	79
80:4	79
80:8	79
80:20	79
81:2–17	167n100
82:1–8	167n100
88:6	87
91:11–16	167n100
95:7–11	167n100
96:13	79
101:2	79
101:7	79
103	79
107:1	79
107:8	79
107:15	79
107:20	148
107:21	79
107:31	79
118:1	79
118:29	79
119:105	148
119:130	148
121	78–79
129	79
136	79
137	78–79
147:13	79
148:5	148
148:15–18	149

Proverbs

	86
1:1	98
1:2–6	99
6:16	122
7:21	79, 92
8	96
28:23	92
30:4	79
30:15–33	120
30:15	121
30:18	121
30:21	121
30:29	121

Job

	86
1:13–22	120
4–7	121
5:19	122
8–10	121
11–14	121
15–17	121
18–19	121
20:8	96
20–21	121
22–24	121
25–26	121
27–31	121
32–37	121
32:1–3	121
38–32	121
38:1	122
42:1–6	121

Song of Songs

1:3	157
1:4	157
1:12	157
1:13	157
2:12	92–93
3:1–4	157
3:4	157
3:10	92
4:12	157
4:16	157
5:1	157

5:2	157
5:6	157
8:1–2	92
8:2	157
8:13	157

Ruth

	113
1:2	113
4:18–22	115

Lamentations

4:15	79

Ecclesiastes

1:5	79
3:2–8	79

Ezra

4:7–23	117n61
9:7	96

1 Chronicles

2:13–15	122, 122n78
29:19	51

NEW TESTAMENT

Matthew

1:1–17	115
3:11	88
3:15	89
8:4	51
12:3	51
15:7	51
19:8	51
22:32	115
22:43	51
26:20	49
27:38	108

Mark

1:8	88
1:19–20	45
3:17	45
7:10	51
14:17	49
15:27	108

Luke

3:16	88
16:26	109n22
16:29	51
16:31	51
20:42	51
22:8	50
22:14	49
23:33	108

John

1	136n125, 138
1:1	83, 118
1:1–2	75–76, 136
1:1–18	59, 116n57, 124, 146
1:3	83, 136, 148
1:4	76, 108, 148
1:4–5	148
1:5	94
1:6–7	83
1:6–8	83, 116, 136
1:7	83
1:8	83
1:9–13	148
1:9–14	136
1:11	55, 94
1:12	83
1:14	50, 59, 108, 118, 124, 147, 151, 153, 153n53
1:15	83, 116, 137n128
1:16	108
1:19	83
1:19–28	125
1:19–34	48, 77, 82
1:19–36	116
1:19–51	77, 78, 124, 136
1:19–53	124
1:19—2:11	116n57
1:19—4:54	77–78
1:20	83

John (cont.)

1:21	47
1:24	83
1:26	88
1:28	83
1:29	59, 88, 94, 118, 137n128
1:29–34	125
1:30	75
1:34	75, 118
1:35	48
1:35–36	77, 125
1:36	59, 118, 138, 139
1:37	83, 138
1:37–39	125n91
1:37–42	77
1:38	108, 118, 137
1:39	83, 89, 138
1:40	83, 88, 139
1:41	118, 137n128, 139
1:41–42	108
1:42	82–83, 88
1:43	137n128
1:43–49	77
1:45	88, 137n128
1:47–51	59
1:48	83
1:49	118
1:50–51	56, 77
1:51	77, 118
2	59
2–4	124
2:1	108
2:1–11	32n96, 82, 83, 157
2:1–12	77
2:1–25	77, 78
2:2	136
2:4	136
2:6	48, 108
2:9	108, 137n128
2:11	48, 50, 55, 82, 98, 106, 108
2:11—12:37	55
2:12	82, 108
2:13	56
2:13–23	83
2:13–25	77
2:16	88, 108
2:17	48, 88, 106
2:19	94
2:21	48
2:22	48, 83, 108
2:23	56, 98
2:23–25	82, 136
2:24	48
3:1	117
3:1–2	83
3:1–15	40
3:1–21	37, 78, 136
3:2	98
3:3	89
3:3–8	94
3:6	75
3:11	75
3:12	83
3:13–21	163, 167
13:13	88n88
3:14	55, 56, 75, 88n88
3:15	83
3:16	94, 156
3:16–19	94
3:16–21	108
3:17	83
3:18	75
3:19	75
3:20	83, 94
3:20–21	83
3:22	83, 108
3:22–36	78, 116, 125
3:22—4:3	116n57
3:23	108
3:23–24	116
3:26	83
3:27–30	157
3:30	75, 76
3:31	75, 83
3:31–36	108, 167
3:32–33	75, 83
3:34	75, 148
3:36	75, 76, 94
4	42, 48, 117, 125–26, 136n125
4–21	40
4:1	48
4:1–26	157
4:1–42	32n96
4:1–45	78

Reference	Page(s)
4:2	83
4:3	48
4:4–42	37
4:5	138
4:5–6	117
4:6	48, 108
4:7	125, 137, 138
4:7–26	126
4:9	47, 108, 125
4:10	125
4:11–12	125
4:12	59
4:13	75
4:13–14	125
4:14	75, 83
4:15	108, 125
4:16	108, 125
4:17	125
4:17–18	125
4:19–20	125
4:21	136
4:21–24	125
4:22	75
4:23	136
4:25	47, 108, 125
4:26	125
4:27	47, 48, 106, 126
4:28	125
4:28–30	126
4:31	48
4:31–38	126
4:34	148, 150
4:35	75, 83, 89
4:36	75, 94
4:39–42	126
4:40	108, 136
4:42	83
4:43	108
4:45	82, 83, 136
4:46	82, 83
4:46–54	78
4:48	82, 98
4:53	90
4:54	83, 98
5	82, 111n35, 126, 131
5–7	124
5:1	56
5:5	108
5:5–9	126
5:8	88
5:10	89
5:10–13	126
5:12	90
5:14	126, 137n128
5:15	88, 126
5:18	107
5:19	83
5:23	148
5:24	83, 148
5:25	136
5:27	88n88
5:28	136
5:29	75
5:30	148
5:31–32	83
5:31–47	116n57
5:36	83, 148, 150
5:37	88n88, 148
5:38	148
5:39	88, 88n88
5:40	88n88
5:41–44	157
5:42	83
5:43	75
5:45	88
5:46	59
6	37, 59, 126
6:1–15	83
6:2	98
6:3	108
6:4	56
6:5–14	126
6:6	48, 108
6:9	108
6:10	83
6:12–13	83
6:14	47, 48
6:15–21	126
6:19	48, 137
6:20	88, 90
6:22	108
6:22–66	126
6:23	83, 108
6:24	108
6:25	108
6:26–66	126n92
6:27	75, 88

John (cont.)

6:29	148
6:32	59, 75
6:32–33	56
6:35	59, 75, 76, 99–100, 118n63, 126n92
6:37	75, 83
6:39	83, 148
6:40	148
6:41–42	126n92
6:44	148
6:46	83
6:54	148
6:55	75, 76
6:57	83
6:60	48
6:61	48
6:64	48, 83, 108
6:66	126n92
6:67–71	126
6:71	83, 136
7:1	48, 83
7:2	56, 108
7:3	108
7:5	107, 108
7:6	75, 138
7:10	83
7:11	83
7:13	94
7:15	47
7:16	83
7:18	83
7:22–23	83
7:23	83
7:27	83
7:28	88n88
7:30	136
7:31	107
7:32	107
7:33	89
7:34	75
7:35	47
7:37	75
7:38	83
7:39	108, 136
7:40	47
7:49	47
7:50	83, 108, 132
7:51	94
8–12	124
8:3	137
8:6	107
8:12	99–100, 118n63
8:12—12:50	124
8:15–16	83
8:16	88n88, 90
8:17	88n88
8:18	83
8:20	108, 136
8:23	75
8:27	107
8:28	56
8:29	88n88
8:31–59	126n92
8:32	75
8:35	75, 83
8:37	94
8:41b–42	157
8:44	75
8:45	83
8:53	59
8:58–59	126n92
9	94, 111n35, 126n92, 131
9:1–7	83
9:2	47, 48
9:6–7	83
9:7	59, 108
9:8	83
9:9	90
9:11	83
9:13	83, 137n128
9:14	108
9:28	83
9:29	83
9:39	75
9:39–41	94
9:41	75
10	82
10:4–5	83
10:6	98, 106, 108
10:9	99–100
10:10	75, 99–100
10:11	75
10:14–15	83
10:16	88n88

Scripture Index

10:21	88	12:23	136
10:22–23	108	12:24	75
10:22–38	124	12:25	75
10:24	94	12:26	75, 108
10:26	75	12:27	136
10:27	75	12:31	75
10:28	83	12:32	56
10:31–39	56	12:34	47, 56
10:38	83	12:35	88
10:40	83, 108	12:35–56	83
10:40–42	82, 116n57	12:37–40	55
10:42	108	12:37–43	108, 136
11–12	82	12:39–41	59, 153n50
11:1–44	83, 157	12:44–45	82
11:2	83	12:46	124
11:3	107	12:47	88n88
11:5	107	12:49	83
11:7	88	12:50	88n88
11:8	48, 108	13	136n125
11:9	75	13–17	124, 149, 150
11:10	75	13–21	55
11:12	48	13:1	48, 136, 150, 156
11:13	48, 106	13:1–3	107
11:15	108	13:1–11	59
11:21	108	13:1–20	156n61
11:23	94	13:3	48
11:25	75, 118n63	13:4	48
11:25–26	100	13:6	137n128
11:29	83	13:9	90
11:30	108	13:11	48, 108
11:31	83, 108	13:13–24	50
11:32	108	13:16	75
11:33	48, 107	13:20	75, 82
11:38	107, 138	13:21	48, 107
11:39–41	83	13:21–30	157
11:40	82	13:21–31	83
11:54	48, 108	13:22	107
11:55	56	13:23	49, 50, 154, 156
12:1	83, 157	13:23–27	108
12:1–8	83, 157	13:24	48
12:2	108	13:24–27	140
12:3	157	13:26	137n128
12:4	83, 136	13:28	48, 108
12:6	94, 108	13:31	83
12:8	75	13:31–35	156n61
12:9	108	13:33	94, 150
12:16	48, 108, 136	13:34–35	157
12:22	137n128	14–17	29

John (cont.)

14:1	82, 83, 88
14:2	75
14:2–5	150
14:3	75, 88n88
14:4	88n88
14:6	100, 118n63
14:7	88n88
14:11	83
14:12	150
14:13	88n88
14:15–24	157
14:16	89
14:17	83
14:19	75
14:20	83
14:21	75
14:26	142
14:27	75, 76, 82, 88
14:28	150
14:29	88n88
14:30	88n88
14:31	88, 108
15	84
15:1	118n63
15:2	75, 83, 94
15:4	83, 90
15:5	83, 88, 100
15:6	83
15:7	83
15:9	83, 156
15:9–17	157
15:10	83
15:12	82, 156
15:13	75, 156
15:13–15	157
15:14	75
15:15	75
15:17	82
15:19	83
15:26	75, 142
16:3	88n88
16:4	83
16:5–10	150
16:7	75
16:8	88n88
16:17	48
16:19	48, 88
16:20	75
16:22	75, 88n88
16:23	88n88
16:24	89
16:25	98
16:27–28	83
16:27–30	150
16:29	48, 98
16:33	75, 82
17	55, 90
17:2	83
17:4	150
17:5	88n88
17:8	150
17:9	88, 90
17:11	88n88, 90, 150
17:12	83
17:13	90, 150
17:15	90
17:17	88
17:19	88n88
17:20	90
17:22	88n88
17:23	90
18–19	59
18–20	124
18:1–11	83
18:2	48, 107, 108
18:3	108, 137n128
18:4	107
18:5	90
18:6	90
18:8	90
18:9	83
18:10	108
18:11	83
18:14	108
18:15	48
18:15–16	49, 50
18:23	48
18:28	138, 139
18:28—19:16	139
18:29	139
18:30–32	139
18:33–37	139
18:36	75, 83, 108
18:38	139

18:40	90, 108
19:3	139
19:4	139
19:5	139
19:6	139
19:7	139
19:9	139
19:10	139
19:12	139
19:13	108
19:14	139
19:15	139
19:17	108
19:18	108
19:23	48
19:25–27	49, 157
19:26	48, 154, 156
19:26–27	50
19:28	48, 150
19:30	55, 150
19:31	108
19:34–35	153
19:35	50, 108
19:39	83, 108, 132
19:41	157
19:42	108
20	82, 136n125
20:1	137n128, 157
20:1–2	82, 157
20:1–8	49
20:1–10	157
20:2	48, 50, 137n128, 154
20:2–8	156
20:2–9	50
20:6	137n128
20:8	82, 108
20:9	48, 108
20:11	157
20:11–18	82, 157
20:12	137n128
20:14	137n128
20:15	82–83, 157
20:16	108, 157
20:17	75
20:18	108, 137n128
20:19	48, 108
20:21	50
20:24	108
20:25	48
20:26	108, 137n128
20:27	75, 108
20:30–31	107, 108, 161
21	131, 136n25
21:1–14	157
21:1–23	124
21:1–25	89
21:2	50
21:3	48
21:4	48
21:5	48
21:6	83
21:7	48, 49–50, 154, 156
21:8	108
21:11	48
21:15–17	157
21:19	108
21:20	48, 50, 137n128, 154
21:20–23	156
21:20–24	157
21:23	108
21:24	48, 51, 108, 124, 153
21:24–25	50, 83, 124, 151
21:25	136

Acts

1:3–4	50
1:13	50
5:30	115
5:32	115
8:14–25	50
11:28	142
19:6	142
21:4	142
21:9	142
21:10–11	142
22:14	115
24:14	115

Romans

4:23–24	114
11:17–24	60, 70

1 Corinthians

7:10	143
7:12	143
7:25	143
10:1–5	114
10:6	114
10:11	114
12:10	142
12:29	142
14	142
14:3	142
14:29–43	144
14:37	144

2 Corinthians

2:17	144
3:1–18	144
5:14	167

Galatians

2:9	50

Ephesians

2:20	142
3:5	142

Colossians

1:15	153n50

1 Thessalonians

5:19	142

2 Timothy

3:16	25

Hebrews

1:1	51, 114, 151
4:12	70
11	114

2 Peter

3:2	144

Revelation

4:7	1

www.ingramcontent.com/pod-product-compliance
Lightning Source LLC
Chambersburg PA
CBHW070250230426
43664CB00014B/2478